Frederick
Douglass

Frederick Douglass

D. H. Dilbeck

FREDERICK DOUGLASS

DOUGLASS

AMERICA'S PROPHET

THE UNIVERSITY OF NORTH CAROLINA PRESS

Chapel Hill

This book was published with the assistance of the John Hope Franklin Fund of the University of North Carolina Press.

Manufactured in the United States of America

Designed by Jamison Cockerham. Set in Arno, by Robert Slimbach; Cutright, by Walden Font Co.; and Sorts Mill Goudy, by Barry Schwartz (after Frederic Goudy). Set by codeMantra.

Cover photograph: Frederick Douglass. Half-length portrait, n.d., unidentified photographer; image no. 35765. Courtesy of the Collection of the New-York Historical Society.

The University of North Carolina Press has been a member of the Green Press Initiative since 2003.

LIBRARY OF CONGRESS CATALOGING-IN-PUBLICATION DATA
Names: Dilbeck, D. H., author.
Title: Frederick Douglass : America's prophet / D. H. Dilbeck.
Description: Chapel Hill : The University of North Carolina Press, [2018] | Includes bibliographical references and index.
Identifiers: LCCN 2017026932 | ISBN 9781469636184 (cloth : alk. paper) | ISBN 9781469636191 (ebook)
Subjects: LCSH: Douglass, Frederick, 1818–1895. | Douglass, Frederick, 1818–1895—Religion. | African American abolitionists—Biography. | African American orators—United States—Biography.
Classification: LCC E449.D75 D55 2018 | DDC 973.8092 [B]—dc23
LC record available at https://lccn.loc.gov/2017026932

To Pearl and Jack

With what shall I come before the Lord
and bow down before the exalted God?

Shall I come before him with burnt offerings,
with calves a year old?

Will the Lord be pleased with thousands of rams,
with ten thousand rivers of olive oil?

Shall I offer my firstborn for my transgression,
the fruit of my body for the sin of my soul?

He has shown you, O mortal, what is good.
And what does the Lord require of you?

To act justly and to love mercy
and to walk humbly with your God.

MICAH 6:6–8

Contents

Illustrations

Frederick
Douglass

A Voice Crying in the Wilderness of Christian Slaveholding America

On 5 July 1852, in the stately Corinthian Hall of Rochester, New York, Frederick Douglass shouldered a heavy burden as he ascended the speaker's platform and looked out on his audience. The burden was by now a familiar one to Douglass. He had grown accustomed to feeling it acutely each July as Americans celebrated their national independence. Douglass had accepted an invitation from the Rochester Ladies' Anti-Slavery Society to take part in their Fourth of July celebrations. On 5 July, well over 500 people gathered at Corinthian Hall to hear Douglass deliver the day's keynote address. Although only thirty-four years old, he was America's most famous abolitionist orator, and the chance to hear him speak that day was well worth the 12½-cent price of admission.

Fourteen summers earlier, Douglass had escaped from slavery in his native Maryland. He knew well the cruelty of the institution he now made a living denouncing. Not long after settling as a fugitive in New Bedford, Massachusetts, Douglass won the attention of the state's abolitionist leaders, who, after hearing him retell his harrowing life story, offered him a paid position on the antislavery lecture circuit. Douglass made hundreds of speeches over the next decade, routinely evoking the horrors of his captivity and ridiculing the defenders of slavery.

But his oration on 5 July 1852 was different. That day, amid boisterous celebrations of American independence, he delivered the greatest speech of his life. Douglass spoke as a man born into bondage in America more than forty years after the Declaration of Independence had proclaimed that all men were equal and endowed by God with liberty. The burden Douglass felt on 5 July 1852 was to speak a word of truth about America in the irony-ridden age of slavery. He tried that day to answer for his overwhelmingly white audience in Corinthian Hall a question posed in the title of his address: "What to the Slave Is the Fourth of July?"

In answering that question, Douglass delivered a scorching sermon that condemned Americans for their hypocrisy, urged them to repent of their sins, and beseeched them to pursue the true righteousness that exalts a nation. Douglass said that on the Fourth of July, more than any other day, slaves saw clearly American duplicity and discrimination. He told his jovial white Rochester audience that to the slave, "your celebration is a sham; your boasted liberty, an unholy license; your national greatness, swelling vanity; your sounds of rejoicing are empty and heartless; your shouts of liberty and equality, hollow mock; your prayers and hymns, your sermons and thanksgivings, with all your religious parade and solemnity, are to him mere bombast, fraud, deception, impiety, and hypocrisy—a thin veil to cover up crimes which would disgrace a nation of savages." Douglass wished he could speak to every white American on Independence Day, and "pour out a fiery stream of biting ridicule, blasting reproach, withering sarcasm, and stern rebuke." He thundered words of judgment to a nation blithely traversing a wicked path. "The hypocrisy of the nation must be exposed; and its crimes against God and man must be proclaimed and denounced."[1]

Sometime in the eighth century BCE, in the Kingdom of Judah, there was born a Hebrew prophet named Isaiah. He prophesied for at least six decades—during the reigns of Uzziah, Jotham, Ahaz, and Hezekiah—to the Lord's chosen people, who had given themselves over to idolatry and evil. The Israelites had divided into two kingdoms, Israel and Judah, and Isaiah lived to see the existence of both threatened by another kingdom, Assyria. The Book of Isaiah, which records the prophet's visions and pronouncements, begins with a condemnation of Judah's wickedness: "Ah sinful nation, a people laden with iniquity, a seed of evildoers, children that are corrupters: they have forsaken the Lord, they have provoked the Holy One of Israel unto anger, they are gone away backward" (Isaiah 1:4).[2] Then the Lord, through Isaiah, exhorts his chosen to pursue true righteousness: "And when ye spread forth your hands, I will hide mine eyes from you: yea, when ye make many prayers, I will not hear: your hands are full of blood. Wash you, make you clean; put away the evil of your doings from before mine eyes; cease to do evil; Learn to do well; seek judgment, relieve the oppressed, judge the fatherless, plead for the widow" (Isaiah 1:15–17).

Less than eight centuries later, another prophet appeared to the same people who had once received Isaiah. At the far eastern edge of the Roman Empire, Jesus Christ preached salvation and liberation: "The time is fulfilled, and the kingdom of God is at hand: repent ye, and believe the gospel" (Mark 1:15). One Sabbath, at the start of his public ministry, Christ entered the synagogue at Nazareth, his hometown. He came to read aloud from the Hebrew scriptures. He opened the scroll to Isaiah and read: "The Spirit of the Lord is upon me, because he hath anointed me to preach the gospel to the poor; he hath sent me to heal the brokenhearted, to preach deliverance to the captives, and recovering of sight to the blind, to set at liberty them that are bruised, to preach the acceptable year of the Lord" (Luke 4:18–19). The crowd gathered at the synagogue erupted in anger when Christ announced that his arrival had fulfilled Isaiah's prophecy. He proclaimed himself the long-awaited Messiah.

Frederick Douglass cherished the words of the prophet Isaiah and the gospel of Jesus Christ. He frequently cited both in his speeches and writings. Near the end of "What to the Slave Is the Fourth of July?," Douglass condemned the American church, in the North and South, for remaining "the bulwark of American slavery." Christian ministers throughout the nation "have shamelessly given the sanction of religion and the Bible to the whole slave system," Douglass said. In doing so, they preached an abominable faith that "makes God a respecter of persons, denies his fatherhood of the race, and tramples in the dust the great truth of the brotherhood of man."[3] To drive home his point, Douglass quoted Isaiah 1:13–17—wherein the Lord chastises wicked oppressors who pray with blood-stained hands in a spirit of false piety. Moments earlier in his speech, Douglass alluded to words Christ spoke to the religious hypocrites of his day, words that closely echoed Isaiah: "Woe unto you, scribes, and Pharisees, hypocrites! For ye pay tithe of mint, anise and cumin, and have omitted the weightier matters of the law, judgment, mercy and faith; these ought ye to have done, and not to leave the other undone" (Matthew 23:23). The time had long passed for America to repent of the sin of slavery, commit itself to true righteousness, and treat all people with mercy and loving-kindness. Douglass warned that the longer America delayed its atonement, the more it tempted wrathful judgment from a just God.

Douglass quoted Isaiah and Christ for more than mere rhetorical effect. He looked to their words not simply for an eloquent turn of phrase that might move the hearts of his biblically literate audience. Douglass's debt to Isaiah and Christ ran far deeper. He affirmed as true what they proclaimed about God and humanity and wickedness and righteousness. They helped him make sense of the world and his place in it. They were the two great pillars that supported his deepest theological and moral convictions. Douglass aspired to speak to America as Isaiah and Christ once spoke—with words of rebuke and warning, exhortation and encouragement, grace and liberty, hope and truth.

This book is a religious biography of Frederick Douglass. My goal is to explain the substance of Douglass's faith and show how it shaped his public career. In the 200 years since his birth, Douglass has attracted many biographers who have admirably recounted the story of his life in thorough detail.[4] My intention is different. I instead focus on one underappreciated part of Douglass's life, his religion, which is vital to understanding who he was, how he thought, and what he did.[5]

Douglass held fast to the Christian faith his entire adult life. He did not adhere to Christianity in an uncritical or unquestioning manner; he was far too independent-minded to remain a conventional Christian churchgoer by nineteenth-century American standards. But any alienation he felt from Christianity was never complete. The fundamental affirmations of the faith remained far too deeply interwoven into his core moral, political, and theological convictions. Douglass first heard the Christian gospel preached by white proslavery ministers on Maryland's Eastern Shore. He later embraced the religion as a teenager under the guidance of black and white Methodists in Baltimore. Like so many Americans in the early nineteenth century, Douglass came to faith within the fold of an evangelical church—the dominant strand of American Christianity in his lifetime.

Douglass never quite abandoned entirely the evangelicalism of his youth, even as he grew beyond it in some ways. He certainly never repudiated his born-again salvation experience in Baltimore, though he referred to it only a handful of times later in life. Still, Douglass spoke often of Jesus Christ. To his final days, he affirmed a largely conventional Christian understanding of the redemption from sin offered through Christ's death—though he always said far more about Christ's moral teachings than his crucifixion and resurrection. Douglass believed in the antislavery, egalitarian spirit of Christ's commandments. He maintained a high regard for the Bible as a great authority on moral and theological matters, though not the only edifying authority. He also undoubtedly had an inclination toward social reform, as was characteristic of so many nineteenth-century evangelicals. In many ways, Douglass's public career was a quintessential example of the evangelical impulse to bring to bear the Christian gospel on a society and thereby transform it.[6]

Even so, Douglass's relationship to organized Christianity was deeply strained. As much as he venerated what he called the "true Christianity of Christ," he also detested how quickly the Christian church in America strayed so completely from what Christ preached. To Douglass, far too many of the nation's Christians appealed to the Bible to justify bondage and bigotry. That fact alone kept him alienated from white Christian congregations in the North and South. But Douglass also had a hard time finding a permanent home even within an African American congregation. In their own way, Douglass thought, these churches also tended to remain quietly complicit in the corrupted Christianity that prevailed in slaveholding America. For his entire adult life, Douglass nurtured his faith in tension—the tension between his assurance of the truth of Christianity and his frustration with how most Americans practiced it.

Douglass never resolved that tension, but it gave meaning to his faith and to how his Christian convictions informed his activism. It is for that reason that I call Douglass "America's Prophet." The key to rightly understanding his religious beliefs and why they mattered to his public career is to appreciate the distinctly *prophetic* character of his faith. I use the words "prophet" and "prophetic" in a very particular way to describe Douglass's Christianity. Traditionally, the Abrahamic religions understood a prophet to be one who revealed God's will, often to a people who had lately abandoned it. In the Hebrew scriptures, the most commonly used word for prophet derives from a verb literally meaning "to bubble up." When a prophet speaks, God's truth bursts into the world.

A spirit of scorn and hope equally defined the sort of prophetic religion that Douglass embraced. He derided Americans for their stubborn wickedness, and warned of imminent judgment, but he also affirmed God's grace for those who repented and lived lives of justice and mercy. Ancient Hebrew prophets like Isaiah stood apart from institutions of political and religious power and called them to account for their hypocrisy and oppression. In doing so, the prophets provided a radical, contrarian vision of righteousness: to care for the marginalized, oppressed, widowed, and orphaned; to heal the brokenhearted; to set free the captives. One modern biblical scholar has written that the vocation of the Hebrew prophets was "to nurture, nourish, and evoke a consciousness and perception alternative to the consciousness and perception of the dominant culture." Prophets existed to offer "an alternative perception of reality," one that might allow people to "see their own history in the light of God's freedom and his will for justice."[7] In his fight against slavery and racial discrimination and inequality, Douglass endeavored to fulfill precisely this sort of prophetic calling in America.

Douglass was neither the first nor the last black Christian to speak a prophetic word to America. Well before Douglass had escaped from slavery in 1838, other African Americans, inspired by the gospel of Christ, testified courageously against prevailing patterns of racial oppression in slaveholding America. In 1816, Richard Allen led the formal founding of the African

Methodist Episcopal Church, America's first independent black denomination. One of the most committed members of the denomination was David Walker, a free black man who in 1829 published *An Appeal to the Colored Citizens of the World*, perhaps the first great prophetic, Christian, antislavery pamphlet. Walker's words inspired many African Americans, including Maria Stewart, who in the early 1830s published her own abolitionist texts, drawing heavily on religious arguments like Walker's, while also blazing a new trail as a black woman who made public antislavery speeches. However controversial Stewart's oratory might have been, the most notorious prophetic foe of slavery in these years was Nat Turner, the deeply religious Virginia slave who led the deadliest slave insurrection in American history— inspired by intense visions of God commanding him to purge the United States of the iniquity of slavery. In his own way, Douglass continued the work begun by Allen, Walker, Stewart, Turner, and others. Many prominent African Americans joined Douglass in carrying forward this prophetic tradition, including Henry McNeal Turner, a bishop in the African Methodist Episcopal Church; Henry Highland Garnet, a leading Presbyterian minister; Alexander Crummell, an Episcopal priest and pioneering pan-Africanist; and Sojourner Truth, the iconic antislavery and women's rights activist. Despite their many theological, denominational, and political differences, they all drew upon their faith to maintain a powerful prophetic witness in the United States.[8]

Throughout the nineteenth century, as America reckoned with slavery and Jim Crow, African American prophetic religion fully blossomed into a vibrant tradition. Although not a systematic theologian, ordained minister, or denominational leader, Douglass was still the most significant spokesman of his day of this black prophetic Christianity. No other voice quite matched Douglass's stature and influence. He commanded the attention of a nationwide audience, white and black, for a half century. Any adequate retelling of American religious history must give ample attention to Douglass and the black prophetic faith tradition that he helped shape.

To that end, and to offer new perspective on Douglass's life and career, I seek to answer three questions in this short book. How and why did Douglass come to embrace a distinctly prophetic Christianity? What were the core moral and theological convictions of his faith, and how did they evolve over time? How did his prophetic Christian religion inform his public activism, first against slavery and later against all forms of racial and gender discrimination? Readers with extensive knowledge of Douglass will note that some elements of his life I mention only in passing, and some I do not really discuss at all—for example, Douglass's family relations and his experiences after the Civil War holding a variety of political posts. But other parts of Douglass's life here receive ample attention, far more than they might otherwise receive in a conventional biography. Along the way, I place a heavy emphasis on the speeches Douglass delivered throughout his fifty-year public career—for in his speeches, more than anywhere else, Douglass most clearly voiced his prophetic theology. My hope is that readers will finish this book with a far better sense of the substance of Douglass's faith and how it gave meaning and direction to his life.

When Douglass published his first autobiography in 1845, he thought it wise at the end to insist that he was not "an opponent of all religion." After all, the most horrific characters in *Narrative of the Life of Frederick Douglass, an American Slave,* are the malicious Christian slaveholders that Douglass encountered as a young slave in Maryland. Douglass wanted readers to know he meant for his seemingly sweeping condemnations of American religion only "to apply to the *slaveholding religion* of this land, and with no possible reference to Christianity proper; for, between the Christianity of this land, and the Christianity of Christ, I recognize the widest possible difference."[9]

Throughout his long public career, Douglass ardently denounced slavery, racism, and bigotry in all its forms. He dedicated much of his life to seeing justice and liberty attained in America by those who had been denied it. But if Douglass pursued any single calling that tied together his entire life, it was simply to force Americans to confront the disjuncture between the Christianity they professed and practiced and "the Christianity of Christ." In that way, he bore a prophetic witness in nineteenth-century America—proclaiming of his nation, as Isaiah once said of his people, "They have forsaken the Lord, they have provoked the Holy One of Israel unto anger, they are gone away backward" (Isaiah 1:4).

To the end of his life, Douglass believed the oppression and injustice he lamented would swiftly pass away if only Americans remained faithful to the religious and political principles they claimed to cherish. Bondage and bigotry could not long endure if Americans truly believed "all men are created equal" and honestly attempted to "do unto others as you would have them do unto you." Douglass lived to see both the end of slavery in America and the onset of Jim Crow—the system of racial discrimination and segregation, upheld both by laws and illegal violence, that relegated African Americans to an unequal caste in American society. When Douglass died in 1895, the United States must surely have seemed as distant as ever from any sort of Promised Land of racial justice and harmony.

Even so, Douglass never wavered in *hope*. The essential element of Douglass's prophetic Christian faith was precisely this deep hopefulness—an abiding confidence that God somehow slowly, mysteriously moved in history to ensure greater freedom and equality for all people. Religious hypocrisy and racial tyranny endured in America. Yet even more immovable was the God who promised to scatter the proud and exalt the humble. In an 1890 speech at the leading black Methodist church in Washington, D.C., Douglass proclaimed that when he despaired about the future of his race and nation, he reminded himself, "God reigns in eternity, and that whatever delays, whatever disappointments and discouragements may come, truth, justice, liberty and humanity will ultimately prevail."[10]

THE SEEKING SLAVE

1818–1838

God and Slavery on
the Eastern Shore

The woods of Talbot County, Maryland, echoed with songs of sadness. Frederick Bailey first heard them as a young slave at Wye House, the great home of the Lloyd family's sprawling plantation on the Eastern Shore. The mysterious melodies captivated Bailey. He sensed the singers' affliction, and yet as a child of six or seven years old he could not fully comprehend the anguished cries. The memory of these sorrow songs haunted Bailey the rest of his life. "Every tone was a testimony against slavery, and a prayer to God for deliverance from chains," he remembered. The songs shaped young Frederick's soul; they were his earliest catechism. But the questions loomed far larger than the answers in these songs, none more unsettling than, "Why has God made me a slave?" Frederick agonized over this question when he realized he too was a slave. He searched for a satisfying answer as a child, while witnessing masters disregard the humanity of their slaves. Before his childhood ended, Frederick had decided that God was not responsible for his enslavement. It was his first momentous theological conviction, and perhaps the most important one of his life.[1]

Frederick Douglass was born Frederick Augustus Washington Bailey in February 1818 along the Tuckahoe Creek at a farm called Holme Hill. Frederick never knew the exact year of his birth. He also never knew the identity of his father. But his skin was far lighter than his mother's and siblings', so from the moment of his birth most people assumed his father was a white man, maybe even his master. As a Bailey, Frederick's Eastern Shore ancestry stretched back well over a century, nearly to the very settlement of Talbot County. His great-great-grandfather Baly was born about 1701, likely either in the British West Indies or in Talbot, and was among the earliest generations of slaves to live in the county. The details of Baly's life are wrapped mostly in mystery, but it is possible to trace his lineage forward to 1818: in 1745, Baly fathered a daughter, Jenny, who in 1774 bore a daughter, Betsey, who in 1792 bore a daughter, Harriet, who in 1818 bore a son, Frederick.[2]

For the first six years of his life, Frederick lived with his grandparents, Betsey and Isaac Bailey, in their small cabin in the woods near Holme Hill. Betsey was a slave, a handsome woman whose striking height matched her stature as a leader among Tuckahoe African Americans. Betsey, like her mother, had been born a slave to the Skinner family. In 1797 Betsey and her two young children were moved to a farm on Tuckahoe Creek by their new master, Aaron Anthony, who had recently married a Skinner daughter.[3]

Around that same time, Betsey married Isaac Bailey, a free black man who earned meager and unpredictable wages as a sawyer. Maryland law did not acknowledge Betsey and Isaac's marriage as legitimate, but that hardly stopped them from making a life together in their single-room cabin of clay, straw, and timber. Betsey and Isaac raised ten children after 1797. She later raised many more grandchildren, including Frederick, whose mother, Harriet, spent her days working the Anthony farm. Douglass never described the religious beliefs or practices of the extended Bailey clan. Betsey, Isaac, and Harriet do not appear to have adhered to the kind of evangelical Christianity that Frederick embraced in Baltimore by age thirteen. Nor do they seem to have participated in any semisecretive religious gatherings of slaves. But Betsey was undeniably the most important figure of Frederick's young childhood. Douglass later wrote that in her care he was "a spirited, joyous, uproarious, happy boy."[4] He loved her deeply, and she enjoyed a rather unusual degree of freedom as an enslaved woman. Anthony let Betsey live with Isaac. He never hired her out as a field hand. He also allowed her to make and sell fishing nets, and even paid for her work as a midwife.

But Douglass still remembered Aaron Anthony as a man of "extraordinary barbarity," even by the exceedingly harsh standards of the Eastern Shore. Anthony was a somewhat unlikely slaveholder. He was born on the Eastern Shore in 1767 to a family of poor farmers who owned neither slaves nor land. His father died before he turned two years old, but through grit and ingenuity Anthony rose beyond his modest birth. By age twenty-seven he was captain of the *Elizabeth & Anne*, the extravagant schooner the Lloyd family used to travel to Annapolis. Three years later, Anthony rose again, this time by marrying Anne Skinner, a scion of an elite Talbot County family. Soon after his marriage to Anne, Colonel Edward Lloyd appointed Anthony chief overseer of the entire Lloyd family estate—which consisted of thirteen farms totaling nearly 10,000 acres, worked by more than 500 slaves. Anthony, Anne, and their young family lived in a house on the main estate of the Lloyd family plantation. As a child, Frederick heard the rumor that Anthony was his father. But his mother never confirmed the rumor before her death. Historians still have not definitively confirmed the identity of Frederick's father.[5]

The first great trauma of Frederick's life came at the age of six, when Anthony moved him from his grandmother's cabin to the chief estate of the Lloyd plantation, the site of Wye House and the Anthony family home. One humid morning in the late summer of 1824, Betsey traveled with Frederick to Wye House. She did not tell him where they were going, and Frederick could hardly know that it would be more than fifty years before he would see his grandmother's cabin again. As they made the twelve-mile journey, Frederick grew so exhausted and anxious that Betsey carried him part of the way. When they came to Wye House, Betsey pointed out Frederick's brother and two sisters in a crowd of children. "Go and play with them," she said. Frederick did as he was told, and his grandmother entered the kitchen of the Anthony home. Soon after, a child ran to Frederick and shouted, "Fed, Fed! grandmammy gone! grandmammy gone!" Frederick frantically searched the kitchen. When he realized his grandmother had left, he collapsed in a fit of inconsolable tears. He sobbed himself to sleep that night.[6]

"Genealogical trees do not flourish among slaves," Douglass wrote in 1855, a truth he learned through bitter experience. The mere whim of a master could separate forever a child from his family. Frederick would later tell the story of his early life as an example of the traumatic terror slavery inflicted on slave families. In his case, it created an emotional and physical chasm between him and his mother, father, grandparents, and siblings. "There is not, beneath the sky, an enemy to filial affection so destructive as slavery," Douglass wrote in his second autobiography, *My Bondage and My Freedom*. "It had made my brothers and sisters strangers to me; it converted the mother that bore me, into a myth; it shrouded my father in mystery, and left me without an intelligible beginning in the world."[7]

As a child, Frederick felt no particularly strong attachment to his mother. Harriet mostly worked on the Anthony farm, and Douglass never remembered her visiting when he lived with his grandmother. When he lived at the Wye House estate, Frederick saw his mother on only a handful of occasions. She had been hired out and worked on a farm twelve miles way. But Douglass recalled how Harriet's "true mother's heart" led her back to her son whenever possible. During one visit, Harriet learned that the slave cook at the Lloyd plantation, Aunt Katy, often refused to provide Frederick with food. Harriet erupted with indignation toward Katy and succeeded in winning food for her son. "That night I learned the fact, that I was not only a child, but *somebody's child*," Douglass wrote years later. But Harriet's absence far outweighed these brief flashes of maternal love. Even in her death, Harriet remained separated from her children. She died not long after Frederick was sent to Wye House, but not once during her illness was he allowed to visit her. Decades later, Douglass still seethed at how slavery denied his mother a "good death," preventing her from gathering her children around her death-bed "to impart to them her holy admonitions." An enslaved woman like Harriet was instead "left to die as a beast," separated from her family even at the moment of her passing.[8]

As a much older man, Douglass drew on his theology to condemn slavery for destroying slave families. He contended that God, "in his wisdom and mercy," had planted in children "germs of affection" for their mother and family, which God intended to blossom into deep familial bonds of loving commitment. But slavery tried to smother these natural feelings of affection and destroy the ties that normally united families. Frederick had never seen his siblings before he arrived at Wye House as a six-year-old. "Brothers and sisters we were by blood; but *slavery* had made us strangers," he later explained. He could only lament that his mother, like so many enslaved women, "had *many children*, but no family!" This was decidedly to the benefit of masters who fathered children with their slaves—as Aaron Anthony may well have done. In this way, slavery stood grossly contrary to the natural order established by God's will. Eventually, as a celebrated orator, Douglass would deploy many religious arguments against slavery. But the one that moved him most deeply was the cruel fact that slavery disregarded "all just ideas of the sacredness of *the family*, as an institution."[9]

Separated from the Baileys, Frederick lived at Wye House on the estate of one of the oldest and wealthiest Maryland families, whose Eastern Shore roots stretched back to the 1660s. By the early nineteenth century, the Lloyds possessed a reputation as particularly harsh and aristocratic-minded slaveholders. When Frederick lived at the Lloyd plantation, the family patriarch was Colonel Edward Lloyd V, a three-time governor of Maryland who also served twice in the U.S. Senate. Despite his political acumen, Colonel Lloyd cared chiefly about managing his vast estate. During Lloyd's lifetime, he largely ended tobacco production on the family farms and instead began growing wheat. The Lloyds produced more wheat than anyone else in Maryland, practically as much as anyone in the United States. When Frederick arrived at Wye House in 1824, 181 slaves worked there, including the 15 owned by Aaron Anthony. Douglass aptly described the Lloyd plantation as "a little nation of its own, having its own language, its own rules, regulations, and customs," utterly isolated and independent from so much of the outside world.[10]

Later in life, when Douglass recounted his childhood at Wye House, he tended to emphasize two points: slaves faced barbaric violence and slaveholding made masters immoral. Young Frederick endured many trials at the Lloyd plantation, and he forever remembered harrowing tales of violence committed by morally degenerate masters. These experiences shaped his early religious outlook. In them he caught a glimpse of how masters used Christianity to justify their violence, even as their actions made a mockery of Christian ideas about the dignity of human life.

Violence on the Lloyd plantation came in a variety of forms—from routine whippings by overseers, to lust-filled beatings of enslaved women by masters, to cold-blooded murder. Douglass remembered learning the Lord's Prayer from "Uncle" Isaac Copper, the cantankerous patriarch of the largest family of Lloyd-owned slaves. Armed with long switches, the old man had little patience with Frederick, and it did not take much to unleash the fury of his lash. Douglass remembered the whippings as a farce, an almost sixty-year-old and nearly crippled slave trying to beat piety into the young enslaved children. The whole affair certainly turned Frederick off, for a time, to the faith Copper preached. Douglass came to see something pathetic but revealing in Copper's inclination to violence against his fellow slaves: "Everybody, in the south, wants the privilege of whipping somebody else," Douglass explained. "The whip is all in all."[11]

Uncle Copper's hickory switch seemed utterly benign compared to the far more depraved acts of physical and sexual violence that Frederick witnessed. None was more terrifying than Aaron Anthony's beating of Frederick's aunt Hester. She was a fifteen-year-old girl of striking beauty, lately courted by Ned Roberts, the son of one of Colonel Lloyd's favorite slaves. As Hester and Ned grew more intimate, Anthony demanded that the two never see each other again. But Hester continued to visit Ned, which incited Anthony's jealous rage. Frederick remembered early one morning waking to Hester's desperate cries. From his bedroom, a closet in the Anthony kitchen, Frederick quietly peered out to see Hester's wrists bound together and her arms tied above her head, fastened to a hook hanging from one of the ceiling's heavy wooden joists. Hester was stripped naked to the waist. Behind her stood Anthony, his three-foot-long cowskin whip in hand. Frederick had never seen anything like this before, and the memory remained with him until the end of his life. Anthony cursed Hester as he methodically delivered blow after blow. Blood flowed down her back. Between her piercing cries she pleaded for mercy.

Frederick watched in stunned and terrified silence as Anthony delivered thirty or forty lashes, before untying Hester and letting her body fall crumpled and bloody and exposed on the kitchen floor.[12]

How is a child, no more than six or seven, supposed to make sense of such violence? At first, Frederick could not fathom why Anthony had so brutally beaten Hester. But in time, Douglass saw Hester's assault as proof of how slavery instilled in slaveholders a violent and lustful spirit, one rooted in the utter disregard of a slave's dignity as a human being created by God. In *My Bondage and My Freedom*, Douglass intimated that Anthony's chief motivation for beating Hester was a toxic mixture of lust and jealousy. If the rumors were true, and Anthony had sexually abused other slave women (Frederick's mother included), it is certainly plausible that Anthony tried to keep Hester from Ned because he wanted her solely for himself. Hester desired nothing more than to marry Ned and make a life and family with him. But Anthony refused. He degraded and oppressed Hester, and by his actions told her she deserved to be treated as something less than human.[13]

Frederick learned on the Lloyd plantation how cheaply white southerners truly valued the lives of enslaved persons, a fact most obvious when masters or overseers murdered a slave. In the plantation-rich world of the Eastern Shore, the murder of a slave—or even a free black—was rarely treated as a crime worthy of prosecution and punishment. Later in life, Douglass repeatedly told the story of the killing of a slave named Demby by the overseer Austin Gore. One day, Gore began to whip Demby, who fled and jumped into a shoulder-high creek. Gore warned Demby he would give him to the count of three to come out of the creek. Demby did not budge. Then without warning Gore fired his musket, killing Demby instantly. "His mangled body sank out of sight," as Douglass described the scene, "and blood and brains marked the water where he had stood."[14]

Demby's murder horrified the Lloyd plantation slaves, not least because Colonel Lloyd and Aaron Anthony accepted Gore's justification: Demby had become an unmanageable slave, and an example had to be made of him. Young Frederick also heard about a Mr. Thomas Lanman who killed two slaves, one by splitting open his skull with a hatchet, only to boast afterward about the crime. A Mrs. Hicks, who lived close to the Lloyd estate, beat a teenaged slave girl to death in a fit of rage because the girl failed to keep Mrs. Hicks's baby from crying through the night. The murder of slaves taught a sobering lesson to Frederick at a young age: Slavery rested on "the reckless disregard of human life," thoroughly tolerated by the supposedly Christian slaveholding South.[15]

"Gore Shooting Denby," from *The Life and Times of Frederick Douglass* (1892).

A bright child like Frederick could see only so many vicious beatings and murders before asking the hardest questions: Why are some people slaves and some masters? Why must slaves like Harriet and Demby suffer such violent oppression, even to death? When and why did slavery begin? Why am I a slave? Frederick pondered these questions while living on the Lloyd plantation. As he did, he confronted the problem of evil: Why did a supposedly all-good and all-powerful God allow evil on Earth? Did slavery's existence mean God was not all-good or all-powerful? Did it mean God simply did not exist?

Frederick posed these questions to slightly older slave children on the Lloyd plantation. Some responded by repeating the submissive proslavery gospel preached by most white southern Christians. One slave told Frederick that God made white people to be masters and black people to be slaves; the present racial social order was God's perfect design. Others merely said that God was a good creator who knew what was best for everyone, and in goodness had destined some people to live as slaves. Frederick was too intelligent and independent-minded to accept these answers. He later remembered wondering, "How did people know that God made black people to be slaves? Did they go up in the sky and learn it?" The claim that a good God ordained certain people to slavery baffled Frederick even more. He found nothing benevolent in being relegated to the life of a slave. The idea that God was responsible for slavery "pained me greatly," Douglass explained. He "wept over it long and often."[16]

Eventually, Frederick crafted his own theodicy, his own justification of the mysterious ways of God. Why were so many people trapped in bondage? "It was not *color*, but *crime*, not *God*, but *man*, that afforded the true explanation of the existence of slavery," Frederick reckoned. He blamed his enslavement not on an indifferent or malicious God but on human beings freely acting in greedy, oppressive, evil ways. Frederick reached this conclusion, in large part, by learning about slaves taken directly from Guinea, men and women "stolen from Africa—forced from their homes, and compelled to serve as slaves." After hearing their stories, Douglass said, "the whole mystery was solved at once."[17] God had not ordained these Africans to be slaves from birth. They were born free, and only later—due to the avarice of other men—were they enslaved.

It is hard to overstate how significant it was that Frederick, in his anger, did not blame God for slavery. Had he done so, he likely could never have embraced Christianity, or any religion. Much of what Douglass later came to believe about God's nature and work in the world bore traces of his earliest conviction that God was not responsible for slavery. The realization

The Seeking Slave

that wicked people, not God, created slavery soon led Frederick to another insight: "What man can make, man can unmake." If slavery was not part of God's inescapable will, but a mere human invention, then perhaps it could be abolished. Just as evil men had made slavery, so too might righteous men destroy it. At the very least, perhaps he, a single slave, could somehow win his freedom.[18]

Though he could not know it at the time, Frederick's life took a dramatic turn in 1826 that decisively set him on a once-unimaginable path to liberty. Aaron Anthony neared death and soon retired from his position at the Lloyd estate. He would no longer live in the house that he and his family and some of their slaves had occupied. The time came to decide what to do with Anthony's slaves. Some were hired out, others were returned to Anthony's farm on Tuckahoe Creek, but a different fate was in store for Frederick. Here Anthony's daughter and son-in-law—Lucretia and Thomas Auld—intervened on Frederick's behalf. Lucretia had for some time taken a special interest in Frederick, a boy she quickly recognized as uncommonly intelligent. She and Thomas arranged for Frederick to live in Baltimore with Thomas's brother and sister-in-law, Hugh and Sophia Auld. He would serve as a playmate and companion to the Aulds' young son, Tommy, as he had done with one of the Lloyd children. Sometime in mid-March 1826, with only three days' advance warning, Frederick set sail for Baltimore and the start of a new phase of his enslaved life.[19]

In his first autobiography, published in 1845, Douglass interpreted his unexpected move to Baltimore as "a special interposition of divine Providence," the first of many indications that God had "marked my life with so many favors." Douglass admitted in 1845 that this belief might strike some as "superstitious, and even egotistical," but it was the deep sentiment of his soul. As Douglass further explained ten years later in My Bondage and My Freedom, he felt certain "there was something more intelligent than *chance*, and something more certain than *luck*," in his departure from the Lloyd plantation. Hamlet expressed it best, Douglass thought: "There is a divinity that shapes our ends, / Rough hew them how we will."[20]

It was not altogether clear to Frederick where God's overruling power ended and human freedom began. Nor could he entirely explain why God intervened to ensure his freedom but allowed millions more to remain enslaved. That question, in one form or another, would remain with Douglass for the rest of his life. But in 1826, as Frederick embarked for Baltimore, he felt great hope that he would not be a slave forever. "This good spirit was from God," Douglass later wrote, "and to him I offer thanksgiving and praise."[21]

2

Religious Awakenings in Baltimore

The *Sally Lloyd* reached Baltimore early on a Sunday morning, docking at Smith's Wharf in the city's central shipping district. The eight-year-old Frederick onboard had never seen a city before. A deckhand on the *Sally Lloyd* showed Frederick the way to the Fells Point neighborhood, where Hugh and Sophia Auld lived. Walking along the city streets astounded Frederick. His "country eyes and ears were confused and bewildered."[1] The rows and rows of houses, the streets full of people freely bustling about and wearing shoes, astonished him. An entirely new world had opened up to Frederick.

All the new sights and sounds and smells that Frederick imbibed on his first day in the city could hardly compare to the even more profound awakenings that he experienced in Baltimore over the next seven years. Here Frederick would secretly learn to read and write. Here he would meet Christ, experience the new birth of salvation, and enter the fold of the African American Methodist church. In Baltimore, Frederick became literate and a Christian—the two most important developments of his late childhood, which remained deeply intertwined. Both convinced Frederick of the liberating power of the word and the truth, especially in the slave's struggle against bondage. He grew immensely in knowledge of the world and himself. Along the way, he found only further confirmation of what he had begun to believe at the Lloyd estate about God, slavery, and humanity.

When Frederick arrived in Baltimore in 1826, the city was the third largest in the United States, behind New York City and Philadelphia. By 1830, Baltimore's population had topped 80,000, a total that surpassed Philadelphia's. The city's free black population hovered around 17 percent. Slightly more than 4,000 residents were enslaved.[2] Baltimore boasted a vast shipping industry, and Fells Point was its epicenter. The shipyards dominated life in the neighborhood; nearly everyone who lived there was somehow connected to the business of building, repairing, or sailing ships. Hugh Auld had settled his family in Fells Point to try to make a fortune in the shipbuilding trade. He cared more about chasing that ambition than watching over the young slave boy sent to him by his brother Thomas. Douglass remembered Hugh as a "sour man, and of forbidding appearance," even though he never treated Frederick very cruelly. It was Sophia's gracious and gentle spirit that first welcomed Frederick into the Auld home. She had never been a slaveholder. She was born to a poor Talbot County family and worked most of her early life as a weaver. Frederick quickly came to regard her more as a mother than a slaveholding mistress. Her "beaming, benignant countenance," Douglass remembered, "seemed ever to say, 'look up, child; don't be afraid.'" Sophia was kindhearted and deeply committed to the Methodism of her childhood. Prayers, Bible reading, and hymn singing filled the Auld house, though Hugh kept his distance from Sophia's religion.[3] Sophia treated Frederick as a child deserving her love.

But eventually not even pious Sophia Auld was immune to the effects slaveholding had on a person's character. She became a far fiercer and colder woman during Frederick's time in Baltimore. Douglass recalled Sophia's transformation as proof that "slavery can change a saint into a sinner, and an angel into a demon." Even as Sophia maintained an outward pretense of Christian piety, she began to treat Frederick terribly, "as a thing destitute of a moral or an intellectual character," he later explained. At the same moment in Frederick's life when he first embraced Christianity, he also witnessed in Sophia how slaveholding could corrupt even well-meaning white Christians, blinding them to the hypocrisy of their mastery over fellow human beings.[4]

Frederick saw repeatedly in Baltimore how professed followers of Christ could ignore the suffering and oppression slaves endured. He never forgot the pitiful sight of Henrietta and Mary, the two young slave women of a Mrs. Hamilton who lived near the Aulds. Henrietta and Mary were "dejected, emaciated, mangled, and excoriated" far more terribly than Douglass had ever seen or thought possible. Mrs. Hamilton regularly whipped the slave girls with a thick cowskin, leaving their faces and shoulders brutally cut open. All this happened, Douglass later scoffed, "in the refined, church going and Christian city of Baltimore."[5] Some white people in the city thought Mrs. Hamilton acted disgracefully, but none bothered to say so publicly, much less intervene on behalf of Henrietta and Mary. Frederick saw this as a terrible sin of omission, a failure of white Christians in the city to love their black neighbors as themselves. So many of Frederick's earliest religious convictions matured in Baltimore, not least of all his growing awareness of the hypocrisy inherent in the faith of white Christians who defended slavery or even tacitly tolerated the sort of abuse endured by slaves such as Henrietta and Mary.

Frederick's main responsibility in the Auld home was to watch over two-year-old Tommy, to play with him and keep him out of harm's way. But Frederick's time in Baltimore nearly ended almost as soon as it started. Just over a year later, after Aaron Anthony's death, Frederick was sent back to the Eastern Shore. Anthony died without a will. His property was to be split equally between his three children, Lucretia Auld and her two brothers, Andrew and Richard. All of Anthony's slaves were gathered together and apportioned to his children. If Frederick had been given to Andrew or Richard, he probably would have never returned to Fells Point. Yet Lucretia won ownership of Frederick, likely through her own request, and promptly sent the boy back to Baltimore. In the end, the whole ordeal was a brief yet harrowing experience that confirmed to Douglass the precariousness of his life, how quickly his fortunes as a slave could change. By late 1826, Frederick was back in Fells Point. Soon after, the Auld family moved to a new house on Philpot Street, where Douglass would live for the next five years. He made friends with a gang of white boys who also lived on the street and whose fathers worked in the shipping business.[6]

Far more consequential to Frederick's life than his new friends in Baltimore and his work in the Auld home was his growing curiosity about a mysterious thing called reading. Douglass later traced his earliest desire to learn to read to the first time he heard the Bible read aloud. Late one Sunday night, after Frederick had fallen asleep under a table in the Auld home, he awoke to the sound of Sophia reading aloud from the book of Job. He heard these words:

> There was a man in the land of Uz, whose name was Job; and that man was perfect and upright, and one that feared God, and eschewed evil. . . . And there came a messenger unto Job, and said, The oxen were plowing, and the asses feeding beside them: And the Sabeans fell upon them, and took them away; yea, they have slain the servants with the edge of the sword; and I only am escaped alone to tell thee. While he was yet speaking, there came also another, and said, The fire of God is fallen from heaven, and hath burned up the sheep, and the servants, and consumed them; and I only am escaped alone to tell thee. While he was yet speaking, there came also another, and

said, The Chaldeans made out three bands, and fell upon the camels, and have carried them away, yea, and slain the servants with the edge of the sword; and I only am escaped alone to tell thee. While he was yet speaking, there came also another, and said, Thy sons and thy daughters were eating and drinking wine in their eldest brother's house: And, behold, there came a great wind from the wilderness, and smote the four corners of the house, and it fell upon the young men, and they are dead; and I only am escaped alone to tell thee. Then Job arose, and rent his mantle, and shaved his head, and fell down upon the ground, and worshipped, And said, Naked came I out of my mother's womb, and naked shall I return thither: the Lord gave, and the Lord hath taken away; blessed be the name of the Lord. In all this Job sinned not, nor charged God foolishly.

Why do the righteous suffer and the evil prosper? Frederick had asked that question as a child who witnessed the horrors of slavery and could not understand why he was a slave. Here, half-awake under the Auld family table, he heard of a man named Job who suffered and asked God the same question. Frederick had to know more about this Job. He reckoned it would require learning to read.

Frederick asked Sophia to teach him. She happily agreed, assuming it would be good for the young boy to know how to read the Bible. She believed it was her duty, as an ardent Methodist, to teach him. The lessons soon began, and Frederick quickly mastered the alphabet. Then he moved on to spelling. Frederick's progress elated Sophia. One day she proudly told a stunned and horrified Hugh, who demanded that the lessons end immediately. Douglass recalled that Hugh then "unfolded to her the true philosophy of slavery." It was unlawful and dangerous to teach a slave to read, he said. "If you give a nigger an inch, he will take an ell," so it was best simply to teach him only the will of his master. "Learning would spoil the best nigger in the world," Hugh continued, because slaves who knew how to read, especially the Bible, became "disconsolate and unhappy." They would inevitably try to run away.[7] Sophia promptly ended the lessons.

Hugh's speech had a strong effect on Frederick. His words were a grand revelation, a piece of essential knowledge in Frederick's childhood quest to understand how white people continued to enslave black people. Frederick assumed that Hugh was correct—that "knowledge unfits a child to be a slave," especially knowing how to read and write. He suddenly realized the surest "direct pathway from slavery to freedom." Learning to read and write took remarkable

"Mrs. Auld Teaching Him to Read," from *The Life and Times of Frederick Douglass* (1892).

determination and ingenuity, particularly under Hugh and Sophia's watchful eyes. Frederick practiced his spelling by writing out letters with a stick in the dirt at the Auld shipyard. In his attic room at night, he labored over worn and well-hidden copies of Webster's spelling book and old Methodist hymnals. Frederick's knowledge of the word came in fragments, arduously pieced together over many years. By the time he was thirteen or fourteen, he could capably read and write, the first of his great awakenings at Fells Point.[8]

Learning to read liberated Frederick. It was fitting that hearing the Bible aloud first inspired him to master reading. The same scripture Douglass heard under the Auld table one Sunday evening eventually shaped his religious sentiments and oratorical prowess. Frederick came to believe that the Bible, like literacy, contained immense power to set a slave free. The Aulds taught Frederick this lesson by doing all they could to keep him illiterate. In time, Douglass looked back on their hostile reaction as an all-too-common example of one of the chief hypocrisies of the Christian slaveholding South: Devout masters did all they could to keep the sacred truth of the Gospel from their slaves. Yet the confounding experience of Job, who heard God in the whirlwind, proved far too compelling to a young boy who had wrestled with the problem of evil. Nothing could keep Frederick from the Bible and from learning to read.

Not long after Frederick mastered reading and writing, he acquired a copy of *The Columbian Orator*, a book second only to the Bible in its significance to Douglass's life. After hearing a group of white boys memorizing passages from the book one day, Frederick bought a copy of the fifty-cent schoolbook. *The Columbian Orator* was an anthology of speeches, poems, and dialogues first assembled by Caleb Bingham in 1797. Bingham, a Massachusetts educator, hoped his primer would instill patriotism and classical republican virtues in the young children of the new American republic, while also providing a model of eloquent rhetoric. American schools widely used the book in the first half of the nineteenth century.[9]

It was quite ordinary for a white boy of thirteen or fourteen to have read passages from *The Columbian Orator*. But the book's lofty excerpts on liberty and democracy were altogether revolutionary in the hands of a literate slave. Frederick read *The Columbian Orator* avidly, and it transformed him. It "added much to my limited stock of language," Douglass explained, "and enabled me to give tongue to many interesting thoughts, which had frequently flashed through my soul, and died away for want of utterance."[10] As a future orator and moral thinker, Douglass received many of his first lessons from *The Columbian Orator*.

Decades later, Douglass remembered several particular excerpts that most affected his heart, soul, and mind: a dialogue between a master a slave, and speeches by Richard Sheridan, William Pitt, and Charles James Fox. None of these selections were conventional theological treatises or sermons, but they were immensely important to Frederick's early moral and theological formation. Collectively, they offered Frederick an answer to the great question of his childhood: Why am I a slave? They corroborated the answer Frederick had first reached at the Lloyd plantation: God ordained no one to slavery. Human oppression and wickedness alone created and sustained the institution.

To Douglass, the excerpt that made this argument most effectively was the imagined "Dialogue between a Master and Slave." The dialogue begins with the master reprimanding his slave for again attempting to run away. At first, the slave does not defend his actions, preferring instead, as he says, to "submit to my fate."[11] But with the master's prodding, the slave eventually launches a full-scale intellectual assault on slavery. His liberty was taken from him without his consent, he says. Slave merchants captured and sold him. After being sent to a foreign land, his master treated him like a piece of livestock, not a human being. The slave has a compelling reply to every argument and rationalization the master can muster. The slave's case is so convincing that the master willingly frees the slave. "It is scarcely necessary to say," Douglass later wrote, "that a dialogue, with such an origin, and such an ending—read when the fact of my being a slave was a constant burden of grief—powerfully affected me."[12] Frederick memorized the entire passage. He longed for the day when he too might converse with his own master on slavery and win his freedom.

At one point in the passage, the master resorts to a classic pillar of the Christian proslavery argument: "It is in the order of Providence that one man should become subservient to another." Frederick had heard this same point made on the Lloyd estate—that God benevolently destined some people to an enslaved life. The slave's witty reply is effectively the same counterargument Frederick had reached at Wye House. "The robber who puts a pistol to your breast may make just the same plea," the slave sarcastically says. "Providence gives him a power over your life and property."[13] Here the dialogue confirmed Frederick's conviction that a good God surely could not sanction slavery, but that evil men certainly could enslave others and justify their greedy actions by appealing to God's will.

After reading *The Columbian Orator*, Douglass said he never wondered if "the Almighty, in some way, ordained slavery, and willed my enslavement for his own glory." The book poured into Douglass's mind "floods of light on the nature and character of slavery," especially that its origin rested in "the power and the avarice of man." Frederick never again entertained the thought that God required some people to submit meekly to slavery. Thereafter, Douglass said, "I almost lost my patience when I found any colored man weak enough to believe such stuff." As Douglass hardened in his belief that God had not established slavery, he also grew angrier over how this false idea could instill in slaves a quietly submissive spirit. Douglass therefore devoted himself to demolishing the myth of God-ordained slavery. Yet, as he had already learned at the Lloyd estate, greater knowledge often leads only to greater suffering. *The Columbian Orator* opened up Douglass's heart and mind but exposed it to pain as much as pleasure. No pain was greater than the utter injustice of his enslavement.[14]

At the age of thirteen, Frederick experienced the second great awakening of his life at Fells Point. He converted formally to Christianity, shepherded along the way by white and black Baltimore Methodists. Frederick's inquisitive mind had long meditated on religious questions, but now he came to believe his debilitating sin left him in "need of God, as a father and protector."[15] He embraced a distinctly evangelical kind of Christianity—with its heavy emphasis on salvation through Christ's death and resurrection, and on the centrality of the Bible as authoritative in the life of a believer. Frederick found liberating truth in the Christian gospel, as a sinner and a slave. In time, as he unleashed his prophetic voice, Frederick turned continually to the Christian faith he first embraced as a child—for he discerned in its precepts, when rightly understood, a powerful witness against slavery, hypocrisy, and oppression.

Frederick found in Baltimore a network of Methodist churches ready to satisfy his spiritual curiosity and hunger for knowledge. He came of age during a momentous rupture in the American Methodist church, the formation in 1816 of an independent black Methodist denomination, the African Methodist Episcopal (AME) Church. Across the late 1790s and early 1800s, dozens of independent black churches were formed throughout the nation, none more famously than Richard Allen's Bethel Methodist Church in Philadelphia. Allen decided to establish the new congregation when in 1792 his existing church finished a new sanctuary and forced its black members to sit in a segregated gallery. By 1794, Allen led the founding of Bethel Methodist Church, a black congregation that still remained part of the white-controlled Methodist Episcopal Church (MEC). It was a common trend within the MEC in the early 1800s. Many major cities, Baltimore included, had semi-independent African American Methodist congregations affiliated with the MEC.[16]

Battles inevitably emerged over just how autonomous such black churches should be. In Philadelphia, white MEC leaders resisted Allen's efforts to secure greater independence for Bethel church, especially over the control of its property and its ability to name its own preachers. Further fueling the conflict was the refusal of Methodist authorities to ordain Allen, which kept him from presiding over the observance of the sacraments at Bethel. The fight reached the courts, but eventually Bethel won its full legal independence from the MEC. Soon after, Allen and others set in motion plans to form the AME Church and thereby secure true religious autonomy for black Methodists.[17] In cities with prominent free black populations, the formation of the AME Church forced a momentous and not always easy decision on African American Methodists. Would they continue to attend MEC congregations or join the AME Church, even if that meant severing existing religious ties and establishing a new congregation in their city?

Black Methodists in Baltimore—a major stronghold of the denomination—certainly faced this dilemma. By 1812 there were three major MEC-affiliated black congregations in Baltimore: Sharp Street, Dallas Street, and Asbury Church. Sharp Street was the largest and most prominent of the three. Its congregation included many competent and compelling lay leaders, black men who had been licensed as exhorters and prayer-meeting leaders. But the church still remained formally under the authority of two white ministers. By 1815, discontent over matters of black ordination, autonomy, and equality in Baltimore's Methodist churches erupted. That year, a group of black churchgoers established the "African Methodist Bethel Church Society." When the AME Church was formally established the next year, the Bethel church of Baltimore was among its founding members. Around 200 of the city's approximately 1,400 black Methodist church members joined the new congregation. Frederick had made friends with some free black boys whose families worshipped at Bethel. But just prior to his conversion, Frederick attended a Sabbath School at Dallas Street. Even so, after his conversion, Frederick joined Bethel, the beginning of a life-long association, often contentious, with the AME Church.[18]

As a spiritually seeking thirteen-year-old, Frederick took his first steps toward conversion after hearing a white Methodist minister named Hanson preach. When or where or how often he heard Hanson (likely an itinerant preacher), Douglass did not record. But he never forgot the substance of the gospel Hanson proclaimed. "He thought that all men, great and small, bond and free, were sinners in the sight of God," Douglass remembered, "that they were, by nature, rebels against His government; and that they must repent

        The Seeking Slave

of their sins, and be reconciled to God, through Christ." There was a certain radical equality in this message that appealed to Frederick. The slaveholding master was no more righteous than his slave. But, initially, Frederick found as much confusion as clarity in this gospel. He accepted fully that he was "wretched, and had no means of making myself otherwise." But Frederick struggled to understand what exactly God required of him as a penitent sinner in search of redemption.[19]

He turned for help to Charles Johnson, a black lay preacher and caulker he had met at Bethel. Johnson, "in tones of holy affection," told Frederick to pray to God for merciful deliverance from sin. But salvation did not come quickly to Frederick. For weeks he remained "a poor, broken-hearted mourner, traveling through the darkness and misery of doubts and fear." Redemption and liberation came only after he cast all his cares upon God, Douglass later wrote. He had found faith in Jesus Christ "as the Redeemer, Friend, and Savior of those who diligently seek Him."[20]

Frederick saw the world anew after his conversion. To him, a "new light" had descended upon all creation, which he now perceived more clearly than ever before. More than anything else, Frederick's heart filled with love unlike any he had ever experienced. "I loved all mankind—slaveholders not excepted," Douglass wrote. At the same time, he abhorred slavery as never before. Frederick always hungered for knowledge, but after his conversion he had an insatiable desire to read and understand the Bible. Acquiring his own copy remained no simple task for a slave, even one living in the home of a Methodist like Sophia Auld. Frederick searched the filthy street gutters of Baltimore for scattered and discarded pages of the Bible. Once found, he would meticulously wash, dry, and read them, hoping to acquire "a word or two of wisdom."[21]

Soon after Frederick's conversion was complete, he forged a close relationship with Charles Lawson, a fellow member of Bethel and the man Douglass called his "spiritual father." "Uncle" Lawson was an elderly free black man who drove a dray for a rope-maker in Fells Point. Douglass never met a more devout man in his entire life. Lawson prayed without ceasing. "His life was a life of prayer," Douglass wrote, "and his words . . . were about a better world." Lawson lived close to the Aulds, and he and Frederick spent many hours together on Sundays. They attended prayer meetings and afterward read together, united by a shared spirit of "singing, praying and glorifying God." More than anyone else, Lawson instructed Frederick in the spirit and truth of the new faith he had embraced. When the Aulds finally became aware of the time Frederick spent at Lawson's place, Hugh demanded that their visits end. Hugh must have reckoned that no good could come from Frederick's spending so many hours with a free black man. Hugh threatened to whip Frederick if he disobeyed, but Frederick continued to meet with Lawson anyway.[22]

As Frederick's "spiritual father," Lawson gave him hope that God had destined him for more than the life of a slave. Lawson told Frederick the Lord had planned for the boy to accomplish a great work. He must be ready to preach the true gospel to a people that needed to hear it, Lawson said, which meant Frederick should continue to diligently study the Bible. Young Frederick could hardy imagine how he might accomplish so much. "The good Lord would bring it to pass in his own good time," Lawson assured him. When Frederick lamented that he would surely remain a slave for his entire life, Lawson replied, "The Lord can make you free." If you want liberty, Lawson said, "ask the Lord for it, *in faith*," and he will provide. Decades later, Douglass realized fully how his time with Uncle Lawson changed his entire "character and destiny." "He threw my thoughts into a channel from which they have never entirely diverged," Douglass explained in 1855. Lawson encouraged Frederick's intense quest for knowledge. He assured the unknown slave boy that he would someday be "a useful man in the world." Douglass's conversion to Christianity likely would not have made him the man he became were it not for Charles Lawson.[23]

Even before Hugh and Sophia Auld learned of Frederick's relationship with Lawson, they certainly noticed the boy's spiritual transformation. Both "seemed to respect my conscientious piety," Douglass thought, perhaps because Sophia remained a professing Methodist. Frederick frequently heard the white Methodist minister Beverly Waugh pray and preach in the Auld home. Waugh became a leading MEC bishop, but at the time he was the presiding elder over the East Baltimore Methodist station, which included the church Sophia attended, Wilk Street. Waugh apparently felt a keen obligation to guard Sophia from backsliding, so he visited the Auld house often.[24] In doing so, he provided Frederick the chance to hear directly from a white MEC clergyman.

When Douglass wrote about his conversion in *My Bondage and My Freedom*, he carefully explained the spiritual debt he owed to Hanson, Johnson, Lawson, and Waugh. He hoped readers would "form an idea of the precise influences which had to do with shaping and directing my mind."[25] Like so many Americans of the early nineteenth century, Frederick came to Christ under the guidance of Methodist ministers and laymen. After his long-coming conversion, Frederick was never again quite the same person. Along with learning to read, it was the second major moment in his young intellectual development, central to the formation of his moral and political convictions.

Even though Douglass nurtured a kind of lover's quarrel with American Christianity, especially African American Methodism, for the rest of his life he never fully departed from the faith he worked out by age thirteen. Despite his many frustrations with the state of religion in America, and his often bitter condemnations of churches and clergy, Douglass could no more abandon Christianity than he could abandon his antislavery witness. Douglass owed so much of the power and clarity of his prophetic voice to his conversion. He became America's prophet because of the religion he embraced in Fells Point. A prophet must know how to speak, a skill Frederick acquired through literacy; but a prophet must also know what to speak, which Frederick discovered in large measure from his Christian faith.

In Baltimore, Frederick left childhood behind. He grew in knowledge of God and humanity and slavery. All the while, Fells Point truly became his home. But in March 1833, Hugh Auld sent Frederick back to the Eastern Shore at the demand of Thomas Auld. It was another great rupture in Frederick's life, and a particularly cruel one to a boy who had improbably found friends and religious mentors in Baltimore. A petty quarrel between Hugh and Thomas prompted the move. Thomas wanted Hugh to care for a crippled slave named Henny as payment for his free usage of Frederick, but Hugh refused. Thomas felt disrespected by his seemingly ungrateful brother, so in retaliation he demanded that Frederick return from Baltimore. "It did seem that every time the young tendrils of my affection became attached, they were rudely broken by some unnatural outside power," Douglass later reflected.[26] He had been away from the Eastern Shore for seven years. He returned an entirely different person, soon to face the darkest moment of his life as a slave.

From the Valley of Shadows to Freedom

During the three years Frederick spent on the Eastern Shore from 1833 to 1836, his new faith in Christ endured a great trial. In light of the evil reality of his enslavement, he could not help but question again God's goodness and the truth of the Christian gospel. Frederick's teenage years on the Eastern Shore were the most demanding and demoralizing of his life as a slave—years that left him physically exhausted and tested his deepest moral and spiritual convictions. Yet after passing through this dark valley, Frederick discovered that the joy and assurance he found in his faith had only deepened. Frederick returned to Baltimore in 1836 as a man, in more ways than one. After three years of hard labor as a field hand, he arrived back in the city bearing an imposing physical stature and newfound religious maturity. He saw clearer than ever the hypocrisy of slaveholding Christianity and the liberating power of literacy and truth. He had seized with unshakeable certainty upon certain convictions about God and slavery that he would never fully abandon and that would shape so much of the rest of his life.[1]

St. Michaels, Maryland, was once a prosperous shipbuilding community, but when Frederick arrived there in 1833 it "wore a dull, slovenly, enterprise-forsaken aspect," he recalled. Most white locals made a living through oyster fishing, though the area still boasted several old plantation estates with regal homes. Thomas Auld and his new wife, Rowena, treated Frederick far worse than the Aulds of Fells Point. Thomas possessed a violent temper and mean spirit. He was "entirely destitute of every element of character capable of inspiring respect," Frederick thought. Thomas acquired his slaves through marriage, and he never quite learned how to be a master. He acted with wild inconsistency toward his slaves, "at times rigid, and at times lax," which only heightened his inclination toward injustice, Frederick remembered. Thomas's lately deceased first wife, Lucretia, had been kind to Frederick, but Rowena was both a religious and pitifully cruel mistress, a doubly awful influence on Thomas, Frederick believed.[2]

Frederick now endured "the painful gnawings of hunger" for the first time in several years. The Aulds provided their slaves a coarse and meager supply of food, a half-bushel of cornmeal each week and little else. The slaves rarely received meat or vegetables. Facing starvation, Frederick and his fellow slaves often had to beg or steal to survive. The Aulds, meanwhile, hoarded for themselves far more food than they could possibly eat before it spoiled. Frederick could not believe how Rowena, "with saintly air, would kneel with her husband, and pray each morning that a merciful God would bless them in basket and in store, and save them, at last, in this kingdom." To offer such hypocritical prayers to the Almighty while her slaves starved seemed to Frederick to tempt an outpouring of God's wrath.[3]

For a brief moment in August 1833, Frederick hoped for a dramatic transformation in his life in St. Michaels. At a Methodist camp revival meeting, in a wooded area about eight miles from the Auld home, Thomas was saved and became a member of a Methodist congregation. Thomas was no stranger to the Methodist community of St. Michaels. Ministers had frequently visited his home to exhort him to repent, but to no avail. Frederick traveled with Thomas to the late summer revival. Though seated in a separate segregated section of the tent that housed the services, Frederick saw one of the preachers lead Thomas to the altar to make his profession of faith. Auld's flushed face, disheveled hair, and quiet groaning seemed like evidence of a true conversion. But something in Thomas's demeanor unsettled Frederick. He never forgot the sight of "a stray tear halting on [Auld's] cheek," which Frederick worried might testify to the half-heartedness of Thomas's transformation. Still, Frederick thought that if Thomas truly had embraced Christ he would emancipate his slaves, for no true Christian could hold another human being in bondage. At the very least, Frederick hoped that Thomas would treat his slaves more kindly.[4]

Auld soon disappointed Frederick. If anything, after his conversion, Auld acted more cruelly toward his slaves. His "whole countenance was *soured* over with the seemings of piety," Douglass remembered. Auld became more "rigid and stringent" to dispel any false hopes that he had gone meek after meeting Christ. Auld grew more violent toward his slaves, and now justified whippings with scripture: "He that knoweth his master's will, and doeth it not, shall be beaten with many stripes." To make matters worse, the Methodists of

St. Michaels warmly welcomed Thomas into their fold. They had no problem calling Thomas a true follower of Christ, despite the fact that he beat and half-starved his slaves. Itinerant Methodist ministers began staying at the Auld home during their travels. The ministers feasted on sumptuous meals, apparently indifferent to both the earthly plight and heavenly fate of the Auld slaves. "They seemed almost as unconcerned about our getting to heaven, as they were about our getting out of slavery," Frederick recalled. The Methodist pulpits in St. Michaels preached to slaves a proslavery gospel of cheerful submission. Frederick remembered ministers exhorting him to obey his master as an act of obedience to God, to accept that the Lord had ordained him to work as a slave, and to look upon his enslavement as "a merciful and beneficial arrangement."[5] The message fell on deaf ears. Frederick had spent too much time with Uncle Lawson and the black Methodists of Bethel Church to accept this proslavery Christianity.

Frederick concluded that Christianity had made Auld only "more cruel and hateful in all his ways." At St. Michaels, Frederick witnessed again much of the proslavery religious hypocrisy he earlier had seen in Baltimore. But now, with Thomas Auld, he saw something even worse: a slaveholder made more evil by his new faith. "The natural wickedness of his heart had not been removed, but only reinforced, by the profession of religion," Douglass explained. Frederick, the recent convert, now faced an unsettling question: Should he still hold to a faith that Christian slaveholders like Auld used so easily to justify violent oppression? Frederick saw more clearly than ever how readily masters could appeal to religion to sanctify their slaveholding. But he also hardened in his certainty that any Christianity that condoned bigotry and oppression was a false gospel.[6]

Frederick did not abandon Christianity when he saw how vicious it made his master and how indifferent it left many white Methodist ministers to the plight of slaves. Instead, his faith inspired him to attend to the intellectual and spiritual well-being of St. Michaels slaves by helping to start a Sabbath School in the area. To the whites of St. Michaels, it was a radically dangerous plan; most of them looked with suspicion on any attempt to teach African Americans, free or enslaved, how to read. A "pious young man" named Wilson asked Frederick if he would like to teach at the school, which would meet at the home of James Mitchell, a free black man. Wilson collected old spelling books and copies of the Bible. About twenty students gathered on Sundays at Mitchell's. "Here, thought I, is something worth living for," Douglass recalled, "here is an excellent chance for usefulness." He hoped to find in the school the same companionship he had known in Baltimore with men like Uncle Lawson.[7]

The Sabbath School hardly went unnoticed by St. Michaels slaveholders. At the school's second meeting, an armed white mob rushed into Mitchell's home and demanded that the group never meet again. One man shouted to Frederick that they would not tolerate on the Eastern Shore another Nat Turner, the slave who in 1831 led an insurrection in Southampton County, Virginia, that killed nearly sixty whites. To the white gang gathered there, teaching slaves to read and write led inevitably to rebellion. Douglass never forgot that at the head of the mob were "professedly holy men," Methodist class leaders and lay dignitaries, including Thomas Auld. Frederick could not understand how these supposed followers of Christ could react with such anger to "simply teaching a few colored children how to read the gospel of the Son of God."[8]

To Douglass, the short-lived fate of the Sabbath School exposed the religious hypocrisy of white slaveholders. Men like Auld professed Christ as Lord, and insisted all men and women needed redemption, yet they denied their slaves the chance to read God's word. As long as the Bible supplied key support to the prevailing proslavery argument, masters surely would deny their slaves the chance to read and interpret scripture for themselves. Christian masters far preferred their slaves "to drink whisky, to wrestle, fight and to do other unseemly things," Douglass argued, than to read the word of God. The violent breaking-up of the Sabbath School depressed Frederick. "The cloud over my St. Michaels home grew heavier and blacker than ever," he wrote. Frederick again faced a familiar question: Could he possibly subscribe to the faith professed by oppressive, hypocritical masters like Auld? Perhaps more than anything, though, the entire episode confirmed a revolutionary truth Frederick had learned in Baltimore: Literacy and the Christian gospel, especially when united, offered liberating power to a slave.[9]

Frederick's determination to start a Sabbath School convinced Thomas that city life had made him a rebellious and troublemaking slave. Thomas tried several times to whip Frederick into submission. When that failed, he sent Frederick away to be "broken." He was to spend a year with Edward Covey, a man known in the region for his talents at breaking insubordinate slaves of their stubbornness. Covey was a poor twenty-eight-year-old former overseer who farmed about 150 acres of rented land. Area slaveholders frequently sent "troublesome" slaves like Frederick to Covey, an arrangement that provided him cheap labor to till his farm. In January 1834, as a bitterly cold wind cut across his face, Frederick walked to Covey's rented land. For the first time in his life, Frederick worked as a true field hand. "I was now about to sound profounder depths in slave life," Douglass recalled, for the rigors of the field and the cruelties of Covey awaited him in 1834.[10]

Covey was an appealing "slave breaker" to men like Thomas Auld because he was a pious Methodist, a devoted church member and class leader. He gathered everyone on his farm together for morning and evening prayers, a time of devotion that began with the singing of a hymn. Covey was a poor singer, so he often called upon Frederick to lead the hymn, who sometimes refused. Frederick saw these moments of supposed Christian fellowship as a gross mockery. Covey's "religion was a thing altogether apart from his worldly concerns," Frederick said. "He knew nothing of it as a holy principle, directing and controlling his daily life, making the latter conform to the requirements of the gospel." To Frederick, Covey was another classic religious hypocrite—a hearer of the gospel and a professor of Christ, but not a *doer* of God's commandments.[11]

Covey purchased only one slave, according to Frederick, and he boasted that he bought her simply "as a breeder." Covey hired another man to live with the slave woman, Caroline, for a year and do all he could to impregnate her. At the end of the year, Caroline gave birth to twins, two children Covey now owned. He and his wife were "ecstatic with joy," Frederick remembered. Having embraced Christianity, Frederick could not fathom how professed believers like the Coveys could shamelessly compel "undisguised and unmitigated fornication, as a means of increasing his human stock."[12] Covey further convinced Frederick that slaveholding thoroughly corrupted a man's moral sensibility, leaving him with a hollow faith far from any true righteousness.

Frederick called Covey "the snake," for he was slyly deceptive and always seeking ways to strike fear into the hearts of his slaves. When Covey checked on his slaves as they worked, he never approached them in a direct and open manner. Instead, he would "creep and crawl, in ditches and gullies; hide behind stumps and bushes," Frederick remembered. Covey's cunning left Frederick and the other slaves always feeling insecure, never quite certain in any moment if Covey was watching them. He would mount his horse and appear to ride away toward St. Michaels, yet thirty minutes later be lying in a ditch or lurking behind a fence spying on the slaves.[13]

Covey inspired fear and anxiety because he resorted often to violence. Frederick received his first whipping less than three days after arriving at Covey's farm, a flogging that left sores on his back for weeks. As some kind of cruel joke, Covey made Frederick drive a yoke of unbroken oxen deep into a forest to gather recently chopped wood. Frederick had never handled oxen before, and Covey gave him no real direction. The oxen set off at a breakneck speed through the forest, eventually smashing the oxcart into a tree and knocking the wheels and body apart. Frederick persevered in repairing the cart and gathering the wood, but on his journey back the oxen crushed a gate erected on the path home. When Covey learned the full story of what had happened, he led Frederick back into the woods, cut off shoots from a blackgum tree, and used them to whip Frederick.[14]

The exhausting work and merciless floggings only continued during Frederick's year with Covey. From dawn to dusk Frederick toiled in the field, long and hard labor that tested the limits of his physical and mental strength. To make matters worse, Covey beat Frederick constantly, at least once a week for the first six months he was on the farm. "Aching bones and a sore back were my constant companions," Frederick recalled. With the relentless work and abuse, Covey succeeded for a time in utterly wrecking Frederick. "I was broken in body, soul, and spirit," Douglass later admitted. "My natural elasticity was crushed, my intellect languished, the disposition to read departed, the cheerful spark that lingered about my eye died; the dark night of slavery closed in upon me." Auld had sent Frederick to Covey hoping to transform him into an unthinking piece of property that submitted wholly to his master's will. Frederick had learned to read; he had learned the meaning of freedom; he had learned the call of the true Christianity of Christ. But now, Covey endeavored to reduce him to a mere brute. Frederick felt as if he had little strength left to resist.[15]

As Frederick walked through this valley, he often looked out from the Covey farm upon the Chesapeake Bay. He would stand alone on the banks of the bay in the stillness of Sabbath mornings and gaze upon the white sails of vessels that had traveled all across the globe. The majestic ships were like "shrouded ghosts" to Frederick. They tormented him, a constant reminder of his wretched enslavement. They nobly departed to open waters, and he remained chained to the Eastern Shore. During his year with Covey, Frederick faced again the spiritual crisis of his childhood. He once again tried to understand why God allowed the injustice of his bondage. Seeing countless ships move freely into the Atlantic Ocean only heightened the dark crisis of faith Douglass endured at Covey's farm.[16]

In his misery one Sabbath morning on the bay's banks, with no audience but God, Frederick uttered his "soul's complaint." He cried out to the ships a psalm of lament:

You are loosed from your moorings, and are free; I am fast in my chains, and am a slave! You move merrily before the gentle gale, and I sadly before the bloody whip! You are freedom's swift-winged angels, that fly round the world; I am confined in bands of iron! O that I were free! O, that I were on one of your gallant decks, and under your protecting wing! Alas! betwixt me and you, the turbid waters roll. Go on, go on. O that I could also go! Could I but swim! If I could fly! O, why was I born a man, of whom to make a brute! The glad ship is gone; she hides in the dim distance. I am left in the hottest hell of unending slavery. O God, save me! God, deliver me! Let me be free! Is there any God? Why am I a slave?

Frederick could not comprehend why God would forsake him. Despair shrouded his quest for understanding, his quest to wrest some kind of meaning from his seemingly senseless oppression. As he cried out to God, Frederick's sorrow slowly transformed into hope for deliverance. He resolved on the banks to do his part to win his freedom: "I will run away. I will not stand it. . . . Only think of it; one hundred miles straight north, and I am free! Try it? Yes! God helping me, I will. It cannot be that I shall live and die a slave."[17]

Not long after this lonely morning on the Chesapeake Bay, Frederick endured the greatest trial and rebirth of his life. One hot August day, Frederick and several other slaves fanned the wheat harvest, a tedious and exhausting process of separating grain and kernels from chaff. Late in the afternoon, Frederick suffered a heatstroke. He collapsed, knocked off his feet by a violent headache and extreme dizziness. The whole process of fanning the wheat came to a halt. Covey arrived and saw Frederick helplessly resting in a bit of shade near a fence. Covey ordered Frederick back to work, but he could barely speak, much less stand on his feet. An agitated Covey then began to beat Frederick, first kicking him in the side and then striking him across the head. The blows cut open Frederick's head and blood flowed heavily across his face. He decided in that moment to flee to Thomas Auld and seek his protection.[18]

Frederick started for St. Michaels almost immediately. He staggered through the woods, head bloodied, still suffering from the effects of the heatstroke. He collapsed more than once, unsure if he could continue the seven-mile journey to Auld. Douglass recalled lying on the hard forest floor for nearly an hour, on the brink of utter defeat, "my mind passing over the whole scale or circle of belief and unbelief, from faith in the overruling providence of God, to the blackest atheism." When Frederick finally arrived at his master's home five hours later, blood and dust and briers and thorns covered him from head to toe.[19]

The Seeking Slave

Frederick hoped his Christian master would show him mercy. For a brief moment, Auld did seem affected by Frederick's presently pitiful condition. Yet Thomas's heart soon turned cold. He eventually defended Covey and condemned Frederick, disbelieving the story of his heatstroke. Frederick had little energy left to argue with Auld. He made one final appeal, suggesting Covey would kill him if he returned. Auld rejected the idea as nonsense—for Covey, he said, was a good religious man. Auld allowed Frederick to stay the night in St. Michaels, but the next morning he sent him back to Covey.[20]

When Frederick arrived midmorning on Saturday, Covey immediately darted after him, cowskin and rope in hand. He intended to tie up and whip Frederick as never before. A panicked Frederick fled quickly through a tall cornfield and into the woods, eluding Covey. Hungry and weary, with blood still caked on his unwashed clothes, life had become a great burden to Frederick. The somber silence of the woods invited prayers to God for deliverance. But Frederick struggled to pray as he had before. The "sham of religion which everywhere prevailed, cast in my mind a doubt upon all religion," he remembered. Once again, the violent hypocrisy of proslavery Christianity made Frederick wonder if *all* religion, Christianity included, was a lie. He felt as if all his "prayers were unavailing and delusive." Frederick could only look above to the quiet heavens and wonder, "What had I done, what had my parents done, that such a life as this should be mine?"[21]

That night, a kindhearted slave named Sandy Jenkins found Frederick in the woods. Sandy was on his way to spend the Sabbath with his wife, a free woman. Sandy and his wife sheltered Frederick in her home that evening. They fed and safely harbored him, despite the risk of floggings or imprisonment. Douglass later called Sandy his "good Samaritan," a man who had "almost providentially, found me, and helped me when I could not help myself." In his later autobiographies, Douglass explicitly said that while Sandy was a "religious man," he also was "a genuine African, and had inherited some of the so called magical powers, said to be possessed by African and eastern nations." The faith Sandy adhered to was not the evangelical Christianity professed by men like Auld or Covey or even Frederick. Sandy entertained some spiritual beliefs that Frederick questioned. Yet Sandy still *acted* in a manner far more faithful to a true and righteous faith, as Frederick understood it, than supposedly sterling slaveholding Methodists like Auld and Covey.[22]

After Sandy and his wife fed Frederick, it came time to discuss what he must do next. Should he return to Covey or attempt to run away? Sandy counseled against fleeing. But he also suggested that Frederick return to Covey's with a special herb, a highly prized root "possessing all the powers required for my protection." If Frederick tucked the root in his right pocket, Covey would not be able to strike him as before, Sandy said. Frederick found the proposal "very absurd and ridiculous, if not positively sinful." It seemed too close to unsacred "dealings with the devil." But Sandy would not relent in the face of Frederick's skepticism. Perhaps it would do Frederick no good, Sandy granted, but it also would do him no harm. Frederick relented and took the root and carried it on his right side. To the very end of his life, Frederick never forgot the compassionate hospitality he received when he needed it the most from Sandy and his wife. Though still tormented by doubts about God's goodness, when he thought of his night with Sandy, Frederick could only conclude, "How did I know but that the hand of the Lord was in it?"[23]

Early Sunday morning, Frederick returned to Covey's farm. When he arrived he found Covey and his wife dressed in their Sunday best, on their way to church. Covey looked kindly on Frederick, inquired how he was, and softly asked him to round up some wayward pigs. For a moment, Frederick wondered if Sandy's herb did possess some magical power. Yet he soon suspected that "the *Sabbath*, and not the *root*," was the real reason for Covey's behavior. The compassion Covey showed Frederick on Sunday alone made more grossly apparent the true hollowness of his faith. "He had more respect for the *day* than for the *man*, for whom the day was mercifully given," Douglass later wrote, "for while he would cut and slash my body during the week, he would not hesitate, on Sunday, to teach me the value of my soul, or the way of life and salvation by Jesus Christ."[24] Covey made a feeble attempt to be like Christ on Sunday. But during the rest of the week, his faith had no bearing on how he treated others, especially slaves.

By Monday morning, Covey was a new man. But so too was Frederick. He resolved to defend and protect himself if Covey tried to attack him. He had cast aside completely the proslavery Christian message he once heard about his duty to submit to his master's will. That morning, as Frederick fed the horses, Covey snuck up behind him in the stable. He tried to knock Frederick off his feet and tie him up. But the "fighting madness" came upon Frederick. He seized a shocked Covey by the throat, and dug in his nails so tightly that blood flowed from Covey's neck. Covey broke free but failed repeatedly to subdue Frederick. He cried out for help to one of his cousins passing by. Yet Frederick swiftly kicked the cousin in the stomach, who then fled doubled over in pain.[25]

By now, in the face of Frederick's resistance, Covey had lost something of his usual tenacity. Covey did not give up the fight, but he could not beat Frederick alone. He called out for help to several other slaves, yet none complied. The struggle continued for two hours. Finally, an exhausted Covey relented and ordered Frederick back to work. His pride wounded after clearly losing the battle, Covey could only sputter, "I would not have whipped you half so much as I have had you not resisted." Covey never again beat Frederick during the remaining six months he lived on his farm. Nor did Covey report Frederick's resistance to Auld or other nearby authorities—which, had he done so, could easily have resulted in Frederick's execution. Frederick assumed that Covey kept his silence about the whole episode to preserve his profitable reputation as a "negro breaker."[26]

Frederick's triumph over Covey was a kind of glorious rebirth in his life as a slave. "It was a resurrection from the dark and pestiferous tomb of slavery, to the heaven of comparative freedom," Douglass later wrote. He may still have been a slave, but he was no longer a trembling, servile coward in Covey's presence. Frederick acquired a new self-respect and self-confidence: "I was *nothing* before; I was a man now." He discovered that by defying a cruel master, he found his dignity as a human being. Frederick never doubted that in resisting Covey he had acted in a righteous manner, as the Lord required. Yet when he told the story of his battle with Covey, Frederick also never explained his victory by crediting God's protection or deliverance. Perhaps God had sent Sandy Jenkins to Frederick in his moment of hopeless despair. But, for the rest of his life, Frederick believed his battle with Covey was *his* victory, the product of *his* hardy resolve and courage and endurance, not simply a miraculous intervention from God.[27]

On Christmas Day 1834, Frederick's time with Covey ended. After a week's rest, traditionally afforded slaves between Christmas and New Year's Day, Frederick proceeded to the worn-out farm of William Freeland, three miles from St. Michaels. Auld had hired Frederick out to Freeland for the upcoming year. Frederick worked to prepare Freeland's farm to grow corn and wheat, an exhausting task. Yet Frederick soon found that Freeland could not have been more unlike Covey or Auld. Freeland possessed some of the vices of his slaveholding class, but he still retained a "sense of justice," Douglass wrote, and none of Covey's "mean and selfish characteristics." Even more important to Frederick, Freeland was not religious. He had made no profession of faith, nor did he attend any church. Douglass believed it was no coincidence that his kindest master was also his least religious. His life as a slave had convinced him that having an ostensibly pious slaveholder for a master was the worst fate any slave could face.[28]

Freeland's example further persuaded Frederick that religion brought out the worst in slaveholders. Christianity as practiced by masters was "a mere covering for the most horrid crimes; the justifier of the most appalling barbarity; a sanctifier of the most hateful frauds; and a secure shelter, under which the darkest, foulest, grossest, and most infernal abominations fester and flourish." The three years Frederick spent back on the Eastern Shore left him certain that religious slaveholders were the cruelest of all. "I have found them, almost invariably, the vilest, meanest and basest of their class," Douglass later wrote. Freeland's character only confirmed this conviction. When Douglass described Freeland in his autobiographies, he also intentionally mentioned the Reverend Daniel Weeden, a Methodist minister who lived on a nearby farm. Weeden's seeming piety was matched only by his violent cruelty toward his slaves. Frederick remembered how Weeden's lash kept the back of one slave named Ceal "literally raw."[29] The comparative humanity of the irreligious Freeland only made more grotesque the violent cruelty of religious slaveholders like Weeden, Covey, and Auld.

Frederick's year with Freeland passed much more smoothly than his year with Covey. Freeland "was the best master I ever had, until I became my own master," Douglass said. He had the opportunity to establish another Sabbath School, which gathered more than forty eager students. "An attachment, deep and lasting, sprung up between me and my persecuted pupils," Douglass recalled as he reflected on the long Sundays spent teaching his fellow slaves how to read. Even so, during 1836 Frederick still felt as acutely as ever the "spirit-devouring thralldom" of his enslavement.[30] He resolved to win his freedom as soon as possible. Frederick devised a plan with five fellow slaves to run away together. But just prior to their intended escape, someone in the group compromised the plan, likely Sandy Jenkins. Frederick and the others unexpectedly found themselves jailed on suspicion of seeking to run away. Thomas Auld led the interrogation of Frederick and the other slaves. He acted to prevent their immediate execution, which some whites demanded out of fear that the suspected plot included violent insurrection. The five men resolutely denied the conspiracy charges. Through it all, looming over them was the terrifying prospect that their masters might sell them to a Deep South plantation.

Thomas let Frederick spend an anxious week in the St. Michaels jail before retrieving him. Thomas could not afford to keep Frederick on his farm; he had acquired a reputation among whites in the area as a dangerous troublemaker. So he decided instead to send Frederick back to Baltimore. He hoped Frederick could learn a trade from Hugh and then make some money for his master by hiring himself out in the city. When Thomas told Frederick of his plan, he also promised that he would free Frederick when he turned

The Seeking Slave

twenty-five. In mid-April 1836, Thomas set Frederick on a boat for Baltimore, a twist of fate Frederick never imagined three years prior.[31]

When he arrived to the Auld home at Fells Point, Frederick soon saw how much he and his former masters had changed in their time apart. Little Tommy had no more use for his former playmate and protector. "The time had come when his *friend* must become his *slave*," Frederick recalled. The old affection between them had grown cold, and Frederick could not help but feel again the sad injustice of his enslavement. The two boys had grown up together, but in slaveholding America, only Tommy could truly become an independent man. Tommy eventually secured employment on a brig and began his career at sea. But Frederick remained "confined to a single condition . . . a minor—a mere boy." Hugh Auld's position had changed too, and for the worse. His shipbuilding business failed while Frederick was away. Hugh had no choice but to work as a foreman in other shipbuilding yards. As a result, Frederick would have to learn his new trade apart from Hugh, at another yard.[32]

Hugh secured for Frederick an apprenticeship learning how to caulk at William Gardner's shipyard. Gardner had won a government contract to build two warships. His crew frantically worked to meet their looming deadline when Frederick first arrived. He discovered bitter racial tensions at the yard. Free whites and blacks had long worked together in the skilled shipbuilding industry, but a recent wave of Irish immigration altered the working dynamic at many shipyards like Gardner's. Irish carpenters, aware of Gardner's tight deadline, threatened to boycott if all the free black employees were not fired. The tactic apparently worked. When Frederick arrived at the yard, he was the only black apprentice. Although the white carpenters did not demand that Gardner fire Frederick (because he was a slave, not a free African American), they still ensured that the young white apprentices tormented him.[33]

Frederick learned how to caulk amid constant verbal abuse and the threat of physical violence. He could hold his own in a fair fight, against any single one of his tormentors, but he could not survive outnumbered. One day, four white apprentices attacked Frederick at once, armed with bricks and handspikes. As they circled Frederick, someone struck him in the head from behind, knocking him stunned to the ground. The attackers rushed in and beat him. Someone kicked his left eye, which felt to Frederick as if it had burst. All the while, no fewer than fifty white carpenters gathered around to watch, some shouting for the apprentices to kill Frederick. When the attack ended, blood covered Frederick's face and severe bruising swelled shut his left eye, but he still managed to stumble home to the Auld house.[34]

The sight of Frederick horrified Sophia. He never forgot how she compassionately washed the blood from his face, bandaged his head, and covered his bruised eye with a fresh piece of beef. She treated him like any loving mother would. Hugh was furious after hearing the full story of what happened. Decades later, Frederick still admired Hugh (even though "he was not a religious man," as Douglass keenly pointed out) for the way he stood up for Frederick after his assault. Hugh's behavior contrasted sharply with the indifferent reaction of Thomas Auld, the pious Methodist, to learning of Covey's attack on Frederick. Hugh "poured curses on the heads of the whole ship yard company," Frederick remembered, though his anger resulted more from the feeling that his *property* rights had been abused than from any outrage committed against Frederick "*as a man*."[35]

Hugh tried to take legal action against the attackers. But a magistrate flatly replied that unless a *white* witness testified to the assault, he could take no action. Frederick's testimony—and his bruised body—was not sufficient evidence against his white assailants. Hugh realized he could do nothing more about Frederick's attack. He withdrew Frederick from Gardiner's yard and then secured a position for him in the yard at which he worked as foreman, a less desirable position but at least one under Hugh's watch. While Frederick worked there, the yard built at least three vessels surreptitiously used in the illegal slave trade.[36]

Frederick tried to restore his former friendships, and build new ones, in black Baltimore. With a group of five free black caulkers, he formed the East Baltimore Mental Improvement Society, a kind of debate club whose members met to consider a wide array of political and theological subjects. The society provided just the sort of intellectual companionship and stimulation that he most craved. Frederick soon met his future wife, Anna Murray, a free black native of the Eastern Shore.[37] Frederick also returned to the world of black Methodism in Baltimore. But his inclination toward fiery discontent with institutional religion soon appeared. Not long after returning to Fells Point, Frederick stopped attending Bethel African Methodist Church, the congregation that had nurtured him as a young convert, the place he had met his spiritual father Charles Lawson. It seems that Frederick left because of an open letter by Bethel's leadership denouncing the abolitionist movement. The letter called abolitionists like William Lloyd Garrison "hot-headed zealots" who threatened to "plunge the country into anarchy and discord," which would prove disastrous for free blacks and slaves alike. Bethel's leaders published the letter in 1835, a moment of rising white suspicion over abolitionism, particularly in slaveholding states like

Maryland. The letter was mostly motivated by a desire to ensure Bethel and its members would not face the kind of violent white backlash that had already occurred against many abolitionists. For that reason, distancing the church from radical abolitionism may have been a prudent act of survival, but Frederick could not tolerate it. There is some evidence, not altogether definitive, that he joined the Sharp Street Methodist Church for a brief time after leaving Bethel.[38]

Either way, Frederick's decision to leave Bethel revealed his growing conviction that the perversions of proslavery Christianity could corrupt even African American churches. As his prophetic voice matured, Frederick at times condemned black churches just as sternly as white churches. If African American congregations failed to stand unequivocally for abolitionism and racial equality in a nation of oppression and bigotry, then Frederick reckoned there was no hope for true Christianity in America.

By late 1837, under Hugh's watch, Frederick had grown quite skilled as a caulker. He earned a decent wage in the shipyard, which went entirely to Auld. Frederick grew ever more dissatisfied with not being able to keep any of his hard-won earnings. So he proposed an alternative to Thomas. He wanted to hire himself out independently and keep a portion of his own pay, while also providing for his own room and board. This sort of arrangement was not that uncommon in Baltimore. Slaves received greater autonomy from their masters, who in return benefited by no longer paying the expense of a slave's room and board. Thomas Auld initially rejected the suggestion, but two months later Hugh agreed to it. Frederick would live alone, secure his own food, clothes, and tools, and pay Hugh three dollars of his weekly earnings at the end of each week. Frederick saw clearly that under this arrangement he still "endured all the evils of being a slave, and yet suffered all the care and anxiety of a responsible freeman." Even so, it was still a step toward freedom, one he took enthusiastically.[39]

Frederick's new independent life began in May 1838 but ended abruptly by August. He made plans one weekend to attend a camp revival meeting about twelve miles outside Baltimore. Frederick unexpectedly had to stay late at work that Saturday evening, and when he finally left he decided not to deliver his weekly payment to Hugh as normal. He planned instead to pay Hugh on his return. Frederick eventually stayed an extra night at the revival. When he returned to the Auld house on Monday evening, Hugh was furious. He immediately ended their arrangement. Frederick could no longer hire himself out, and had to live again with the Aulds. Frederick lost the meager freedom he had gained.[40]

Soon after, Frederick decided to run away. Over the next three weeks, he carefully plotted his escape. He returned to work and saved as much of his earnings as he could, a mere seventeen dollars in all. Anna sold a featherbed and drew from her own savings to provide Frederick the rest of the money he would need to make it to New York City. If he arrived there safely, he intended to send for Anna, marry her, and begin a new free life together. Frederick planned to escape by train, but he needed some way to convince a conductor or any other authority that he was a free man and not a slave. He eventually secured a "seaman's protection" from a former sailor, a document that certified its holder was a free American sailor. Although Fredrick did not look like the man described on the document, he gambled that the conductor would not carefully examine it. The risk paid off. Frederick boarded a train and boldly presented himself as a sailor to the conductor who passed through the cabin. The man gave only a passing glance to Frederick's paper.[41]

The entire long journey north was full of close calls, improbable moments when Frederick crossed paths with acquaintances who knew he was a slave but did not have the chance to expose him as a runaway. He took a train to Wilmington, Delaware, then a steamboat to Philadelphia, then a train to New York City. He arrived there early in the morning on 4 September 1838. He walked through the city exhausted and hungry and impoverished, but Frederick recalled the sensation of "peace and joy" that still thrilled his heart. He had long wondered if God had ordained him to remain forever a slave. But now he wondered no more: "The chain was severed; God and right stood vindicated."[42]

The city was still a confusing and unsettling place. Frederick feared he could trust no one. He had arranged to arrive at the home of David Ruggles, the leader of a group that helped fugitives escape farther north, but he did not know how to get there. Eventually, with the help of a stranger, Frederick made it to Ruggles's residence. Ruggles warmly hosted Frederick and assisted him in the next leg of his journey to freedom. Frederick sent for Anna, and once she arrived the two were married in the city. When Ruggles learned Frederick was a caulker, he decided to send him and Anna to New Bedford, Massachusetts, a major whaling town full of work for a man with Frederick's skills. With his new wife at his side, Frederick made his way to Massachusetts, trading forever his former life as a slave for all "the rights, responsibilities, and duties of a freeman."[43]

THE ZEALOUS ORATOR

1839–1852

The Young Abolitionist Orator

Douglass never forgot the day, soon after arriving in New Bedford, when he earned two silver half-dollars. He had failed to find work at the wharves one morning, and on his way home he noticed a pile of coal outside a Unitarian minister's home. Douglass asked the minister's wife if he could carry the coal inside. She accepted his offer. Not long after he began she placed into his hands two silver half-dollars as payment for his labor. Anyone who had not been a slave could not understand "the emotion which swelled in my heart as I clasped this money," Douglass wrote.[1] He would not have to give the wage to his master; he could finally enjoy the full fruits of his labor. In New Bedford, Douglass found a freedom he once scarcely imagined as a slave boy on the Eastern Shore. He was free not only to earn a living but also to pursue truth and practice his faith as he best saw fit.

By 1845, Douglass had emerged as a leading abolitionist with a distinct prophetic message for America. The first years of his free life in New Bedford prepared him intellectually and morally to embark on a public antislavery career. In New Bedford, Douglass directly encountered both northern Christianity and abolitionism for the first time. In the former, he experienced some of the same bigotry he had seen in southern proslavery religion; in the latter, he discovered an ideology and movement that squared with his deepest religious convictions and his desire to work for justice and equality. By 1841, Douglass spoke regularly on the abolitionist lecture circuit, and across the early 1840s the core elements of his emerging prophetic voice had cohered into a powerful message about the state of slavery and Christianity in America.

New Bedford in 1838 was a thriving port town with a population greater than 12,000. The city was hardly free of racial prejudice, as Frederick quickly discovered. But it also potentially offered far greater opportunity for a black man than Douglass had ever known, even in Baltimore. A Quaker couple, Nathan and Mary Johnson, first helped the Douglasses settle in New Bedford. Soon after their arrival, Frederick nearly won a job as a caulker in a boat-yard that paid two dollars a day, but the yard's white workers appear to have refused to allow a black man into their ranks. Even though he knew a skilled trade, Douglass had to work a variety of unskilled jobs—sawing and shoveling and digging and loading and unloading. Frederick and Anna lived in great poverty in their first months in New Bedford, with a child on the way. Eventually, Douglass found steadier work, first at a whale-oil refinery and then at a wharf. He also made friends with members of the city's small African American community, which numbered around 1,000 people.[2]

When he first reached New Bedford, Douglass especially desired to find a church to join as a member. He had not abandoned his Methodist faith, but, he later recalled, he had "become lukewarm and in a backslidden state."[3] The tribulations of his final years in slavery dulled something of his young ardor for Christianity. But now free and far separated from slaveholding religion, Douglass sought to rededicate himself to the faith he cherished. He attended two Methodist congregations in New Bedford—first, briefly, the white-led Elm Street Methodist Church, then later, for several years, the town's AME Zion Church. At Elm Street, he discovered that white congregations in the North easily exhibited familiar patterns of racial prejudice, and even helped perpetuate slavery and the religion that sustained it. Douglass hoped to find refuge in the AME Zion Church, which in many ways he did. But in time, he grew somewhat disillusioned with northern black Christianity too. He feared that congregations like New Bedford's AME Zion Church could at times remain too silently passive in the face of the nation's prevailing white supremacist Christianity.

Douglass had hoped that Elm Street Methodist would be free of the "unholy feeling" of racial prejudice, but the majority-white congregation quickly disappointed him. Church leaders, including the pastor, the Reverend Isaac Bonney, forbade Douglass from sitting on the main floor of the sanctuary. They forced him to sit in the segregated balcony, justifying the action as "an accommodation of the unconverted congregation who had not yet been won to Christ and his brotherhood." That is, the white church leaders said that if not-yet-converted white attendees had to sit with black members in integrated seating, some might leave offended before ever hearing the gospel. For a time, Douglass accepted as sincere the church's justification for segregated seating. But he soon grew convinced that the church's white minister and members did not truly recognize their fellow black believers as "children of the same Father, and heirs of the same salvation, on equal terms with themselves."[4]

The church revealed its true character in how it administered the Lord's Supper. One Sunday, after Bonney preached, he dismissed everyone from the sanctuary except church members. Now that the unconverted had left (making irrelevant the argument for segregation), Douglass expected to see the "holy sacrament celebrated in the spirit of its great Founder," but he saw instead only the spirit of bigotry and condescension. The half-dozen black members descended from the balcony but still sat separated in a distant corner of the sanctuary floor. "They looked like a sheep without a shepherd," Douglass remembered. Bonney first called forward to the altar the church's white members to receive the bread and wine. Only after he had served them all did Bonney then look to the black members and earnestly proclaim, "Come forward, colored friends!—come forward! You, too, have an interest in the blood of Christ. God is no respecter of persons."[5]

The words rang hollow in Douglass's ears. To his dismay, the "poor, slavish" black members went forward to the altar as commanded. "I went *out*, and have never been in that church since," Douglass wrote more than a decade later. He had no desire to associate with any congregation so completely beholden to "wicked prejudice." Douglass concluded that the Elm Street church was no "Christian church, at all."[6] The Sundays he worshipped at Elm Street convinced him that northern churches were not immune to the prejudice and hypocrisy he had seen in the Christian slaveholding South.

Douglass and his family wandered for a time among the other churches of New Bedford before joining a congregation affiliated with the AME Zion Church. African American churchgoers in New York, led especially by James Varick, established the AME Zion denomination in the early 1820s. From its very beginning, the denomination was a regional and institutional rival of Richard Allen's African Methodist Episcopal Church, despite minimal theological differences. The AME Zion church of New Bedford met in a small schoolhouse in the town. Douglass became heavily involved in the church, serving as a sexton, steward, class leader, and clerk for the congregation.[7] In 1839, Douglass was formally licensed to preach, and often did so on Sundays at the request of the church's minister. Douglass later recognized how his membership in the Zion church profoundly affected the course of his antislavery career. In preaching to the congregation, he first honed his skills as an orator and began to acquire a distinct style as a speaker. Nearly sixty years later, mere months before he died, Douglass called his time with the New Bedford Zion congregation "among the happiest days of my life."[8]

At roughly the same time Douglass joined the local Zion church, he also received a subscription to America's leading abolitionist newspaper, William Lloyd Garrison's *Liberator*. Douglass avidly read the newspaper. He received both political and moral instruction from it. The newspaper "took its place with me next to the bible," Douglass later wrote. "I *loved* this paper, and its editor," he continued, for they enriched his mind and soul by educating him in the tenets of abolitionism. As Douglass's suspicions of institutional Christianity increased, he came to believe that the abolitionist movement embodied all that was best about the Christian faith, rightly understood. He hoped that by somehow joining the abolitionist cause he might truly live out the faith he proclaimed.[9]

The *Liberator* had been at the forefront of the American antislavery movement since William Lloyd Garrison and Isaac Knapp published the first issue on 1 January 1831. American abolitionism always remained a diverse and often fractious movement, yet since the early 1830s Garrison had offered significant intellectual and institutional leadership within the world of nineteenth-century antislavery activity. He founded and edited the movement's leading newspaper, and also helped establish its leading organizations—first the New England Anti-Slavery Society in 1831 and then the American Anti-Slavery Society in 1833.[10]

Abolitionists did not always agree about the best strategies and tactics to achieve their shared goal. Garrison advocated "moral suasion" as the only pure and effective way of ending slavery in America.[11] He and other like-minded abolitionists sought to achieve a kind of moral awakening in America. They hoped to open the eyes of white northerners to the utter barbarity of slavery and thereby convince them to support abolition. Practically speaking, this commitment to moral suasion led many abolitionists to reject both conventional political activity and the use of violence as counterproductive to the antislavery cause. Garrison liked to say that the U.S. Constitution—and the government it created—was hopelessly proslavery, a pact with Hell that abolitionists had to reject outright. But about the time Douglass began reading the *Liberator*, members of the American antislavery movement increasingly fought among themselves over the question of political participation. Some abolitionists had established the Liberty Party, an independent third party expressly devoted to ensuring the end of slavery. The Garrisonian abolitionists continued to reject such political activity as both less effective than moral suasion and also as a sinful complicity in a proslavery political and constitutional order.

Douglass called the *Liberator* "a paper after my own heart." It preached against "hypocrisy and wickedness in high places" and appealed to "human brotherhood" in its demands for immediate emancipation. Like *The Columbian Orator*, the *Liberator* offered Douglass new language and arguments to wield against slavery. As a still unknown fugitive in New Bedford, Douglass came to revere Garrison. At the time, he thought "few men evinced a more genuine or a more exalted piety." Garrison seemed to Douglass to exemplify the consistent practice of a true faith. "Not only was Sunday a Sabbath" to Garrison, Douglass wrote, "but all days were Sabbaths, and to be kept holy." Unlike the Christian slaveholder, Garrison's professed religious and moral commitments pervaded his entire life. Douglass later admitted that in the early 1840s, he had worshipped Garrison as a hero worthy of "love and reverence." Douglass's admiration for Garrison in these years reveals how thoroughly he had come to believe that the abolitionist movement epitomized the true gospel of Christ in action—perhaps even far more than any organized Christian church in America.[12]

In New Bedford, Douglass first confronted questions about the compatibility of institutional Christianity and abolitionism. Could an ardent abolitionist remain faithful to the antislavery cause while also still remaining a member of an organized church, whatever the denomination? Douglass believed that his time as a member of New Bedford's AME Zion church prepared him for "the work of delivering my brethren from bondage." But in time, he felt he had to formally separate even from the Zion church to maintain his faithfulness to his abolitionist calling. Douglass did not reject Christianity outright; he continued his entire life to revere what he fondly called the true Christianity of Christ. But he grew ever more wary of how the American church, as an institution, perpetuated slavery and racial prejudice.

Eventually, Douglass believed he had a kind of Christian duty "to remain separate from the church, because bad men were connected with it." Even the Zion church in New Bedford, Douglass once wrote, often "consented to the same spirit which held my brethren in chains." Douglass never explained what exactly he meant, though he may well have desired from the congregation a more directly confrontational attitude toward proslavery religion. For the sake of the gospel and the antislavery cause, Douglass kept a certain distance from the organized Christian church—all in the hope that he might best fulfill his prophetic calling.[13]

Still, it was within the AME Zion church in New Bedford that Douglass honed his fledgling skills as an orator. There he began to speak publicly on racism and slavery. At a March 1839 meeting, church members gathered to discuss colonization schemes that proposed to free America's slaves and remove them to Africa. Douglass spoke against the plans and proceeded to describe his life as a slave and argue for immediate emancipation. As he read the *Liberator* and grew bolder in his pronouncements at the Zion church, Douglass also began attending antislavery meetings in New Bedford. Initially, he sat in silence and merely listened. Yet Douglass could hardly contain "the truths which burned in my breast," and in the summer of 1841, he made his first great antislavery speech, which forever changed the course of his life.[14]

In August of that year, the Massachusetts Anti-Slavery Society held a grand convention in Nantucket, a port city made lately prosperous by the whaling industry. Douglass had never taken time off from work since his escape, but he traveled to Nantucket that summer. William C. Coffin, a successful bookkeeper and abolitionist from New Bedford, invited Douglass to attend the convention after hearing him speak at the Zion church. The Anti-Slavery Society planned to hold the meeting in Nantucket's Athenaeum. But on the eve of the convention, the Athenaeum's trustees refused to let the society use the building, especially after learning that black northerners had been invited to attend and even speak. The convention met instead in a large building known as the Big Shop, owned by members of the Coffin clan and mostly used to build boats for whalers.[15]

Not long after Douglass arrived on Nantucket Island, William Coffin found him among the gathering crowd. As they walked through the city together, Coffin urged Douglass to speak at the convention, if he felt so moved. Douglass had not intended to speak, but Coffin's offer intrigued him. Douglass had seemingly prepared for such an opportunity since he first acquired copies of the Bible and *The Columbian Orator*. When Douglass arrived at the Big Shop in the early evening of 16 August, a sizeable crowd had already assembled. The building was packed to capacity, with people even sitting atop the rafters in the ceiling. The audience included some of America's most notable abolitionists, leading figures within the American Anti-Slavery Society including William Lloyd Garrison, Wendell Philips, and John A. Collins. As was customary at such meetings, the convention considered formal resolutions and heard speeches. Garrison offered the first resolution, which condemned racial prejudice in the North. Several speeches followed. In the twilight hours of the evening, Douglass finally rose to speak.

He had never addressed an audience this large, and his nerves got the better of him. "I trembled in every limb," Douglass remembered, straining to stand confidently upright. The man who later spoke with compelling, effortless eloquence struggled that evening to string together a sentence "without hesitation and stammering." The text of Douglass's address has not survived. No one thought to record it verbatim. Nearly fifteen years—and hundreds of speeches—later, Douglass admitted that he could not remember "a single connected sentence" he spoke that evening. But based on recollections of convention attendees, Douglass appears to have told his life story. His words filled the rapt audience with quiet excitement, for there stood a man who had endured the worst of slavery and escaped to tell of it.[16]

What Douglass most remembered was the response that followed his speech. William Lloyd Garrison spoke next with "unequaled power," Douglass later said, "sweeping down, like a very tornado, every opposing barrier, whether of sentiment or opinion." Another person at the Big Shop that evening recalled Garrison asking the audience, "Have we been listening to a thing, a chattel person, or a man?" He continued, "Shall such a man be held a slave in a Christian land?" The audience shouted "No!" in reply, and Garrison answered, "Shall such a man ever be sent back to bondage from the free soil of old Massachusetts?" By now, the whole convention had sprung to its feet and drowned out Garrison's voice with fervent cries of "No! No! No!"[17]

When the meeting adjourned later that night, a new life began for Douglass. John A. Collins, then the leader of the Massachusetts Anti-Slavery Society, offered Douglass a job as a lecturer for the society. He hoped Douglass would strike a blow against slavery by publicly retelling his life story. Douglass could now earn a wage not as a caulker but by traveling the antislavery lecture circuit and delivering speeches. Douglass soon moved his family from New Bedford to Lynn, Massachusetts, just north of Boston, and began his career as an antislavery orator "in the full gush of unsuspecting enthusiasm." Douglass later recalled how ardently he believed that the antislavery cause would soon triumph, because the "God of Israel"—the "Almighty Disposer of the hearts of men"—surely favored those who labored for emancipation.[18]

Years later, Douglass looked back on his first year on the lecture circuit as a time of great passion and great naïveté. He did not fully appreciate how arduous the antislavery struggle would be. Yet the first speeches Douglass delivered as a Massachusetts Anti-Slavery Society agent, in late 1841, contained more than youthful idealism. They also reveal that some of the quintessential elements of Douglass's prophetic voice had already taken shape. Although Douglass described his experiences as a slave in these speeches, he devoted extensive attention also to exposing the religious hypocrisy that bolstered slavery and racism in America.

In one of Douglass's earliest recorded speeches, delivered in Lynn in October 1841, he condemned slaveholders for their false piety and the way they distorted Christianity to justify slavery. This October speech, though brief, foreshadowed many of the main themes in Douglass's first autobiography, published four years later. Douglass said his master, Thomas Auld, whipped slave women while quoting from the Bible to justify the violence. Despite his cruelty, Auld had a reputation as a model Methodist in his church—a testament to the duplicity of Auld and his congregation. Douglass also mocked the proslavery sermons he heard preached from southern pulpits. Ministers tortured the Bible to make their arguments, but the absurdity of their justifications went even deeper. Douglass recalled a white minister telling the slaves to look at their own hands "and see how wisely Providence has adapted them to do the labor." In contrast, the minister continued, the hands of white masters were obviously far more "delicate" and "not fit for work." Douglass snidely added, "Some of us know very well that we have not time to cease from labor, or ours would get soft too." As soon as he began his career on the antislavery lecture circuit, Douglass tried to expose Christian slaveholders as cruel tyrants and discredit the biblical proslavery argument as a dishonest sham.[19]

In early November 1841, Douglass attended the quarterly meeting of the Plymouth County Anti-Slavery Society in Hingham, Massachusetts. There he delivered two speeches that similarly captured the essence of his prophetic oratory during his first months a Massachusetts Anti-Slavery Society agent. Attendees at the meeting included Garrison and Collins, among other notable Massachusetts abolitionists. The society crowded a church in Hingham to consider several resolutions, which offered Douglass the chance to speak twice. That afternoon, he rose in support of a resolution that identified slavery, and not the abolitionist movement, as the true threat to the Union's future. Speaking on behalf of the resolution, Douglass made a wider point about northern complicity in slavery. Douglass condemned both northerners who helped return runaway slaves to bondage and the disastrous "union" between northern and southern churches. Eventually, in the years to come, Douglass would refine this critique of northern Christians who maintained forms of fellowship with proslavery southern churches, explaining in far greater detail how such actions helped perpetuate slavery. But even by November 1841, Douglass already saw how northern Christians bore real responsibility for the preservation of slavery in America.[20]

When the Plymouth County Anti-Slavery Society reassembled later in the evening, it debated a resolution denouncing racial prejudice as "cruel and malignant, utterly at variance with Christianity, in direct violation of the word of God." The gathered crowd, overwhelmingly white, did not immediately approve the resolution. Garrison argued strenuously in support of it, as did Edmund Quincy, a leader in both the Massachusetts Anti-Slavery Society and the American Anti-Slavery Society. Quincy summoned Douglass to speak for the resolution. As he described his experience with racial prejudice, and ably denounced it, Douglass's rhetorical skills disproved any assumptions of black inferiority still accepted by members of the audience. Douglass alluded to several examples of racial discrimination he had faced in the past, none more unsettling than what he encountered at New Bedford's Elm Street Methodist Church. The congregation's white Methodists simply could not embrace their black brothers and sisters in Christ as true equals, a betrayal of the spirit of the gospel, Douglass suggested. "The grand cause is slavery," Douglass granted, but no less important, in the long run, was the prejudicial spirit than inflicted the North and South and corrupted American religion. Eventually, the society adopted the resolution, but only after members were forced to vote in a thoroughly public manner, by standing.[21] In late December 1841, Douglass delivered a revised and expanded version of this speech that spoke even more boldly against southern slavery and northern racial prejudice as two sides of the same sin. Douglass ridiculed white Americans of all regions for saying that "they like colored men as well as any other, *but in their proper place!*" The problem, Douglass continued, was that "they assign us that place. . . . They will not allow that we have a head to think, and a heart to feel, and a soul to aspire." This kind of prejudice pervaded American society, Douglass said, and "goes even into the church of God," where it least belongs.[22]

For the next four years, Douglass lived an itinerant orator's life, traveling widely on the abolitionist lecture circuit. He continued to speak in Massachusetts, but he increasingly journeyed throughout New England and other free states to plead the cause of antislavery and racial equality. In 1842, Douglass and several other Massachusetts Anti-Slavery Society agents spoke extensively in Rhode Island against a provision in the state's new proposed constitution that would have limited the right to vote only to all white men. The year 1843 was the "Year of One Hundred Conventions," a joint effort among New England abolitionists to hold 100 antislavery conventions throughout several northern states, from Indiana to New Hampshire. "I have never entered upon any work with more heart and hope," Douglass recalled. He believed he could rally white Americans to abolitionism if only they heard for themselves the horrors of slavery. Douglass journeyed first to western New York, then Ohio, and then Indiana, where he encountered great hostility. Soon after Douglass and fellow abolitionists began to speak in Pendleton, Indiana, a mob of several dozen men demanded that they stop. When they refused, the mob assaulted the lecturers. Douglass broke his right hand in the ensuing melee.[23]

Undaunted by the violence and opposition he faced throughout the North, Douglass continued to travel the antislavery lecture circuit in the early

1840s. His surviving speeches from these years demonstrate how thoroughly Douglass was a Garrisonian in his sentiments. He defended moral suasion over explicit political action as the tactic best suited for the antislavery cause. At a January 1842 meeting of the Massachusetts Anti-Slavery Society, Douglass asked his fellow abolitionists to name a single thing the state legislature had done "that has caused you to recognize my humanity." Instead, only the persuasive pleading and moral example of the abolitionists had convinced any white northerner to set aside prejudice and embrace "a holy zeal for human rights."[24] Such a change in a person's heart and mind could not be enacted by a piece of legislation. Douglass told Garrison in 1844 that only "a great moral and religious movement" could end slavery in America—a kind of spiritual awakening independent of the nation's political machinations. If abolitionists remained dedicated to "the simple proclamation of the word of Truth," Douglass continued, "and in faith believing that the God of truth will give it success," then the antislavery cause would surely triumph.[25]

Not surprisingly, Douglass also embraced the Garrisonian view of the U.S. Constitution as a "covenant with death." In May 1845, the same month he published his first autobiography, Douglass asked attendees of an American Anti-Slavery Society meeting, "God says thou shalt not oppress: the Constitution says oppress: which will you serve, God or man?"[26] Douglass assumed that the Constitution's irredeemably proslavery character left abolitionists no other choice but to remain independent of the nation's existing political order—and thereby ensure they would not compromise their commitment to truth and justice.

On occasion, Douglass also voiced approval for nonviolent resistance to slavery, another key pillar of Garrisonian abolitionist orthodoxy. But Douglass's commitment to nonviolence was always somewhat less fervent, if not altogether tenuous, even by the early 1840s. After all, he had battled Edward Covey and felt no remorse about doing so, even after learning the abolitionist arguments against violent resistance. In 1843, Douglass attended the National Convention of Colored Citizens, his first major meeting of African Americans. There he heard Henry Highland Garnett deliver a passionate call for violent rebellion by slaves. Garnett, like Douglass, had been a slave on Maryland's Eastern Shore before escaping to freedom. He eventually studied theology at the Oneida Theological Institute, and in 1843, at the age of twenty-eight, pastored an African American Presbyterian church in Troy, New York. Garnett called upon the convention to adopt a resolution endorsing violent resistance. Douglass spoke strongly against the resolution, which eventually failed. But based on the limited record of the convention's proceedings, his opposition to Garnett's resolution does not exactly appear motivated by pure pacifism. Instead, more pragmatically, Douglass insisted that insurrections failed to end slavery and only inspired disastrous reprisals. He never quite fully embraced Garrisonian nonviolence in the early 1840s.[27]

Still, Douglass believed that only the American abolitionist movement, especially its Garrisonian wing, stood any real chance of bringing about the end of slavery. "There was no hope for the slave in Church, or State, or in the working of society, framed as it now is," Douglass proclaimed in May 1843 in a speech to the American Anti-Slavery Society in New York City. He had little confidence in the nation's existing political and religious institutions to destroy slavery. Yet organizations like the American Anti-Slavery Society, Douglass continued, remained "above either Church or State," and, more important, were "*moving both*, daily, more and more." Through the power of moral suasion—an uncompromised prophetic witness—the antislavery movement continued to make meaningful strides toward eradicating slavery.[28] This, Douglass believed, was the great work he had undertaken as he joined the abolitionist lecture circuit in the early 1840s. In completing this work, Douglass hoped to truly live a just and righteous life.

As Douglass traveled and spoke throughout the 1840s, more than anything else he told the story of his own life and escape—the same story that had first captivated abolitionist leaders on Nantucket Island in August 1841. Eventually, fellow antislavery activists, especially Wendell Phillips, urged Douglass to publish his tale. In June 1845, the "Anti-Slavery Office" in Boston published *Narrative of the Life of Frederick Douglass, an American Slave*, Douglass's first great autobiography. The book sold 5,000 copies by the end of the year, and 30,000 within five years.[29] The *Narrative* is a tale of harrowing oppression and heroic triumph, one man's unsparing account of the horrors of slavery and how he resisted them and escaped from bondage. The *Narrative* is more than merely an autobiography. It also delivers, by design, a prophetic word to America, particularly its professed Christians. Douglass spent years on the lecture circuit honing his religious critique of slavery. In the *Narrative*, he distilled that message into a compelling condemnation of the hypocrisy of religious slaveholders and the hollowness of proslavery Christianity.

In the "Appendix" of the *Narrative*, Douglass most explicitly denounced the "corrupt, slaveholding, women-whipping, cradle-plundering, partial and hypocritical Christianity of this land," a false faith not even deserving the name Christian. Douglass appealed to what he called "the Christianity of Christ"—"good, pure, and holy"—to condemn proslavery religion. The two

Frederick Douglass, ca. 1847. *Courtesy of the Art Institute of Chicago.*

were fundamentally unalike. Douglass hoped readers of his *Narrative* would not "suppose me an opponent of all religion," despite the harsh words he had for many American Christians and their churches. "What I have said respecting and against religion," Douglass explained, "I mean strictly to apply to the *slaveholding religion* of this land, and with no possible reference to Christianity proper." Douglass worked to vindicate true Christianity from the corrupt version of the faith used to justify slavery.[30]

The Zealous Orator

He also appealed to the spirit of "the Christianity of Christ" to expose the false righteousness and oppression of slaveholding religion. The religion of the slaveholding South, Douglass said, was full of "pomp and show" and "horrible inconsistencies." The cruelest slaveholders were also the most ardent churchgoers. "The man who wields the blood-clotted cowskin during the week fills the pulpit on Sunday," Douglass scoffed, "and claims to be a minister of the meek and lowly Jesus. The man who robs me of my earnings at the end of each week meets me as a class-leader on Sunday morning." All the major villains of the *Narrative* corroborated Douglass's charges of religious hypocrisy. After Thomas Auld converted and joined the Methodist Church, he only became crueler toward his slaves. Edward Covey, the violent "slave-breaker," was also a respected member of his local Methodist congregation.[31]

Yet for Douglass, the tragedy of American religion went deeper than the fact that individual slaveholders often professed Christianity but used the faith to justify slaveholding. Far worse was how, at an institutional level, slavery and the Christian church remained inextricably connected. "The slave auctioneer's bell and the church-going bell chime in with each other," Douglass lamented, "and the bitter cries of the heart-broken slave are drowned in the religious shouts of his pious master." Slaveholders and clergymen maintained a mutually beneficial relationship, to the detriment of Christianity in America. Masters give their "blood-stained gold to support the pulpit," Douglass explained, "and the pulpit, in return, covers his infernal business with the garb of Christianity." To Douglass, both the slaveholder and the minister who sanctioned slaveholding stood equally guilty of debasing and shaming the Christian faith.[32]

Near the end of the *Narrative*, Douglass quoted at length from the twenty-third chapter of the Gospel of Matthew to compare slaveholding Christians to "the ancient scribes and Pharisees." In the biblical passage Douglass cited, Jesus Christ—speaking in full prophetic fashion—exposed the religious leaders and seemingly pious men of his day for practicing a false and oppressive faith. "They bind heavy burdens, and grievous to be born, and lay them on men's shoulders, but they themselves will not move them with one of their fingers," Christ says in Matthew 23. So too, Christ continues, do the scribes and Pharisees put on a pious pretense—praying in a loud and showy manner—while utterly failing to do what the Lord required, to act with true humility and kindness and righteousness. "Woe unto you, scribes and Pharisees, hypocrites," Christ proclaims. "For ye are like unto whited sepulchers, which indeed appear beautiful outward, but are within full of dead men's bones, and of all uncleanness. Even so ye also outwardly appear righteous unto men, but within ye are full of hypocrisy and iniquity." Douglass quoted these verses in his *Narrative* and then insisted that Christ's words still held true for "the overwhelming mass of professed Christians in America." Seemingly pious slaveholders "attend with Pharisaical strictness to the outward forms of religion," Douglass declared, "and at the same time neglect the weightier matters of the law, judgment, mercy, and faith." They had utterly abandoned the true Christianity of Christ, which Douglass predicted only invited the wrath of a just and avenging Lord.[33]

Douglass's *Narrative* won great renown on both sides of the Atlantic, especially in antislavery circles. Key leaders in the American Anti-Slavery Society, especially Garrison and Philips, thought Douglass should capitalize on the publication of his autobiography by traveling to Great Britain for an extended speaking tour. The foreign trip promised also to help Douglass avoid immediate recapture. He had divulged a great deal of information about his identity and escape in his *Narrative*. An enterprising hunter of escaped slaves could conceivably track him down and return him to the Eastern Shore. Even as Douglass began his famed career as an author and orator against slavery, he remained a fugitive slave, suspended between bondage and true freedom.

Bearing Witness in Great Britain

Even after a long passage across the Atlantic Ocean, Douglass could not quite escape the proslavery Christianity of his native land. For eighteen months, Douglass journeyed throughout Ireland, Scotland, and England, speaking tirelessly on behalf of the American slave. He appealed to British Christians to abandon every form of fellowship with slaveholding Christians of the American South. Association of any kind with slaveholders made Britons complicit in the sin of slavery, Douglass argued, and compromised the integrity of their Christian witness. Douglass hammered home this message while speaking extensively on two major church-related controversies in Britain—one concerning the upstart Free Church of Scotland, the other involving a group known as the Evangelical Alliance. Both controversies, at their core, centered on the same question: Could a slaveholder be a true Christian?

Douglass seized the chance to speak on this question in Great Britain. By doing so, he sought to expose the hypocrisy of proslavery religion, strip it of its respectability, and thereby strike an important blow against American slavery. The year and a half Douglass spent abroad ultimately proved quite consequential in the development of his prophetic faith. When he returned to America in April 1847, Douglass saw more clearly than ever before the thorough corruption slavery had unleashed in the Christian church—not just in the slaveholding South but throughout the entire United States and the world.

Douglass admitted that after he published his *Narrative*, the chance of being returned to slavery "haunted me by day, and troubled my dreams by night." He looked for temporary refuge in Great Britain. Douglass sailed the Atlantic on the *Cambria* with James N. Buffum, a prosperous carpenter and abolitionist from Lynn, Massachusetts. Buffum and Douglass were denied a passenger cabin on the ship. America's sacred "color test and condition," Douglass wrote, triumphed even on a British vessel crossing the ocean. Buffum and Douglass had no choice but to accept a cheap steerage cabin, the sort of treatment Douglass had come to expect in northern free states.[1]

Douglass still managed to converse frequently with his fellow passengers on slavery and abolitionism. At the end of the voyage, the ship's captain even invited Douglass to deliver a public lecture on slavery. As Douglass described the plight of American slaves, some passengers tried to silence him with threats and shouts of condemnation. A few slaveholders onboard, having enjoyed a bit of brandy, even promised to throw Douglass overboard if he did not stop speaking. "Yes, they actually got up a mob," Douglass sarcastically wrote to William Lloyd Garrison, "a real American republican, democratic, Christian mob."[2] Eventually, the captain suppressed the mob by threatening to put them in irons for the rest of the trip. Douglass gleefully reported the whole event to his British crowds, for he thought it captured how insecure proslavery forces tried to stifle all discussion of slavery.

Once he arrived in Great Britain, Douglass worked for the next eighteen months at a characteristically frenetic pace. He spoke publicly on nearly 200 occasions—quite often delivering remarks that stretched on for several hours. Douglass arrived first at Liverpool on 28 August, but he immediately traveled to Ireland, where he spent the next four months. Douglass stayed a month in Dublin before moving south to the port town of Cork. By mid-November, Douglass moved north to Limerick and then to Belfast, where he remained until early January 1846. From there, Douglass traveled to Scotland. He spoke in Glasgow, Dundee, Edinburgh, and several other leading Scottish towns until leaving for England in late May. Throughout the remaining months of 1846, Douglass's speaking itinerary grew only more frantic. He mixed major stops in England with visits back to Scotland and Ireland. By late November 1846, Douglass returned to England and stayed there for the remainder of his trip. Even so, in his final months abroad, Douglass still traveled extensively throughout England—from Newcastle upon Tyne to Bristol, and all the major cities in between.[3]

Having honed his skills as an orator since 1841, Douglass used them to great effect in Britain to plead the antislavery cause. He addressed a wide range of topics, but on nearly every occasion that he spoke, Douglass worked to turn British public opinion against American slavery. "The main object to which my labors in Great Britain were directed," Douglass explained, "was the concentration of the moral and religious sentiment of its people against

American slavery."[4] Douglass delivered his speeches extemporaneously, without a prepared text or notes. As he spoke his deepest convictions about slavery, Douglass's prophetic voice resounded throughout Britain. Taken altogether, Douglass's speeches reiterated many key themes he had developed in his *Narrative*: the cruelty of slavery, the hypocrisy of proslavery religion, and the need for a revival of *true* Christianity.

Douglass later said that the best example of the kind of speech he typically delivered in Britain was his 12 May 1846 address in London's Finsbury Chapel. English abolitionists invited Douglass to speak at a large meeting hosted by the British and Foreign Anti-Slavery Society. Well over 2,000 people gathered to hear Douglass's three-hour-long address. He began by evoking the horrors of American slavery. Although God gave each enslaved person an "intellect" and "moral perception," masters worked to stamp out both and make a slave a mere "brute beast." Masters denied their slaves the chance to receive an education, to marry, or even to read the Bible. No weapon was too cruel for slaveholders to enforce their reign: "Starvation, the bloody whip, the chain, the gag, the thumb-screw," among others. This was the plight of American slaves, Douglass told his listeners, the millions in bondage who lived and suffered in a nation "boasting of its liberty, boasting of its humanity, boasting of its Christianity, boasting of its love of justice and purity."[5]

For the rest of his speech at Finsbury Chapel, Douglass dwelt on the tragic disconnect between the boasts of Christian America and the fate of its slaves. Here he spoke in full prophetic form. Southern religion remained "the great supporter, the great sanctioner" of all the "bloody atrocities" American slaves endured. Support for slavery had become an essential pillar of Christian orthodoxy as practiced in the white South, Douglass said. Ministers of Christ's gospel were the *most* ardent defenders of the institution. Each Sunday they stood in the pulpit and lent their support to slavery, delivering sermons that "torture the hallowed pages of inspired wisdom." Douglass concluded that the "darkest feature of slavery" was the unequivocal support it received from the white southern clergy, which exposed any critic of the institution to "the charge of infidelity." The ultimate irony of proslavery Christianity was that it labeled slavery's opponents heretics and its supporters orthodox.[6]

But rather than disregard Christianity altogether, Douglass sought to preach boldly the real religion of "our blessed Savior." He refused to allow slaveholders to distort Christ's message unchallenged. Douglass proclaimed that the same Christ who "poured out his blood on Calvary, cared for my rights—cared for me equally with any white master."[7] At the end of his speech at Finsbury Chapel, Douglass reminded his listeners that the heart of the

Christian gospel was a radically antislavery message: "the glorious principle, of love to God and love to man; which makes its followers do unto others as they themselves would be done by." The kind of love to which Christ calls his followers, if truly practiced, would destroy "the slaveholding, the woman-whipping, the mind-darkening, the soul-destroying religion" of the American South.[8] Douglass assured his British audiences that he never wavered in his faithfulness to the Christianity of Christ, rightly understood. "I love it," he told an audience in Cork, Ireland, in October 1845. "I love that religion which is from above, without partiality or hypocrisy—that religion based upon that broad, that world-embracing principle, 'That whatever you would that men should do to you, do ye even so to them.'"[9] Douglass forever found in the gospel of Christ a powerful weapon against southern proslavery religion.

In a speech in Belfast in late December 1845, Douglass frankly described the prophetic work he sought to undertake in his British speaking tour. He wanted to reveal to the world the "corruption and sinful position" of America's churches on slavery. Even so, Douglass confessed to his audience that "any attempt to expose the inconsistencies of the religious organization of our land is the most painful undertaking." It pained Douglass that the American church—though a natural reservoir of "the love of virtue and of justice"—could abandon Christ's teachings and uphold slavery. To purify American Christianity, and eradicate the institution of slavery, Douglass believed he had to shine "the light of truth" into the church's "dark recesses," and "expose her deeds to the light." But Douglass hoped no one would mistake his fiery prophetic voice for hostility to Christianity. "Let no man rank me among the enemies of the church, or of religion, because I dare to remove the mask from her face," Douglass said. He spoke ultimately out of *love* for Christianity and America's churches. Douglass labored not only for the abolition of slavery but also for the "salvation and purification" of the American church.[10] "If Christianity were allowed to have a full and fair hearing," Douglass predicted, "slavery would be abolished for ever."[11]

Douglass called on the British to help end American slavery, a task "of interest to every member of the human family."[12] Yet he knew that many Americans disapproved of "exposing the sins of one nation in the ear of another," as he wrote in a public letter to newspaper editor Horace Greeley. However, slavery was no ordinary evil, especially as it existed in America. It was "such a giant sin—such a monstrous aggregation of iniquity," that abolitionists had no choice but to appeal to the whole world for aid in destroying it. The British could best assist the antislavery cause by treating slavery (and the religion that justified it) as utterly "disreputable." If subjected to the opprobrium of the world, American slavery could not long endure.[13]

As he appealed to the British to assist the American slave, Douglass preached a message of hope. "I have been asked if I supposed the slavery of the United States would ever be abolished," he said to an audience in Paisley, Scotland, in March 1846. "It might as well be asked of me if God sat on his throne in heaven. So sure as truth is stronger than error, so sure as right is better than wrong, so sure as religion is better than infidelity, so sure must slavery of every form in every land become extinct." God had decreed slavery's death, which would inevitably come to pass. But this did not mean that opponents of slavery could passively wait for God to destroy slavery. Douglass said they should instead rally to action and assist God in the noble work of expanding freedom and eradicating bondage.[14]

During the eighteen months Douglass spent abroad, among the many speeches he delivered and topics he tackled, two particular religious controversies in Britain attracted his attention: first, the decision by the Free Church of Scotland, founded in 1843, to accept financial donations from American slaveholding Presbyterians; and second, the 1846 decision by the Evangelical Alliance, an international organization of evangelicals, to accept slaveholding Christians as members. Douglass repeatedly addressed both controversies in his speeches, and often at great length. He did so because the issues offered him the chance to exhort British Christians to flex their moral might against slavery by severing all ties with slaveholding believers. Douglass preached this message from the very moment he arrived in Britain. In one of his first speeches, in Dublin on 1 October 1845, Douglass called on Irish Christians to "hold no Christian intercourse" with slaveholders and man-stealers. "Be faithful friends in your Christian testimony against such profanation of Christianity," Douglass encouraged his listeners.[15] Communion with American slaveholders not only profaned the British Christian's faith but also helped perpetuate slavery in America—by granting respectability to an institution and religion that deserved only contempt.

The controversy surrounding the Free Church of Scotland and the Evangelical Alliance ultimately centered on a momentous theological question: Were slaveholders true Christians or did they practice a false faith and deserve to be cast out of Christ's church? As Douglass traveled to Britain, this question bitterly divided the leading evangelical denominations in America. By 1845, both Baptists and Methodists had split along sectional lines. In the run-up to the separation, the Baptists fought over appointing a slaveholder as a missionary; the Methodists divided over whether it was acceptable for a bishop to own slaves. Ultimately, southern Baptists and Methodists formed their own independent denominations, freeing themselves from direct anti-slavery agitation and condemnation.[16]

The same fundamental questions that broke apart the Baptist and Methodist denominations in America also fueled the controversy that raged over the Free Church of Scotland and the Evangelical Alliance. Should slaveholders and nonslaveholders continue to fellowship as common followers of Christ? Douglass took a strident, uncompromising stand on this question. "I do not believe a slave owner can be a Christian," he told an audience in Taunton, England.[17] He also assumed that if true believers maintained any sort of "Christian intercourse" with slaveholders, they compromised the integrity of their Christian witness. Even more tragically, Christians who associated in any way with slaveholders helped *perpetuate* slavery—for their association tacitly granted a legitimacy to proslavery religion and the institution it bolstered. This was why the stakes were so high to Douglass in the controversies over the Free Church of Scotland and the Evangelical Alliance. Hanging in the balance was the ability of faithful Christ-followers to maintain an uncompromising witness against slavery.

The Free Church of Scotland was established in 1843, only three years prior to Douglass's arrival in Britain. That year, the Reverend Thomas Chalmers led a party of 450 evangelical clergymen out of the established Church of Scotland, an action eventually known as the Disruption of 1843. The schism had several complex underlying causes, and anger about the status quo in the established church had been building among some Scottish Presbyterians for more than a decade. The ministers who formed the Free Church of Scotland particularly detested the Church of Scotland's patronage system, which effectively allowed a local church's wealthy landowning patron to select its parish minister, even if the majority of the congregation disapproved. A bitter fight over this issue erupted by the late 1830s. As Scottish courts grew increasingly involved in the matter, clergymen also fought over old questions about the Church of Scotland's independence from the state. By May 1843, more than one-third of the total ministers of the established church joined Chalmers to withdraw and form the Free Church of Scotland.[18]

The breakaway evangelicals had created a new church, but now they had to finance it. When the ministers left the Church of Scotland they forfeited their salaries and control of existing church property. Chalmers's plans to secure a firm financial position for the Free Church included a fundraising campaign among American Presbyterians. Representatives from the church traveled to the United States to plead for support. Altogether, they raised 3,000 pounds, mostly from Presbyterians in the slaveholding South, especially South Carolina. Christian slaveholders in the American South knew full well that their critics at home and abroad often denounced them as rank heretics and hypocrites. They were sensitive to the charges. For many Presbyterian slaveholders, donating to the Free Church of Scotland seemed like a chance to acquire a certain respectability—perhaps even admiration—in the eyes of at least some of their fellow Christians throughout the world.[19]

Chalmers gave the Presbyterian slaveholders ample reason for such hope. In a public letter to a Charleston minister who had helped raise money for the Free Church of Scotland, Chalmers said, "I do not need to assure you how little I sympathize with those who—because slavery happens to prevail in the Southern States of America—would unchristianize that whole region." Chalmers's letter outraged abolitionists in Britain and America, who heaped scorn on his church for compromising its integrity by maintaining ties with slaveholding Presbyterians. As the controversy intensified, Chalmers penned another public letter defending his actions. He flatly called slavery a "great evil." Yet he rejected his critics' argument that a slaveholder could not be a Christian. He also strongly resisted what he labeled "the proposed excommunication of all slaveholders." Ultimately, Chalmers did not budge on the theological issue of greatest concern to abolitionists like Douglass: He refused to call slaveholders non-Christians and end his fellowship with them.[20]

Douglass spoke throughout Scotland at the precise moment the controversy over the Free Church reached a fever pitch. Not surprisingly, he extensively addressed the issue, which offered a perfect opportunity to deliver the prophetic message he had already formulated. Douglass's first major speech on the matter came on 20 January 1846 in Dundee. He began by reading from the first chapter of the Book of Isaiah: "Ah sinful nation, a people laden with iniquity, a seed of evildoers, children that are corrupters: they have forsaken the LORD, they have provoked the Holy One of Israel unto anger, they are gone away backward." Douglass said the verse perfectly described the United States, especially the churches of the slaveholding South—the same congregations the Free Church of Scotland had lately embraced. Every one of the church's meetinghouses was "built with the price of blood," Douglass said, funded by profits from slave labor. As long as Chalmers and the church continued to "fellowship with man-stealers, woman-whippers, cradle-robbers, and plunderers," they compromised their Christian witness and ensured slavery would endure.[21]

Over the next several months, Douglass spoke repeatedly on the Free Church of Scotland, condemning in great detail its association with American slaveholders. The church's actions offended one of Douglass's deepest religious convictions: "that man-stealing is incompatible with Christianity—that slave-holding and true religion are at war with each other," as he told an audience in Arbroath, Scotland.[22] In fellowshipping with slaveholders, the Free Church of Scotland granted that slavery and Christianity *were* compatible, that the slave-master could be a genuine Christian. For this reason, the church was guilty of a "damning heresy." It proclaimed "that a man may be a Christian whatever may be his practice, so his creed be right," Douglass argued.[23] As long as the church accepted slaveholders' money and used it to pay ministers and build churches, it scarcely deserved to be called a Christian church at all. Douglass detested the thought of church representatives traveling to the American South and not saying a word against slavery. The church's agents ardently courted potential donors from among the Presbyterian slaveholding class. But even after looking firsthand upon slaves "divested of every right, stripped of every privilege, and denied the right of reading the Word of God," the agents "did not raise a whisper."[24] They kept their silence for the financial benefit of the Free Church of Scotland, a crass and selfish abandonment of their Christian witness.

Above all, Douglass insisted that the church, by its actions, "made itself responsible for slavery."[25] In accepting slaveholders' money, the church strengthened slavery in America. "Whatever tends to make slavery respectable, tends to perpetuate it," Douglass explained, and the church lent respectability to slaveholders by acknowledging them as Christians worthy of fellowship.[26] Douglass went so far as to argue that the church did "more for infidelity and atheism than all the infidels in Scotland combined."[27] By associating with slaveholders, the church dealt an immense blow to both the antislavery cause and the cause of Christ.

Only one option remained for the Free Church of Scotland to right its wrongs: "Send Back the Money!" Douglass repeated this refrain nearly every time he spoke on the church. "Let this be the theme in every town in Scotland," he once said.[28] It certainly was the driving appeal of Douglass's speeches on the controversy. Like a revivalist preacher, he roused his Scottish audiences to shout the slogan and condemn the church's actions. Douglass believed sending back the money would "do more to unrivet the fetters, to break the chains of the bondsman, and to hasten the day of emancipation, than years of lecturing by the most eloquent abolitionists."[29] By returning the money, the Free Church of Scotland would proclaim unequivocally that slaveholders were not respected members of the global Christian community, and if they ever desired to be, they must first free their slaves.

Ultimately, Douglass's oratory and the "Send Back the Money" campaign failed completely. Leading members of the Free Church of Scotland resented Douglass's strident critiques. Even some antislavery advocates worried that

Douglass spoke too harshly on the matter. Despite the public attention and outcry Douglass helped provoke, the church stood its ground. It refused to return the money. Ten years later, Douglass concluded that the church "lost a glorious opportunity for giving her voice, her vote, and her example to the cause of humanity, and to-day she is staggering under the curse of the enslaved, whose blood is in her skirts."[30] The Free Church of Scotland controversy convinced Douglass that Christian congregations *outside* the slaveholding South could easily act in ways that helped preserve American slavery.

Douglass also learned this lesson from the second major controversy that attracted his attention while abroad, which concerned membership in the Evangelical Alliance. The Evangelical Alliance was an international and interdenominational organization of evangelical Christians founded in 1846. It brought together a fairly wide array of Protestants, primarily American and British, though somewhat tenuously. They disagreed on no small number of issues, such as what exactly the alliance should do and how it should respond to the nineteenth century's latest intellectual developments, namely, Darwinian biology and biblical higher criticism.[31]

The first great internal debates of the Evangelical Alliance erupted at the moment of its formation over whether slaveholders should be admitted as members. In early 1846, prior to the alliance's official founding, British organizers of the group gathered for a preliminary meeting in Birmingham. There, one attendee presented a resolution barring slaveholders from joining the alliance, once formally organized. The rest of the attendees agreed to the resolution. When word reached the United States, a group of slaveholding evangelicals decided to attend the first alliance meeting anyway. They insisted that the preliminary resolution had no binding power over the organization. When the alliance convened formally in August 1846, around 900 delegates attended. Nearly 800 were from Britain, fewer than 50 came from continental Europe, and 77 were Americans—including slaveholders such as Thomas Smythe, a South Carolinian clergyman who had helped raise money for the Free Church of Scotland.[32]

Initially, the Evangelical Alliance went about its business without open conflict over slavery. Attendees first worked to draft an official doctrinal statement. No one referenced slavery until near the end of the deliberations, when one London delegate brought a resolution excluding slaveholders from membership in the alliance. The courteous spirit that had thus far prevailed disappeared almost instantly. The American slaveholders in attendance threatened to withdraw completely from the association if the resolution was not immediately dismissed. After the angry and confused debate that followed, a committee was established to consider the matter. The committee deliberated for six days and nights. It eventually produced a compromise resolution, which stipulated that the alliance would not grant membership to persons "who are slaveholders by their own fault, and through their own interest."[33]

The Americans initially agreed to this compromise but reversed their position two days later. They instead demanded separate national branches of the alliance—one in America, the other in Britain—that could independently govern their requirements for membership. The issue returned again to the special committee for its reconsideration. Ultimately, American intransigence triumphed. The alliance agreed to "adopt such organization in their several Countries, as, in their judgment, may be most in accordance with their peculiar circumstances." Slaveholders could now join the American branch of the Evangelical Alliance, unbothered by the scorn they received from some British antislavery Christians.[34]

Douglass loathed how American slaveholding evangelicals acted at the alliance meeting. Their petulance was matched only by their hypocrisy, he thought. To Douglass, the question before the Evangelical Alliance was simple: "Whether a manstealer ought to be regarded as a standing type and representative of Christ, or not?" No slaveholder, regardless of the circumstances of his slaveholding, could faithfully follow Christ, Douglass believed. He therefore detested the "compromise" resolution the special committee drafted. The resolution perpetuated a "deceitful idea," Douglass said, "that a man could hold a slave, not by his own fault, but that the blame might lie with another party." The resolution treated "Christian" slaveholders as "objects of commiseration rather than condemnation," which Douglass feared only strengthened slavery in America.[35]

Douglass thought the Evangelical Alliance betrayed the gospel of Christ in how it regulated its membership. The alliance excluded Quakers and Unitarians but "welcomed to their communion the man-stealer." In effect, the group privileged fellowship with proslavery evangelicals more than fellowship with antislavery Christians outside the evangelical fold. Douglass believed the alliance "strained at gnats and swallowed camels." That is to say, the alliance obsessed over the gnat-sized theological differences separating Christian evangelicals and nonevangelicals, yet tolerated the camel-sized sin of slaveholding *among* evangelicals.[36] Douglass condemned the Evangelical Alliance for its "infidelity" to God's commandments. Amid the extended debates over the organization's membership, the majority of attendees "never raised a whisper in condemnation" of slavery, he said. Their silence made them guilty of "unfaithfulness and disobedience" to the religion they professed.

"They proved themselves to be false to God, to Christ, and to his people," Douglass concluded, "but friend to slavery and the slaveholder." For that reason, the alliance "acted like a band of infidels rather than of Christians."[37]

Douglass explicitly linked the controversy over the Free Church of Scotland and the fight over membership in the Evangelical Alliance. Both matters confirmed for Douglass the absolute necessity of rejecting Christian fellowship with slaveholders for the sake of the fight against slavery. In late September 1846 in Glasgow, Douglass argued that both the Free Church and the Evangelical Alliance stood "on the side of the oppressor." There was no neutral middle ground on the issue of slaveholding, Douglass insisted. Individuals and organizations were either proslavery or antislavery, either friends or enemies to the slave, for one could not legitimately tolerate slavery and worship "at the shrine of liberty at the same time."[38]

The Free Church and the Evangelical Alliance acted as if they could associate with slaveholding Christians and somehow avoid complicity in the sin of slavery. But Douglass believed that when Christian groups like the Free Church and the Evangelical Alliance fellowshipped in any way with Christian slaveholders, they merely strengthened slavery's hold in America. Association with foreign Christians granted a certain respectability to American slaveholders—at the very least, it tacitly recognized them as true Christians, despite their slaveholding. This allowed the slaveholder to "go on in his usual career," continuing to hold men and women and children in bondage.[39]

Ultimately, as in the controversy over the Free Church, Douglass achieved no real victory in his campaign against the Evangelical Alliance. The organization maintained its membership policy regarding slaveholders, despite condemnation from Douglass and other abolitionists. Douglass masterfully used the tactic of nonviolent moral suasion to try to force change in the Free Church and the Evangelical Alliance. But he did not succeed. Once Douglass returned to America in 1847, his commitment to both nonviolence and apolitical moral suasion waned fairly quickly. Douglass's experiences in Britain did not, by themselves, cause this shift in thinking. Yet his campaign against the Free Church and the Evangelical Alliance certainly revealed the limits to the power of nonviolent moral suasion in the battle against slavery.

In his final months in Britain, Douglass tried to maintain an incredibly frantic schedule. He spoke nearly every night, often for several hours. By March 1847, the grueling pace had taken its toll. Douglass decided it was time to return home. His friends held a public sendoff for him in London, attended by well over 1,000 people. There, Douglass made a final farewell address to the British people. It was his last opportunity to deliver a prophetic word in Britain, and he did not disappoint. Undoubtedly anticipating his return to America, Douglass reserved his sternest words for his native country. America "is one great falsehood, from beginning to end," he said. The nation's venerated political and religious principles and institutions were hollow at the core, corrupted by slavery. "I am going back, determined to be honest with America," Douglass told his audience; he returned "to unmask her pretensions to republicanism, and expose her hypocritical professions of Christianity." Douglass's eighteen months in Britain allowed him to see clearly a sobering truth about human bondage in the United States: "The church in America is, beyond all question, the chief refuge of slavery." Christian ministers, North and South, remained the most "bold, brave, and uncompromising" defenders of the institution. In America, religion and slavery remained "woven and interwoven together," which made all the more arduous the task awaiting prophetic antislavery voices like Douglass's. For abolitionists to succeed, they had to expose proslavery religion for what it really was—not merely a source of oppression, but also a perversion of genuine Christianity.[40]

In determining "to be honest" with America, Douglass had resolved to preach the gospel of Christ to a people who claimed to follow his commands but in reality only mocked them with their words and deeds. On 20 April 1847, Douglass's transatlantic voyage ended. He arrived in Boston and hurried to his home. Douglass returned with a deep zeal to change America with his prophetic message. But in the immediate future, he—not his home nation—would be the one to undergo a transformation.

An Antislavery Constitution and a Righteous Violence

Douglass returned to America an emboldened crusader for the antislavery cause. With encouragement (and financial support) from friends in England, Douglass established his own newspaper, the *North Star*, which published its first issue in early December 1847. Douglass's ambitions had grown larger than the opportunities afforded by the American Anti-Slavery Society. To his surprise, William Lloyd Garrison and several other society leaders strongly opposed his newspaper plan. They much preferred to keep Douglass tightly within the American Anti-Slavery Society fold, under their close watch, than to see him strike out on his own as a possible rival. Douglass proceeded with his plans anyway and was soon relieved of his position as an American Anti-Slavery Society lecturer. He then moved his family from Massachusetts to Rochester, New York, on the state's western frontier, along Lake Ontario. Within a year's time, Douglass the fledgling editor became a political activist in ways abhorrent to abolitionists committed to "moral suasion" alone. In 1848, he attended the political convention that formed the Free-Soil Party, and he had great hopes for what it and the other antislavery third parties might accomplish.[1]

Across the late 1840s and early 1850s, Douglass's ties to the American Anti-Slavery Society and the Garrisonian wing of abolitionism rapidly frayed—institutionally, geographically, and intellectually. As he embarked on a new phase in his public life, he reconsidered certain elements of the antislavery ideology he had accepted since his escape. These years marked "a radical change in my opinions," Douglass later explained, especially about the character of the U.S. Constitution and the role of violence in the struggle against slavery.[2] Distinctly theological considerations ultimately played a major role in motivating Douglass to see the Constitution as antislavery and violent resistance as potentially necessary and moral.[3] While revising his outlook on these two topics, Douglass also continued to broaden his prophetic vision. As the slavery crisis intensified, and the nation plunged into a war with Mexico, Douglass denounced as pointedly as ever *all* of America, not just slaveholders or white southerners, for its guilt in sustaining slavery.

Douglass was not a lawyer or judge, but he was a careful reader of the Constitution. Since his fugitive days in New Bedford, he had accepted the Garrisonian view that the Constitution was hopelessly proslavery. After Douglass arrived home from Great Britain in the spring of 1847, he continued to affirm this reading of the Constitution for more than a year. "Its Bill of Rights is to practise towards us a bill of wrongs," Douglass wrote Thomas Van Rensselaer, a fellow black abolitionist and newspaper editor. "Its self-evident truths are self-evident lies. Its majestic liberty, malignant tyranny. The foundation of this government—the great Constitution itself—is nothing more than a compromise with man-stealers."[4] As long as he viewed the Constitution as inescapably proslavery, Douglass also continued to remain aloof from overt political activity within the system created by the Constitution. "For my part I had rather that my right hand should wither by my side than cast a ballot under the Constitution," Douglass told a Syracuse, New York, audience in September 1847.[5] "I have no love for America," Douglass confessed several months earlier, just after his arrival from Britain. "The institutions of this Country do not know me—do not recognize me as a man. . . . I am not thought of or spoken of, except as a piece of property belonging to some *Christian* Slaveholder."[6]

Yet in 1849 and early 1850, Douglass began to rethink these opinions. He studied the issue more seriously than ever before, including "the just and proper rules of legal interpretation" and also the "origin, design, nature, rights, powers, and duties of civil governments," as he later recalled.[7] In early 1849, Douglass took his first clear step away from a straightforward reading of the Constitution as proslavery. He made a subtle yet important distinction between the *intent* of the drafters of the Constitution and the *letter* of the law they had written. Although the Founders originally intended for the Constitution to preserve slavery, a plain reading of the text of the Constitution itself did not necessarily demand a proslavery interpretation alone, Douglass now believed. In February 1849, he granted to a fellow abolitionist, "On a close examination of the Constitution, I am satisfied that if strictly 'construed according to its reading,' it is not a pro-slavery instrument."[8]

Even so, Douglass still believed that the proslavery intent of the Framers irredeemably corrupted the Constitution. The founding generation had widely supported slavery, which infused the Constitution they drafted with a certain inescapably proslavery sentiment. "We are told of the wisdom and goodness of our ancestors," Douglass said in a January 1850 debate over the Constitution held by the American Anti-Slavery Society. "*I know they were slaveholders. This one fact is enough for me.*" Following the Garrisonians, Douglass continued to affirm that the "unholy, unrighteous" Constitution written in 1787 should be discarded and replaced entirely—for any supreme law that "does not love Justice and Liberty for all, does not love Liberty and justice."[9]

As Douglass began to reconsider his views on the Constitution, he became good friends with Gerrit Smith, a wealthy New York reformer and antislavery activist. Smith corresponded often with Douglass in the late 1840s and early 1850s. He played an important role in convincing Douglass of the antislavery character of the Constitution. In many ways, Smith occupied a wing of the American abolitionist movement decidedly different from the one associated with Garrison. He argued for both an antislavery reading of the Constitution and also for overt political activity, namely, support of the upstart Liberty Party.[10]

Smith tried to convince Douglass that if he truly believed the Constitution "construed only in the light of its letter, is not a pro-slavery instrument," then he had to embrace entirely an antislavery reading of the text. Smith argued that the Founders' proslavery intentions did not matter because the letter alone of the Constitution clearly was not proslavery. If a plain reading of the Constitution revealed its meaning, then there was no need to look outside the text for insight. As Smith put the point, "If the Constitution is capable of being construed in the light of its letter, it is utterly contrary to the laws of interpretation to attempt to prove it in any other light."[11] That is, Douglass should not let the Founders' proslavery intentions shape his interpretation of a text that, taken alone, was not proslavery. "If the Constitution is incapable of being construed according to its letter, there is, of course, liberty to go outside of it for help to construe it," perhaps by making a historical argument about the authors' original intent, Smith further explained. "But you admit, that it is capable of being interpreted in the light of its letter," Smith wrote to Douglass, and according to sound rules of textual interpretation, if it is possible to understand the Constitution "in the light of its letter, it is utterly contrary to such rules to attempt to interpret it in any other lights, or by any other helps."[12]

By March 1849, Douglass granted that Smith's argument was probably valid. After summarizing Smith's position in the *North Star*, Douglass concluded that he had found "many rules of interpretation favoring this mode of understanding the Constitution of the United States, and none against it, though there may be such."[13] Even so, Douglass still—in the same editorial—denounced the Constitution and the government it created as "a most foul and bloody conspiracy against the rights of the three millions of enslaved and imbruted men." Smith's arguments drew Douglass away from an understanding of the Constitution as strictly proslavery, but they did not entirely convince him that the document was antislavery.

Douglass came closer to embracing an interpretation of the Constitution as antislavery once he accepted that the foundational principles of the document—ever-present in its text—stood utterly contrary to slavery. At this point, Douglass's experience reading the Bible as antislavery proved absolutely pivotal in convincing him to read the Constitution in the same way. The same methods of interpretation Douglass first used to find an antislavery message in scripture, despite its seeming support of slavery, he eventually used to read the Constitution as fundamentally antislavery.

Douglass had long insisted that at the heart of the Bible was a radical message of liberty and human dignity—a spirit that overrode any particular passages that appeared to condone slavery. In an 1846 speech in Belfast, Douglass insisted that "faith, hope, and charity sparked on every page [of the Bible], all of which deal death to slavery." Douglass contended that the "fundamental principle running through and underlying" the entire Bible was a radically antislavery sentiment: "Whatsoever ye would that men should do unto you, do you even so unto them." Proslavery clergy might offer tortured readings of particular chapters and verses to sanction slavery. But to Douglass, all efforts to make the Bible proslavery failed miserably in light of the overriding spirit of the text.[14]

Eventually, Douglass applied this same hermeneutic—this same method of interpretation—to reading the Constitution in an antislavery manner. The Constitution's preamble thus became immensely important to Douglass: "We the People of the United States, in Order to form a more perfect Union, establish Justice, insure domestic Tranquility, provide for the common defence, promote the general Welfare, and secure the Blessings of Liberty to ourselves and our Posterity, do ordain and establish this Constitution for the United States of America." The opening lines of the Constitution revealed its fundamental spirit and governing principles, especially a deep reverence for justice and liberty for all people, Douglass argued in an April 1850 editorial in the *North Star*.[15]

Yet in the same editorial still Douglass did not completely embrace an interpretation of the Constitution as antislavery. He assumed instead, for a time, that a "fundamental contradiction" rested at the heart of the nation's founding document: Its foundational principles were antislavery, even though some of its particular articles were explicitly meant to sustain slavery.[16] As late as January 1851, Douglass still had difficulty reading the Constitution as antislavery, largely because of the obvious proslavery intentions of the Founders. As Douglass asked Gerrit Smith, "Is it good morality to take advantage of a legal flaw and put a meaning upon a legal instrument the very opposite of what we have good reason to believe was the intention of the men who framed it?"[17]

A scandal erupted in May 1851 when Douglass publicly announced at the annual meeting of the American Anti-Slavery Society that he now believed in the wholly antislavery character of the Constitution. As a result, Douglass also affirmed that American abolitionists should not rely only on moral suasion to end slavery but also on outright political action. At one point in its May meeting, the American Anti-Slavery Society considered a resolution withholding its formal endorsement from any antislavery newspaper that did not affirm the proslavery nature of the Constitution. Amid the debate, Douglass informed stunned attendees that if the resolution passed his paper would no longer be eligible for the society's endorsement. Douglass always remembered the condescending, insulting way Garrison cried out in reply, "There is roguery somewhere"—as if Douglass could not have sincerely and independently reached such a conclusion. With Garrison's backing, the society still passed the resolution, and Douglass's relationship with the Garrisonians grew more toxic.[18]

Days later, in an editorial in the *North Star*, Douglass further explained that, properly interpreted, the Constitution could "be made consistent in its details with the noble purposes avowed in its preamble." Douglass evoked the plainly antislavery *spirit* of the Constitution, contained in its opening lines, as the key to rightly understanding the document's *letter*, its articles. Here Douglass relied on the method of interpretation that he had long used to read the Bible in an antislavery way—by appealing to the spirit of a text as necessary to comprehending its letter. Consequently, Douglass again also affirmed that every American had an obligation "to use his *political* as well as his *moral* power" to end slavery.[19]

Douglass told Gerrit Smith that he abandoned his earlier objections to reading the Constitution as antislavery once he realized that "I am only in reason and in conscience bound to learn the intentions of those who framed the Constitution *in the Constitution itself*." The full intentions of the Framers on slavery varied, and ultimately even remained somewhat mysterious. But the meaning of the Constitution was plainly evident, strictly construed according to its spirit and letter.[20] Douglass assumed that if the Constitution proclaimed that its purpose was to establish justice and secure the blessings of liberty—the noble sentiments of the preamble—it could not also "have been designed at the same time to maintain and perpetuate a system of rapine and murder like slavery."[21]

At the same time Douglass began interpreting the Constitution as antislavery, he also came to believe violence could be necessary and appropriate in the struggle against slavery. Well into the late 1840s, Douglass had largely supported nonviolent resistance as advocated by the Garrisonian abolitionists. "I am not a man of war," he told an antislavery crowd in Syracuse, New York, in September 1847. "I would not hurt a hair of a slaveholder's head."[22] But Douglass's commitment to strict nonviolence disappeared in the wake of the Fugitive Slave Act of 1850. The act sought to appease southern slaveholders by making it easier to recapture escaped slaves. Most infamously, it required all citizens and U.S. marshals to assist in hunting down fugitives. Anyone who refused faced large fines or imprisonment.[23] Douglass contended that the act truly nationalized slavery by marshaling support for the institution from "all the powers of the American government."[24] In light of the new law, Douglass saw more clearly than ever how the tyrannical "Slave Power" dominated nearly every facet of American life: "If I go to the Church, it is almost entirely on the side of oppression; if I go to the Press, it is almost entirely on the side of oppression; if I go to the great political parties, they are both on their knees to the Slave Power, begging for the votes of slaveholders!"[25]

Abolitionists faced a difficult dilemma in determining how best to react to the new law they considered plainly unjust. Less than a month after the passage of the act, Douglass admitted to a crowd at Faneuil Hall in Boston that American slaves and their allies could not completely prevent the execution of the new law, if the majority of Americans supported it. "But after the fullest deliberation," Douglass said, "we one and all—without the slightest hope of making successful resistance—are resolved rather to die than to go back." Douglass promised to do all he could to keep fugitive slaves beyond the reach of professional slave catchers, even if it meant the cobblestones of Boston flowed with blood. One of two outcomes seemed likely now: "the slave-hunter will be here to bear the chained slave back, or he will be murdered in your streets."[26]

In early January 1851, opponents of the Fugitive Slave Act from across the North gathered in Syracuse, New York, for a four-day convention. When

The Zealous Orator

Douglass spoke on the first day of the meeting, he offered an uncompromising defense of violent resistance to the law. "I am a peace man," he said, but the extraordinary circumstances demanded something more than nonviolence. The only way to end the injustice sanctioned by the act was to make slaveholders believe they faced "bodily harm if they come here, and attempt to carry men off into bondage." Fugitive slaves and their allies must be willing to shed the blood of slaveholders and slave catchers. Douglass predicted that "two or three dead slaveholders will make this law a dead letter."[27] Douglass further contended that violence resistance to an unjust law was a truly moral action, a way of "doing God service." He also unapologetically concluded that the "slaveholder has no right to live." Any man who would "so far sink his manhood as to become a wolf, a tiger, a bloodhound"—and hunt down a fellow human being who had finally attained freedom—did not deserve to live. To Douglass, the *liberty* of the fugitive slave was more valuable than the *life* of a slaveholder or slave catcher.[28]

Throughout 1851, Douglass grew stronger in support of violent resistance to the Fugitive Slave Act—largely because of three particular episodes in which escaped slaves struggled to remain free. Henry Long had fled from slavery in Richmond, Virginia, in 1848 by hiding away on a vessel headed for New York City. He safely lived there for more than a year before a Richmond resident spotted him one day and informed his master. By early January 1851, Long's owner recaptured and sold him to a Georgia slave trader. Long's fate "shrouded my spirit in gloom," Douglass told a Rochester, New York, audience in mid-January. "His hopes and aspirations, plans and purposes, have been cut off and destroyed." If the people of New York City had come to his aid, Long might still enjoy his freedom, Douglass said. But his return to slavery proved "that nothing short of physical resistance will render the colored people of the North safe from the horrible enormities which must result from the execution of the fugitive slave law."[29]

Three months later, in the abolitionist hotbed of Boston, an escaped slave from Georgia named Thomas Sims was arrested. Despite a vigorous legal defense arranged by Lewis Hayden, a leader in the city's African American and abolitionist communities, a Boston court returned Sims to slavery. U.S. Marines escorted Sims through Boston's streets before loading him on a ship for Georgia. Douglass spoke for many northerners when he wrote that Sims's capture left him "shocked and sorrow stricken." If such a horror could happen in Boston, it could happen anywhere. Douglass here again affirmed that armed resistance might best keep African Americans in the North from a similar fate. "In these troublous times no colored man should be without arms in his house, if not upon his person," Douglass wrote in an April editorial. "A law that cannot be executed but by exposing the officers authorized to execute it to deadly peril, cannot long stand."[30]

Douglass's most direct involvement in outright resistance to the Fugitive Slave Act came amid the so-called Christiana incident of September 1851. William Parker, a former slave who farmed near the Pennsylvania village of Christiana, harbored several fugitive slaves who had escaped from Maryland. When their master, Edward Gorsuch, learned that they were likely hiding at Parker's farm, he and several U.S. marshals descended on the farmhouse to recapture the runaways. Parker refused to hand over the men to Gorsuch and the marshals, and then had his wife alert their neighbors that they needed help resisting the slave catchers. In the melee that followed, Gorsuch was killed and Parker and two fugitives fled north. As they journeyed on the Underground Railroad, they stopped for a time at Douglass's home in Rochester, where they hid before taking a boat to Canada. As he boarded the boat, Parker gave Douglass the gun he had used to kill Gorsuch.[31]

Shortly thereafter, Douglass defended the violent resistance at Christiana in his newspaper. If Parker and the escaped slaves acted immorally, Douglass wrote, then "the whole structure of the world's theory of right and wrong is a lie." Because Gorsuch tried to reenslave the fugitives and deprive them of their lives and liberties, he had forfeited his own right to life. "The man who rushes out of the orbit of his own rights, to strike down the rights of another," Douglass argued, "does, by that act, divest himself of the right to live; if he be shot down, his punishment is just." By violently resisting the Fugitive Slave Act, a man like Parker might break a human-made (and unjust) law, but he upheld a higher "law of nature."[32] A few months later, Douglass again similarly suggested that violence was sometimes necessary to resist an oppressive law and restore true justice: "I believe that the lines of eternal justice are sometimes so obliterated by a course of long continued oppression that it is necessary to revive them by deepening their traces with the blood of a tyrant."[33]

Still, Douglass was not by nature prone to violence. He certainly did not rejoice in shedding blood for the slave's sake. He far preferred for America to experience a transformative moral and religious awakening—a dramatic realization of the injustice of slavery. Douglass hoped to inspire such an awakening by speaking a hard prophetic truth to the nation. As he revised his opinions about the Constitution and violent resistance, Douglass also deepened his commitment to fulfilling a prophet-like role in slaveholding America. In the late 1840s and early 1850s, especially in the wake of America's war with Mexico and the passage of the Fugitive Slave Act, Douglass spoke to America as sternly as ever. He explicitly preached his prophetic word to *all* of America as never before. He wanted northerners especially to realize their hypocritical complicity in slavery.

Douglass believed the Mexican-American War of 1846–48 offered a prime example of how most American churches, in particular, remained profoundly responsible for the preservation of slavery. Douglass called war "one of the greatest curses of mankind," but he thought the Mexican-American War was especially horrible because it opened the possibility of slavery's expansion into the far western part of the American continent.[34] Yet despite its obvious wickedness, many American Christians and clergymen approved of the war, blessing it with all sorts of religious justifications. Douglass concluded that America had collectively "resolved to rush on in her wicked career, though the road be ditched with human blood, and paved with human skulls."[35] It made Douglass sick to hear churches throughout the North celebrate America's victory in the war and "boast of it as a triumph of Christianity!"[36] To Douglass, the war warranted shame and contrition from Americans. It had revealed how thoroughly the nation's Christian churches remained the greatest bulwark of slavery. They lent support for a war that served to strengthen slavery in America, Douglass thought, and "sustain the pro-Slavery and negro-hating religion of the country."[37]

In a similar way, following the Mexican-American War, Douglass condemned the northern clergy for widely supporting the Fugitive Slave Act. He loathed how "hypocritical Doctors of Divinity" could so easily "torture the pages of the Holy Bible to sanctify popular crimes."[38] The act rested on a plainly un-Christian assumption, Douglass said, "that law can make property of man—a marketable commodity of the image of God." Yet Christians on both sides of the Mason-Dixon Line failed to see the gross contradiction between the law's demands and Christ's teachings. The Christian churches of the North and South, united in their support of the act, together practiced a "caste-religion," always proclaiming in word and deed that black Americans were inferior to white Americans.[39]

Douglass considered the Fugitive Slave Act a dire threat to religious liberty in America because it effectively made it illegal to truly live like Christ. Christians had an obligation to love their neighbor, to care for the marginalized and oppressed, yet the Fugitive Slave Act forced them to do exactly the opposite—to participate in the recapture of escaped slaves. The law criminalized any true attempt "to carry out the principles of Christianity," Douglass said in an August 1852 speech in Pittsburgh.[40] A few weeks later, in an address in Ithaca, New York, Douglass explained that while Christ commanded his followers to "feed the hungry, clothe the naked, and take in the stranger," the Fugitive Slave Act made "it penal to obey Christ." The law might not "interfere with the forms and ceremonies of the Christian religion," Douglass granted, but it still posed a terrible threat to the faithful practice of the Christian faith. It outlawed "the fundamental principles of Christianity . . . the weightier matters of the law, judgment, mercy, and faith."[41] Douglass argued that no true follower of Christ—no true believer in a just and loving God—could submit to such a law. "I do not believe that human enactments are to be obeyed when they are point blank against the laws of the living God," Douglass wrote in his newspaper in October 1851. The Fugitive Slave Act contradicted the moral duties incumbent on Christians, so no truly faithful person could comply with it.[42]

Douglass used the controversy surrounding the Mexican-American War and Fugitive Slave Act to speak a prophetic word to the entire nation, not simply the slaveholding South. He sought to expose the hypocrisy of American Christianity and, at the same time, vindicate the true Christianity of Christ as a bitter foe of bigotry and oppression. Douglass called on all American Christians to more faithfully practice the faith they proclaimed by actively working to destroy slavery.

But at present, most churches remained too thoroughly complicit in slavery's continued existence. At the May 1849 meeting of the New England Anti-Slavery Society, Douglass said, "a Church countenancing or fellowshipping Slavery in any of its aspects was not a Christian Church, but a sinning Church," an iniquity he found in no short supply in America.[43] Douglass suspected that slavery endured in America because "we are too religious as a nation." By that he meant that Americans "substituted religion for humanity—we have substituted a form of Godliness, an outside show for the real thing itself." Like the scribes and Pharisees of Christ's day, American Christians put on a facade of righteousness. But their refusal to oppose slavery revealed the hollowness of their faith.[44] White Christians everywhere denied "the brotherhood of the human family" and failed "to do their duty towards *man*." Consequently, Douglass continued, the worship they offered to God was "unacceptable in His sight."[45] Douglass even believed that many African American churches, in their own way, failed to fully combat slavery and racism as Christianity required. Northern black churches that did not host antislavery meetings acted as "the tyrant as readily and as bitterly as do our white oppressors," for in their silence they occupied the "slaveholding position."[46] Douglass had particularly little patience for African American ministers who preached messages of otherworldliness. He hated to hear a black minister conclude from biblical texts like "Seek ye first the kingdom of heaven" that African Americans everywhere, slave and free, should simply "wait for God to help them." Douglass believed such teachings amounted to passive acceptance of slavery and racial oppression. He still assumed that God actively worked on behalf of American slaves, but even by the late 1840s he also insisted that African Americans had an active role to play in securing their own freedom and elevation. They could not simply wait to receive it.[47]

But even as he criticized American churches for their moral failure on slavery, Douglass also offered a constructive vision of how to live as a faithful Christian in slaveholding America. Douglass cared little for quibbles over arcane theology and more for putting the Christian faith into practice. To live like Christ, he believed, was to care for the outcast and marginalized and oppressed—the orphan, widow, and slave. True Christianity "takes off fetters instead of binding them on . . . lifts up the bowed down," Douglass said, so followers of Christ must always "sympathize with the oppressed, and act our part in breaking their bonds."[48] Although he had formally left the Methodist Church, Douglass still believed in the Christian vision of a righteous life. In core Christian dogma, Douglass discovered ideas radically opposed to slavery. The Bible proclaimed that every human being was made "in the image of God," equal in dignity and value.[49] And at the center of true Christianity was *love*—a love of God that led to a fervent love of one's neighbor, slave and free alike. "God, the foundation and source of all goodness, must be loved in order that we may love our fellow-man," Douglass once said. If only Americans would love God rightly and love their neighbors lavishly, then slavery would disappear, for the institution remained so fundamentally contrary to the most basic Christian commandment: "Love your neighbor as yourself."[50]

But at the present moment, Douglass found too little love in the American Christian church. It remained beholden to the Slave Power and complicit in its oppression. Douglass concluded in 1850 that "the judgment-day of slavery is dawning."[51] America would surely soon face a terrible reckoning, a bitter day of judgment from the Lord for its iniquity. Long-forgotten ancient empires far stronger than America "have been shattered by the bolts of the wrath of a *just* God," Douglass wrote in the *North Star*, and he predicted that if the United States continued in its present path of wickedness, it would soon face the same fate.[52]

No single speech more completely captured the prophetic voice Douglass had refined throughout the late 1840s and early 1850s than his "What to the Slave Is the Fourth of July?" More than 500 people gathered at Corinthian Hall in Rochester, New York, on 5 July 1852 to hear what they surely thought

Frederick Douglass, 1856. *Courtesy of the Art Institute of Chicago.*

would be a typical, celebratory address venerating America's independence and founding. Instead, in the style of an ancient Hebrew prophet, Douglass delivered a fiery sermon—condemning America for its wickedness and oppression, calling upon it to atone for its sins, and pleading with its people to pursue the path of true righteousness by living according to its highest political and religious ideals.

Douglass's speech began in a conventional way. He recalled the lives and legacies of America's Founders, a generation of "brave men" who boldly defended the principles they believed in and achieved their great goal of national independence. Douglass praised the Declaration of Independence as "the ring-bolt to the chain of your nation's destiny." The soaring words of the declaration contained "saving principles," and America must remain "true to them on all occasions."[53] On the surface, the first third of Douglass's speech resounded with the congratulatory tone all-too-common in the era's Fourth of July addresses. But if Douglass's audience listened closely, they would have detected the true sentiment of his sermon. The most powerful and unsettling element of the opening of Douglass's speech is his frequent use of the pronoun *your*. To his overwhelmingly white audience, Douglass referred to *your* national independence, *your* political freedom, *your* nation, *your* fathers. The Founders succeeded in creating a new nation, Douglass said, "and to-day you reap the fruits of their success. The freedom gained is yours; and you, therefore, may properly celebrate this anniversary."[54]

But what, then, to the slave was the Fourth of July? It was a day whose celebrations laid bare all the terrible hypocrisy, discrimination, and oppression that poisoned America, North and South. For that reason, Douglass could not help but resent the Rochester Ladies Anti-Slavery Society for asking him, a black man and former slave, to deliver a celebratory speech for the occasion. "Do you mean, citizens, to mock me, by asking me to speak to-day?" Douglass asked. The cruel ordeal reminded him of Psalm 137, which he quoted in part to the gathered crowd:

> By the rivers of Babylon, there we sat down. Yea! we wept when we remembered Zion. We hanged our harps upon the willows in the midst thereof. For there, they that carried us away captive, required of us a song; and they who wasted us required of us mirth, saying, Sing us one of the songs of Zion. How can we sing the Lord's song in a strange land? If I forget thee, O Jerusalem, let my right hand forget her cunning. If I do not remember thee, let my tongue cleave to the roof of my mouth.

Just as the ancient Israelites, in exile and bondage, had been called upon to sing for their Babylonian captors, so too did Douglass feel coerced into performing on the Fourth of July for the captors and oppressors of his people.[55]

Douglass had no desire to make again the same self-evident antislavery arguments that he and others had made innumerable times. He had wearied of trying to reason with Americans, to convince them through patient logic that it was wrong to enslave a human being. "At a time like this," Douglass said, "scorching irony, not convincing argument is needed." He decided to trade the rational argument of the philosopher for the ominous judgment of the prophet: "For it is not light that is needed, but fire; it is not the gentle shower, but thunder."[56] With the thunderous tone of a prophet, Douglass denounced America's crimes against God and humanity. He decried the nation's internal slave trade as "fiendish and shocking."[57] He condemned the Fugitive Slave Act as unprecedented "in the annals of tyrannical legislation." It "nationalized" slavery, he said, and robbed African Americans everywhere of liberty and justice. The act effectively outlawed Christ's command to care for the least, but most churches and ministers remained too "stupidly blind, or most wickedly indifferent" to recognize the contradiction between the law and true Christianity.[58]

Instead, the American church callously "made itself the bulwark of American slavery." Nearly every Christian minister either explicitly defended slaveholding or refused to speak against it, a betrayal of the Christian faith. "They strip the love of God of its beauty," Douglass cried, by preaching a religion that "favors the rich against the poor" and "exalts the proud above the humble." These same ministers and their congregations presumed to worship the Lord in spirit and truth, but God looked with anger on their worship as an abomination. Douglass quoted the prophet Isaiah to warn the American church that if it did not soon abandon its present path of wickedness and hypocrisy, it would face the wrath of God. In the first chapter of Isaiah, which Douglass cited to his audience, the Lord spoke to his chosen people: "When ye spread forth your hands I will hide mind eyes from you. Yea! When ye make many prayers, I will not hear. Your hands are full of blood; cease to do evil, learn to do well; seek judgment; relieve the oppressed; judge for the fatherless; plead for the widow." When Douglass considered the state of Christianity in slaveholding America, he saw not a spirit of justice, compassion, and mercy but a spirit of oppression, indifference, and hypocrisy.[59]

Imitating Hebrew prophets like Isaiah, Douglass issued his own stern warning to America at the end of his speech. "A horrible reptile is coiled up in your nation's bosom," he said, and "the venomous creature is nursing at the tender breast of your youthful republic." The terrible serpent of slavery exposed "your Christianity as a lie," Douglass continued, and also threatened to ruin America. The nation could not afford to delay any longer. It had to crush the head of the terrible snake that endangered its very existence, or tempt a terrible judgment from the Lord.[60]

Douglass offered a dark diagnosis of America's spiritual state, yet he still ended his speech in Rochester on a note of hope. "I do not despair of this country," he concluded, because he detected in the unfolding hand of history "forces in operation, which must inevitably work the downfall of slavery." The "great principles" of the Declaration of the Independence, the nation's founding charter; the "obvious tendencies of the age," enlightened and eman-cipatory in its spirit; and the benevolent, providential work of God all encour-aged Douglass that slavery could not long endure in America. He ended by reciting a poem written by William Lloyd Garrison, a kind of prayer to end his prophetic sermon, whose opening refrain pleaded with God to "speed the year of jubilee / The wide world o'er!"[61] As dark days of sectional crisis descended in the 1850s, Douglass relied more than ever on this spirit of Chris-tian hope to maintain his resolve in the fight against slavery.

THE HOPEFUL PROPHET

1853–1895

The Crisis of the Union

When the American Anti-Slavery Society gathered for its annual meeting in 1853 in New York City, the abolitionist movement was passing through a season of frustrating setbacks and bitter internal divisions. Slavery's defenders appeared to grow more powerful each year, while tensions among abolitionist factions grew fiercer. Despite the prickly treatment he had received at the previous year's convention, Douglass decided to attend the 1853 meeting anyway. "There are many societies, but there is but one cause," he wrote in his newspaper, explaining the decision.[1] Douglass spoke briefly during the first day of the meeting, between speeches by New York minister Henry Ward Beecher and William Lloyd Garrison. "There has been much said as to the hopeful and fearful side of this great controversy with Slavery," Douglass told his audience. "For my own part, I feel a little of both. I feel hopeful, and I feel fearful." Slaveholders had gained effective control of the nation's leading institutions—the state, church, and press. They lately seemed wildly successful in their effort to make slavery permanent and respected in America. Yet Douglass had not lost hope that a new dawn of freedom would soon commence. "I am distressed, and yet I have faith," Douglass said at the end of his short speech. "I believe Slavery will come down," and with its demise would arrive "that day when there shall be no slave, no chain to clank in our ears."[2]

Eight years later, America's Civil War erupted, which tested the very future of the Union and strengthened Douglass's faith that American slavery was nearing its end. At the onset of the war, in May 1861, Douglass wrote: "However timid men at this junction may alternate between hope and fear, one thing is certain—slavery is a doomed institution." Douglass predicted that slaveholders' rash support for secession and war only made more likely slavery's imminent death. But he also expected that before then, "the land may yet be drenched in human blood." Douglass hoped God would avert such a catastrophe, "unless there can be no other way opened for the redemption of the now crushed millions!" Opponents of slavery could now only place their faith in "Him who is 'mighty to save, and strong to deliver.'"[3]

For abolitionists, the late 1850s occasioned great fear and optimism. Slavery strangely seemed more powerful and imperiled than ever before. In these years, Douglass held fast to a distinctly Christian *hope*—a set of convictions that revived his soul with the assurance that American slavery would not long endure. Douglass's theology of hope shaped how he understood and responded to the major events of the sectional crisis of the 1850s. He rooted his hope in a distinct understanding of who God was and what God was doing in history. Douglass anticipated slavery's immanent death because he believed God was just, merciful, powerful, and actively at work in human affairs. The abolitionist cause faced many setbacks, yet Douglass still believed that God and truth would prevail—humbling the haughty slaveholder, setting free the captive, and establishing liberty and righteousness in America.[4]

When the Civil War finally began in the spring of 1861, Douglass relied on this same theology of hope to interpret the war's direction and define its purpose. He discerned God using the conflict to bring about slavery's demise. Douglass also considered it his duty as America's prophet to call the loyal citizenry to atone for slavery and take part in its destruction. If America failed to do so, Douglass warned, a wrathful God would surely bring upon the nation apocalyptic judgment and destruction.

Douglass's hope drew strength and substance from a Christian understanding of God as a good and all-powerful being at work in history. At the 1853 American and Foreign Anti-Slavery Society meeting, Douglass reminded wary abolitionists to remember that a "God of mercy and justice is enthroned above all created things."[5] Douglass spoke often of God as the author and protector of eternal *truth*, and he confidently believed "all the truths in the whole universe of God are allied to our cause."[6] God's truth, everywhere present in the world, stood starkly opposed to human bondage—nowhere more obviously than in the fact that all people were created in God's image, full of dignity and a "right to liberty." Douglass found reason to hope for slavery's eventual demise whenever he remembered that "truth, like the great God from whose bosom it emanates, is from everlasting unto everlasting, and can never pass away."[7] Despite temporary setbacks to the antislavery cause, Douglass affirmed that God worked in powerful and often mysterious ways to destroy American slavery: "I recognize an arm stronger than any human arm, and an intelligence higher than any human intelligence, guarding and guiding this Anti-Slavery cause, through all the dangers and perils that beset it."[8] A righteous God still reigned over all the earth and labored to "see *Truth* triumphant over all foes."[9] Douglass anticipated "the final triumph of the great Principles which underlie the Abolition movement," because "truth is mighty, and will prevail."[10]

Still, Douglass never denied the tremendous challenges facing the antislavery cause, especially the immense power of slaveholders and their allies. He spoke often of the "Slave Power," a pervasive, poisonous influence in American life, dead-set on halting abolitionism. Douglass defined the Slave Power as "that force which operates unceasingly through all the channels of social and political influence from Slavery and for Slavery."[11] The Slave Power kept a stranglehold on the nation's leading political and religious institutions, blunting the "moral sense" of the nation and leaving Christianity in America especially "marred, battered, defaced, and utterly perverted."[12] The Slave Power's triumphs made it hard for many abolitionists to maintain a hopeful spirit. But Douglass assured his fellow antislavery activists that, however disheartening events might appear, they need not despair. "I will walk by faith, not by sight, for all grounds of hope founded on external appearance, have thus far signally failed and broken down under me," Douglass wrote in the summer of 1860. He looked back on the 1850s as a decade full of victories for defenders of slavery, who sought to expand the institution and make it permanent. "Nevertheless," Douglass continued, "God reigns, and we need not despair, and I for one do not."[13] God, in full wisdom, might for unknowable reasons decide to delay the emancipation of American slaves. But abolitionists should take heart, for the almighty God of liberty and justice still actively worked in the world to destroy slavery.

Douglass voiced this prophetic Christian hope throughout the sectional crisis of the late 1850s, particularly during the controversies surrounding the Kansas-Nebraska Act of 1854, the Supreme Court's 1857 *Dred Scott v. Sandford* decision, and John Brown's failed insurrection at Harpers Ferry, Virginia, in 1859. These three events left many antislavery activists worried about the future, but Douglass responded with a word of hope—fully confident that a righteous God still governed human affairs, and that truth and justice would eventually prevail.

In 1854 the long-standing controversy over slavery's future in America's western territories returned with a vengeance. That year, Illinois Democratic senator Stephen Douglas introduced a measure for organizing the northern half of the Louisiana Purchase into two new territories, Kansas and Nebraska.

The Missouri Compromise of 1820 had excluded slavery from any section of the Louisiana Purchase north of the 36°30′ parallel, the southern border of Missouri. Even though the new territories of Kansas and Nebraska fell north of that line, Douglas's act left open the possibility that slavery could extend into one or both of the territories. The guiding principle of Douglas's Kansas-Nebraska Act of 1854 was popular sovereignty, which empowered residents of a given territory to decide for themselves whether to enter the Union as a slave or free state. Douglas's act elicited intense opposition from a wide range of northerners, all wary over the possibility of slavery extending far north in the United States. The act proved disastrous for the Whig Party, irrevocably dividing it along sectional lines and destroying it as a national party. Antislavery activists across the nation denounced the act as an ominous abandonment of the Compromise of 1820 that amounted to a moral capitulation to slavery.[14]

Douglass saw the Kansas-Nebraska Act as another example of how the Slave Power worked to suppress all antislavery discussion, extend slavery into the western territories and beyond, and "make slavery respected in every State in the Union."[15] He blamed its passage on the "audacious villainy of the slave power, and the contemptible pusillanimity of the North."[16] Slaveholders and their northern allies so easily disregard the Missouri Compromise because they had none of the integrity that it took to fulfill a bargain, Douglass said. They were selfish and deceitful people, and only a fool would put faith in "the honor of a man who has broken faith with God by enslaving man, the image of God."[17] Douglass fully expected the Slave Power to eventually disregard and replace the Kansas-Nebraska Act, if it ever proved inadequate to the task of preserving slavery.

Douglass believed the time had come for northerners to take an uncompromising antislavery stand. Instead of again conciliating slaveholders, northerners should insist that slavery had no legitimate constitutional or moral justification to exist *anywhere* in America. In the face of the Kansas-Nebraska Act, Douglass said, enemies of the Slave Power must finally rally together and proclaim, "Slavery, like rape, robbery, piracy or murder, has no right to exist in any part of the world."[18] The act was yet another instance of the Slave Power imposing on the nation a law "against the plainest dictates of the Christian religion." Ministers had an obligation to resist the act and thereby "arrest the nation in its downward progress, and save it from the deep damnation to which it is sinking." The time for evasion and equivocation on the slavery issue had definitively passed. A choice now stood before all Americans, Douglass said: "The banner of God and liberty, and the bloody flag of slavery and chains shall then swing out from our respective battlements and rally under them our respective armies, and let the inquiry go forth now, as of old, Who is on the Lord's side?"[19]

But regardless of how Americans answered that question, Douglass remained confident that God would ensure the end of slavery in America. In an extended speech on the Kansas-Nebraska Act in Chicago, Douglass told his audience, "Truth is eternal. Like the great God from whose throne it emanates, it is from everlasting unto everlasting, and can never pass away." The abolitionist movement defended the rights and dignity of all human beings, and in that way it remained aligned with God's eternal truth. Douglass anticipated "the ultimate triumph of free principles in this country," because he placed his faith in "the wisdom of that great God, who has promised to overrule the wickedness of men for His own glory—to confound the wisdom of the crafty and bring to naught the counsels of the ungodly."[20]

To Douglass, the "counsels of the ungodly" appeared most blatantly in the Supreme Court's 1857 *Dred Scott v. Sandford* decision. Dred Scott was a slave who moved with his master from the slave state of Missouri to the free state of Illinois and then the free territory Wisconsin. In 1846, Scott filed a lawsuit claiming that his residence in the free state and territory had freed him from slavery altogether. Eventually, the suit made its way to the U.S. Supreme Court. Chief Justice Roger Taney attempted to resolve once and for all the crisis over slavery in the *Dred Scott* decision. He hoped to pacify slaveholders and render pointless any further abolitionist agitation. The Court ruled 7–2 against Scott, and Taney's majority opinion delivered several major blows against the antislavery movement. Taney's ruled that Scott was not entitled to his freedom simply because he resided for a time in a free state and territory. He also declared that Scott, because he was an African American, was not a citizen of the United States and could not legitimately sue in federal court. Those two pronouncements alone sufficiently addressed the matter at the heart of the *Dred Scott* case. But Taney went even further in his decision. He declared that the Missouri Compromise of 1820 was unconstitutional because Congress had no authority to restrict slavery's expansion in any way in the western territories. Taney had effectively declared unconstitutional one of the foundational aims of the fledgling Republican Party, leaving uncertain the very future of the antislavery movement.[21]

Two months after the Supreme Court delivered the *Dred Scott* decision, Douglass spoke on the ruling at a meeting of the American Anti-Slavery Society in New York City. He acknowledged that the decision revealed some of the clear advantages that the Slave Power had over the abolitionists.

Church, state, and court alike seemed utterly beholden to the proslavery ideology. Many "difficulties and discouragements" presently beset the antislavery movement, Douglass confessed. "I see them clearly, and feel them sadly."[22] Yet he still believed abolitionists did not labor in vain. "David, you know, looked small and insignificant when going to meet Goliath," Douglass reminded his audience, "but looked larger when he had slain his foe." The antislavery movement might appear weak when arrayed on the battlefield against the mighty Slave Power. Defenders of slavery had the nation's political, religious, and judicial institutions on their side, but the opponents of bondage had the support of the almighty Lord. "My hopes were never brighter than now," Douglass boasted.[23]

He remained hopeful because he believed the *Dred Scott* decision plainly contradicted God's eternal law and therefore could not forever stand. "The Supreme Court of the United States is not the only power in this world. It is very great, but the Supreme Court of the Almighty is greater," Douglass insisted. Chief Justice Taney's power had its limits. "He cannot reverse the decision of the Most High," Douglass said. "He cannot change the essential nature of things—making evil good, and good evil." Taney tried to do exactly that in *Dred Scott*, but he did not truly succeed—even though the ruling seemed to hand a victory to the Slave Power. Douglass called the Court's decision "an open rebellion against God's government." God created all people in his image and desired none to live enslaved; the Court's ruling attempted to "undo what God has done." Douglass believed God would not allow the decision to stand. Defenders of slavery might pressure the Supreme Court to disregard "the black man's cry for justice," but they could not "shut up the Court of Heaven" to his cry. "All that is merciful and just, on earth and in Heaven," Douglass said, "will execrate and despise this edict of Taney."[24]

The work and will of God might remain somewhat mysterious, but Douglass kept hope that God used even the *Dred Scot* decision to end slavery in America. "I am superstitious enough to believe that the finger of the Almighty may be seen bringing good out of evil," he confessed to his American Anti-Slavery Society audience. Douglass thought God might be using the decision to keep the nation fully aware of the tyranny of the Slave Power and the terrible character of slavery. "It is another proof that God does not mean that we shall go to sleep, and forget that we are a slaveholding nation," which Douglass assumed would only help spread antislavery sentiment throughout the nation. *Dred Scott* appeared to secure slavery's existence in America to a far greater degree than any previous law or court decision. Yet Douglass, in a spirit of prophetic hope, reflected on the nature of God and God's eternal law and concluded instead that "slavery is a doomed system," regardless of what the Supreme Court ruled.[25]

In an America dominated by the Slave Power, Douglass found very few people eager to do whatever was necessary to end slavery. But there was at least one man, in a nation of millions of indifferent souls, still willing "to count his own life as worth nothing in comparison with the freedom of millions."[26] John Brown, New England's militant abolitionist and fiery Calvinist, inspired hope in Douglass in the late 1850s, for his stern words and courageous deeds were a prophetic call to action. Douglass first met John Brown in 1847 at Brown's home in Springfield, Massachusetts. Brown immediately made "a very deep impression upon my mind and heart," Douglass later recalled. "Certainly I never felt myself in the presence of a stronger religious influence than while in this man's house." Everything in Brown's austere home—from the furniture to the meal served—seemed to Douglass to reflect the man's zealous commitment to "stern truth, solid purpose, and rigid economy." Douglass remembered Brown as a lean, hard-worn, and sturdy man, like "mountain pine," whose blue-gray eyes "were full of light and fire." His words demanded attention. In 1847, Douglas had not yet fully abandoned Garrisonian nonviolence, but Brown offered a compelling moral alternative: the righteous use of violence in the fight for freedom.[27]

During their first meeting, Brown described to Douglass his goal of raising a guerrilla force to strike swiftly and secretly throughout the South. While the force would liberate some slaves, it mostly would seek to induce terror in the hearts of slaveholders. "Slavery was a state of war," Brown said to Douglass that day, which meant slaves could do whatever was necessary, even by violent means, to secure their freedom. Brown hoped the terrifying prospect of bloody insurrection would convince slaveholders to voluntarily abandon the institution. Douglass later pointed to his first meeting with Brown in 1847 as a pivotal moment in his waning commitment to nonviolence. "My utterances became more and more tinged by the color of this man's strong impressions," Douglass recalled. He had found in Brown a man of unquestioned religious zeal who offered a compelling justification for the use of violence in the antislavery struggle.[28]

More than ten years after their original meeting, Brown arrived at Douglass's Rochester home one day in February 1858. He had lately traveled throughout New England raising money for his latest antislavery scheme. Two years earlier, in the violence-ridden Kansas Territory, Brown led a small band of antislavery radicals who murdered five supposedly proslavery settlers in the territory. Brown eventually lived in Douglass's home for several weeks, constantly writing letters to raise financial support for an emancipatory operation whose details remained hidden. Initially, Douglass learned only fragments of Brown's intentions. But in August 1859, Brown revealed his plans in full to Douglass in the hopes of persuading him to participate.

Brown and twenty-one accomplices intended to capture the federal arsenal at Harpers Ferry, Virginia, free and arm nearby slaves, then press further south down the Appalachian Mountains, emancipating slaves and terrorizing slaveholders. Brown's plan astonished Douglass. Even though he admired the old man's ardent antislavery zeal, he could not join the raid, a direct attack on the property of the federal government. He fully expected the raid to fail. Douglass's wariness about Brown's plan proved well founded. Although Brown successfully captured and raided the arsenal at Harpers Ferry, the rest of the plan unraveled. Brown did not inspire widespread slave insurrection. Eventually a company of U.S. Marines subdued Brown and his men, killing or capturing most. Brown was promptly tried and convicted of murder, conspiring a slave rebellion, and treason against Virginia. The jury deliberated less than one hour. On 2 December 1859, Brown was hanged.[29]

Ralph Waldo Emerson infamously declared that Brown would "make the gallows glorious like the cross," a sentiment Douglass echoed. He too praised Brown as a "noble, heroic, and Christian martyr." Brown lived and died for the Christian faith, rightly understood; his raid to free slaves was "animated by a desire to do unto others as he should himself be done unto," Douglass said.[30] Brown "translated into heroic deeds the love of liberty and hatred of tyrants" at the heart of both the Bible and the Declaration of Independence. Douglass believed Brown was a man of "spotless integrity" whose awe-inspiring actions on behalf of American slaves won him eternal "glory so bright and enduring."[31]

Having earlier accepted violence as sometimes necessary in the antislavery struggle, Douglass defended Brown's effort to spark an armed insurrection. Brown "attacked slavery with the weapons precisely adapted to bring it to the death," Douglass argued. "Moral considerations have long been exhausted upon slaveholders," so abolitionists everywhere had to accept the necessity of brute force to crush the Slave Power. Douglass believed that Brown rightly realized that slavery "shields itself behind *might*, rather than right," and therefore "must be met with its own weapons."[32] Brown, through his words and actions, convinced Douglass completely that moral suasion alone would never conquer slavery in America. "I have little hope of the freedom of the slave by peaceful means," Douglass wrote in June 1860, for slaveholders "have neither ears nor hearts for the appeals of justice and humanity." Only violence—"the fear of death"—might compel masters to free their slaves.[33]

The Hopeful Prophet

Riot in Tremont Temple, Boston, 3 December 1860. From *Harper's Weekly*, 15 December 1860.

Although the raid on Harpers Ferry failed to incite mass slave insurrection, Douglass still saw in Brown's deeds reason for hope. Douglass expected that Brown's bold and uncompromising rebellion against slavery would serve as a clarion call to the Christian North to embrace the cause of emancipation. Like the words of a prophet, Brown's actions would "rouse a dead Church and dumb Ministry to the duty of putting away this dark and dangerous sin," slavery. In the immediate wake of Brown's capture, Douglass wrote, "The infuriated demon of Slavery never seemed to me more certain of extirpation than now."[34] Brown's raid might appear to some as another failure and setback for the abolitionist movement. But Douglass saw it as evidence of the moral might of the antislavery cause and the certainty of its triumph.

In the run-up to the 1860 presidential election, Douglass expressed some ambivalence about the new Republican Party and its nominee, Abraham Lincoln. He rightly worried that Lincoln and most Republicans, though antislavery, were not immediate abolitionists.[35] After Lincoln's election, Douglass castigated southern slaveholders who rashly called for immediate secession from the Union. "There is no sufficient cause for the dissolution of the Union," Douglass wrote in his newspaper in December 1860. He predicted slavery would be safer within the Union than in a newly independent southern nation.[36] But by early February, seven slaveholding states had seceded and formed the Confederacy. Some sort of ominous conflict seemed on the horizon, and in early 1861 Douglass rejoiced in its imminent arrival. He believed God worked through the climactic events of the sectional crisis to set in motion slavery's final death. After the fall of Fort Sumter in April 1861, and the formal start of the Civil War, Douglass confessed he had "no tears to shed, no lamentations to make." Instead, he proclaimed, "God be praised!"[37] Slavery's final death throes had arrived.

During the four long years of the Civil War, Douglass relied on a spirit of prophetic hope to make sense of the conflict—to discern its ultimate meaning and God's purposes in it. From the very start of the fighting, Douglass insisted that God was using the war to destroy slavery, and the Union must take part in God's righteous work. Loyal citizens and their armies should fight not simply to preserve the Union but also to end slavery, Douglass argued. If they failed to do so, they imperiled their nation's future and invited the judgment of a just God. Douglass saw in the war a momentous theological question about the relationship between divine and human effort in ending slavery. Was emancipation a triumph of God's active work in history, or the labor of long-suffering abolitionists, or some strange mixture of both? Douglass confronted those questions head-on throughout the Civil War as he tried to ensure that the Union committed itself to abolishing slavery amid its conflict against the Confederacy.

At the onset of the Civil War, the Spring Street AME Zion Church in Rochester held weekly antislavery lectures, at which Douglass frequently spoke. In the days immediately after the Confederate attack on Fort Sumter in April 1861, Douglass addressed the audience at the Zion church and offered a prophetic and hope-filled vision of the war. "I have never spent days so restless and anxious," Douglass confessed to his listeners. "Our mornings and evenings have continually oscillated between the dim light of hope, and the gloomy shadow of despair." The war inspired new hope for the possibility of emancipation, yet new reason for despair given the nation's uncertain future.[38]

Many northerners now feared that the crisis over slavery had spiraled out of human control, Douglass acknowledged. "There is a general feeling amongst us, that the control of events has been taken out of our hands," he said, "that we have fallen into the mighty current of eternal principles—invisible forces, which are shaping and fashioning events as they wish, using us only as instruments to work out their own results in our National destiny." Even though in April 1861 the Union government had not embraced emancipation as an official war aim and therefore was "not yet on the side of the oppressed," Douglas predicted "events mightier than the Government [are] bringing about that result."[39] Less than a year later, Douglass confidently declared that a great providential force continued to move the war toward the abolition of slavery: "Through the certain operation of the *changeless laws of the universe*," he said during a speech in Rochester, "Emancipation, which has long been a great and solemn national duty, pressing heavily on the national conscience has at last become a great and all commanding national necessity."[40]

But even as Douglass anticipated slavery's death, he also offered near-apocalyptic predictions about the terrible fate that awaited the nation if it failed to purge itself of slavery. In early 1862, months before President Abraham Lincoln issued the preliminary Emancipation Proclamation, Douglass said that if American remained a "cunning, cowardly, and selfish nation given over—as other nations have been before us—to hardness of heart and blindness of mind, it needs no prophet to foretell our doom."[41] To Douglass, the Civil War was only the latest manifestation of an eternal, cosmic struggle between "right and wrong, good and evil, liberty and slavery, truth and falsehood, the glorious light of love, and the appalling darkness of human selfishness and sin."[42] The Union now had to decide on which side of this conflict it stood, a decision determined by how it dealt with the issue of emancipation. If the Union wavered on abolition, it invited terrible divine judgment and possible national ruin. In refusing to strike a swift deathblow against slavery, and therefore continually "disregarding and trampling upon the self-evident rights and claims of human nature," the Union repeated the errors of a "long list of ruined nationalities and Empire," Douglass said, "which have forgotten that righteousness alone exalteth a nation, and that the violated justice will surely bring destruction."[43]

Naturally, then, as soon as the war began, Douglass called upon Union leaders to act in accordance with God's will and make emancipation an explicit goal of their war effort. "Is not abolition plainly forced upon the nation as a necessity of national existence?" Douglass asked in the pages of *Douglass' Monthly* in September 1861.[44] As a military strategist, Douglass argued that the Union would only triumph in the conflict if it directly attacked slavery, "the primal cause of that war," as he called it in May 1861.[45] "This war with the slaveholders can never be brought to a desirable termination until slavery, the guilty cause of all our national troubles, has been totally and forever abolished," Douglass explained one month later.[46] He argued that striking a deathblow against slavery required the enlistment of African American soldiers in the Union military, particularly former slaves. The Union desperately needed additional manpower, a need met by creating new black regiments. "Men in earnest don't fight with one hand, when they might fight with two," Douglass reasoned, "and a man drowning would not refuse to be saved even by a colored hand."[47] Escaped slaves would eagerly fight against their former masters, and the Union would reject their service at its own peril. "Let the loyal army but inscribe upon its banner, Emancipation and protection to all who will rally under it, and no power could prevent a stampede from slavery, such as the world has not witnessed since the Hebrews crossed the Red Sea," Douglass predicted in July 1862.[48]

To Douglass, emancipation was both a military necessity and essential to redeeming the moral character of the Union. He likened slavery to a "moral blight," a kind of "soul plague and withering curse, which is now raining desolations upon the land." The ravages of epidemics such as cholera, small pox, or yellow fever paled in comparison to the devastation of the disease of slavery, which the Union must now "scatter with all its guilty profits to the wind."[49] Douglass saw wartime abolition as just and vital to national existence, so he harshly castigated the Lincoln administration through the first year of the war for not immediately committing the Union to emancipation. In a January 1862 address in Philadelphia, Douglass proclaimed of the Union war effort, "it would seem, in the language of Isaiah, that the whole head is sick, and the whole heart is faint, that there is no soundness in it." He had in mind President Lincoln's reluctance to "tell the world what he is fighting against," the oppressive and rebellion-inspiring institution of slavery. Federal leaders claimed to fight for the preservation of the Union, but their dithering on slavery and emancipation only threatened to destroy the Union. "After-coming generations will remark with astonishment this feature in this dark chapter of our national history," Douglass predicted, eight months before Lincoln issued the preliminary Emancipation Proclamation.[50]

Douglass's calls for emancipation in the early months of the Civil War often included a prophetic warning of impending divine judgment. In May 1861, he wrote in *Douglass' Monthly*, "During the last twenty years and more, we have as a nation been forging a bolt for our own national destruction. . . . We have sown the wind, only to reap the whirlwind." Instead of working for the abolition of slavery, Americans collectively "plunged our souls into new and unfathomed depths of sin, to conciliate the favor and secure the loyalty of the slaveholding class." Even worse, the Union continued this pattern of conciliation after the start of the Civil War. But even if Lincoln and the Union leadership did not immediately pursue emancipation as formal policy, "the inexorable logic of events will force it upon them in the end," Douglass predicted. He anticipated that the "irrepressible conflict, long confined to words and votes, is now to be carried by bayonets and bullets," and that God almighty would "defend the right" and ensure the abolition of slavery.[51]

Douglass did not shy away from tackling perplexing theological questions about how exactly God's active work in history to destroy slavery fit together with the activity of abolitionists. Throughout the war, Douglass insisted that ultimately, however mysterious, both divine providence and human effort together secured emancipation. This meant that foes of slavery had to persevere in their good work, while also retaining hope that God ordained their triumph.

In a revealing June 1861 editorial in *Douglass' Monthly*, Douglass told his readers that "Providence will bring freedom to the slave out of this civil war." But he also tried to avoid unintentionally fostering in them a passive spirit. Douglass feared that his prediction that God used the Civil War to destroy slavery might lead some abolitionists to neglect to continue their own vigorous antislavery efforts. "All the Divine powers of the universe are on the side of freedom and progress," Douglass proclaimed, which should offer enemies of slavery everywhere great confidence. Yet, Douglass continued, "our faith is at once to be suspected the moment it leads us to fold our hands and leave the cause of the slave to Providence." This had been the "great and deadly sin" of the American church and its clergy for too long.[52]

Americans too often passively set aside the struggle for freedom and justice for slaves, preferring to "leave slavery to Divine Providence." To Douglass, this was precisely the wrong response to the fact that God moved in history to destroy slavery, which should instead compel all righteous people to join in God's work. "We, too, are hopeful, but look not for miracles," Douglass wrote. "We are not expecting to see the waters roll asunder, and give to those now in bondage a dry road to freedom, and then roll back again and swallow up the pursuing hosts of our modern Pharaohs." Abolitionists must instead "deal with stubborn facts, and with fixed laws," and know that their labors played an essential role in God's grand work of dismantling slavery. "Nothing should be left to chance or to accident," Douglass implored his readers. Their great struggle to end slavery continued even during a war that manifested the will of God.[53]

Douglass rejoiced when President Lincoln announced the preliminary Emancipation Proclamation in September 1862 after the Battle of Antietam. The Proclamation, which would take effect on 1 January 1863 if Confederates did not surrender, declared free the slaves in all areas in rebellion. The Emancipation Proclamation revived Douglass's hopes. He believed more confidently than ever before that the war would bring slavery's total downfall. On the final Sunday of December 1862, Douglass delivered a celebratory address at the Zion Church, calling upon the congregation to join him in a spirit of "joy, thanksgiving and praise." The "Eternal Power of the Universe" finally fulfilled its promise to America's slaves, and helped ensure the demise of the institution that held them in bondage. Even so, Douglass said, "this is no time for the friends of freedom to fold their hands and consider their work at an end." The struggle for liberty and equality continued. Everyone who had labored to end slavery now needed to work with equal fervor against racial bigotry and injustice.[54]

Even after the Emancipation Proclamation took effect in January 1863, the future of slavery remained somewhat uncertain—not least if the Union lost the Civil War. Douglass had ample reason to contemplate the sacred purpose and significance of the war, as well as the relationship of divine and human effort in the long work of ending American slavery. Douglass meditated on these questions at greatest length in a January 1864 speech titled "The Mission of the War," delivered at the Cooper Institution in New York City. "The mission of this war is National regeneration," Douglass said. He had in mind both the abolition of slavery and a meaningful "moral growth," the trading of an oppressive institution for higher principles of true justice and mercy. "I look for no miraculous destruction of Slavery," Douglass admitted early in the speech. Americans still had a role to play in the cosmic history of emancipation. God's will alone would not fully determine the course of the story.[55]

"The war looms before me simply as a great national opportunity," Douglass explained, "which may be improved to national salvation, or neglected to national ruin." The war posed to Americans a grand moral choice: either dismantle slavery and regenerate the nation, or fail to free those in bondage and face the terrible consequences. Douglass believed that God eventually would destroy American slavery, regardless of what the Union leadership did during the Civil War. Yet he also insisted "it is cowardly to shuffle our responsibilities upon the shoulders of Providence." Knowing full well that the Lord desired to see slavery's death, Americans should actively work to accomplish that goal. Douglass called upon Union leaders to align their vision of the "mission of the war" with God's purposes—and see the Lord's will realized in America through emancipation and the defeat of the Confederacy. "Justice and humanity are often overpowered—but they are persistent and eternal forces—and fearful to contend against," Douglass proclaimed. "Let but our rulers place the Government fully within these trade winds of Omnipotence, and the hand of death is upon the Confederate Rebels."[56]

The Hopeful Prophet

In the uncertain months between the issuance of the Emancipation Proclamation in January 1863 and the end of the war in April 1865, Douglass looked ahead to the future trials and opportunities awaiting African Americans. "A mightier work than the abolition of slavery now looms," Douglass said in December 1863 at an American Anti-Slavery Society meeting in Philadelphia. With slavery nearing death, it came time now to fight for "the elevation of the colored people," and in particular to ensure that "the colored man is admitted a full member in good and regular standing in the American body politic."[57] Douglass saw that the next great challenge facing African Americans was the battle for genuine political and civil equality after emancipation. Even before the Civil War ended, Douglass advocated for full and equal citizenship for African Americans as the only just conclusion to the great war to end slavery.

In May 1863, at a speech in New York City at the Brooklyn Academy of Music, Douglass posed what he thought was the defining question awaiting America after the Civil War: "Can the white and colored peoples of this country be blended into a common nationality, and enjoy together, in the same country, under the same flag, the inestimable blessings of life, liberty and the pursuit of happiness, as neighborly citizens of a common country?" Douglass adamantly answered "yes," and he insisted that racial harmony and national prosperity in America required full civil and political equality for African Americans.[58] The kind of equality Douglass had in mind was "the complete abolition of every vestige, form, and modification of Slavery," which would above all require equality "before the law, in the jury box, [and] at the ballot-box."[59]

Douglass delivered his most moving wartime appeal for black equality in November 1864 in Baltimore. He gave the brief speech after returning to his home state following its passage of a new constitution abolishing slavery. It was the first time he traveled back to Maryland since his escape in 1838. "The spirit of liberty has been here," Douglass rejoiced at the outset of his speech, "and like the breath of the Almighty, has touched our chains, and left them broken." Douglass visited Maryland not simply to celebrate the end of slavery in the state but also to appeal to white Marylanders to embrace the principle of full civil and political equality for all its citizens, regardless of race. "Don't put this new wine of liberty into the old bottles of slavery," he pleaded. "Don't mend this new garment with old cloth." He called upon Maryland to explicitly guarantee the right of African American men to vote and hold elective office. In eradicating slavery Marylanders placed their state "in harmony with the eternal laws of the moral universe," Douglass said. Yet the possibility remained that the state could fall out of harmony with the divinely established truths of liberty and justice, especially if it systematically denied African Americans the full freedom and equality they deserved.[60]

The same Christian hope that carried Douglass through the crisis of the 1850s and the Civil War also sustained him through an uncertain post-war era. As the fighting ended, the work of piecing the nation back together commenced. At the heart of that work, as Douglass rightly anticipated, was defining the meaning of freedom and equality for African Americans after slavery. Ominous signs soon appeared that staunch resistance awaited any effort to establish meaningful civil and political liberty for black southerners. But Douglass still had faith that a mighty and merciful God would see the work of deliverance fully completed.

Even so, Douglass hoped that the nation would willingly atone for its sins of racial oppression and turn from the wicked legacy of slavery. "Oh! That the heart of this unbelieving nation could be at once brought to a faith in the Eternal Laws of justice," Douglass once prayed during the Civil War, "justice for all men, justice now and always, justice without reservation or qualification except those suggested by mercy and love."[61] Slavery was dead. But America needed Douglass's prophetic vision as much as ever as it lurched toward the Reconstruction era and determined the fate of true justice, mercy, and love in America.

8

Reconstruction Battles over Racial and Gender Equality

In May 1866, less than a year removed from the Civil War, a small group of women's rights activists met in New York City and established the American Equal Rights Association. Not even six months earlier, the Thirteenth Amendment to the U.S. Constitution was ratified, abolishing slavery in America. The new association's stated purpose was "to secure Equal Rights to all American citizens, especially the right of suffrage, irrespective of race, color or sex." The Civil War had unleashed all sorts of revolutionary consequences in America. Not surprisingly, as soon as the war ended, many women's rights advocates thought an opportune time had come to press for true gender equality. The American Equal Rights Association shrewdly linked the cause of women's suffrage with the postwar effort to establish civil and political equality for African American men.[1]

Frederick Douglass traveled to New York City in May 1868 to attend the association's second anniversary meeting at the Cooper Institute. Douglass supported the work of the association because he believed the abolition of slavery did not mark the end of his prophetic calling. He devoted his attention in the years immediately following the Civil War to expanding the boundaries of freedom and equality in America. He fought in particular to secure for African Americans and women the full civil and political equality they deserved. To Douglass, the causes of gender and racial equality were inseparable.

He gladly made the journey to New York City from Rochester in May 1868 to join fellow supporters of the American Equal Rights Association. Douglass sat onstage with an illustrious group of suffragists and listened attentively as several activists spoke, including Elizabeth Cady Stanton, the presiding officer. Before the morning's end, Douglass also addressed the crowd. "I know of no argument that can be adduced in favor of the right of man to suffrage which is not equally forcible, and equally applicable to woman," he began. Surely any argument for suffrage based upon notions of the dignity of men applied also to women. Douglass then made a distinctly religious argument for universal suffrage. He appealed to his decidedly optimistic vision of human nature to endorse the right of all people, regardless of race or gender, to vote. "If I believed in the doctrine that human nature is totally depraved and unmixed with good," Douglass explained, then perhaps he could accept a restricted suffrage. "But I believe that men are rather more disposed to truth, to goodness and to excellence, than to vice and wickedness," he continued, "and for that reason I wish to see the elements of humanity infused throughout all human government." This held true for men as well as women, Douglass hastened to add, and was perhaps even truer of women than men.[2]

The attendees of the American Equal Rights Association stood far outside the mainstream of American society. A great many white Americans in 1868 only tepidly supported black suffrage and many more rejected outright the prospect of women voting. Despite the radical transformations made possible by the Civil War, the meaning of equality in America remained in flux. The most important and contentious battles of the Reconstruction era shaped the future of citizenship in America. Douglass actively participated in these public debates, and in the process he consistently affirmed a vision of human nature both optimistic and universal, true of every race and gender. Throughout the era of Reconstruction, Douglass drew on this understanding of human nature to argue for true civil and political equality for all people— the next great battle in his public career as America's prophet.[3]

The end of slavery hardly guaranteed civil and political equality for African Americans. In the immediate postwar South, the nature of the freedom now enjoyed by former slaves was not entirely clear. Almost as soon as the firing ceased, politically powerful white southerners attempted to preserve something like the racial control and oppression of antebellum slaveholding society. In May 1865, Douglass presciently predicted how events would unfold in the former Confederate states if the South's white political elites regained power: "But let the civil power of the States be restored, and the old prejudices and hostility to the Negro will revive."[4]

President Andrew Johnson's approach to reconstructing the nation after Union victory did little to quell Douglass's concerns. Johnson, a Tennessean and self-proclaimed champion of poor whites, loathed the slaveholding aristocratic planters of his native region. But he had no desire to inaugurate a radical social transformation of the South beyond the abolition of slavery and the renunciation of secession. Johnson made some effort to prohibit ex-Confederate leaders from participating in the provisional governments and constitutional conventions assembled in 1865 throughout the former Confederate states. But he did not intervene as these same constitutional conventions began restoring the South's antebellum racial order. Each one explicitly limited suffrage to white men, and some refused to immediately ratify the Thirteenth Amendment. When new state legislatures met throughout the South, they quickly passed what became known as Black Codes, laws that imposed a wide range of social and economic restrictions on black southerners. White political leaders designed the Black Codes to trap former slaves in a subordinate and unequal status in southern society, not far removed from slavery. With ample reason, Douglass said in September 1865, "the present is a critical moment for the colored people of this country." But the future remained decidedly uncertain: "Heaven only knows what will be in store for our people in the South."[5] The ominous turn of events immediately after the war in the former Confederate states convinced Douglass that "slavery is not abolished until the black man has the ballot."[6]

Douglass watched with apprehension as life for former slaves in the postwar South failed to live up to the glorious promises of emancipation. In February 1866, he had an opportunity to voice his hopes and concerns directly to President Johnson. Douglass was part of a delegation selected by the National Convention of Colored Men, then deliberating in Washington, D.C., to meet with Johnson in the Executive Mansion. The thirteen-man delegation included Douglass, his son, and George T. Downing, a successful restaurateur and former antislavery activist from Rhode Island.[7]

Johnson shook hands with each member of the delegation as they entered his office. Downing began the meeting with a succinct summation of the frustrations and aspirations shared by members of the National Convention of Colored Men. "We are in a passage to equality before the law. God hath made it by opening a Red Sea," he said. But African Americans desperately needed the assistance of Johnson and the power of the federal government to guarantee their equality. Downing contended that the mere ratification of the Thirteenth Amendment was inadequate. "We [wish] it enforced with appropriate legislation," he explained. In practice, despite the letter of the Constitution, too many ex-slaves remained trapped in oppressive and unequal positions in southern society. "The Fathers of the Revolution intended freedom for every American," Downing continued, "that they should be protected in their rights as citizens and equal before the law." Downing did not attempt to define in detail what equality before the law for African Americans actually meant, what sorts of rights in particular it encompassed. He simply implored Johnson in general terms to act to protect the rights of the nation's African American citizens. "We are Americans, native born Americans," Downing said. "We are citizens."[8]

When Downing finished, Douglass briefly interjected before Johnson could reply. "In the order of Divine Providence you are placed in a position where you have the power to save or destroy us; to bless or blast us. I mean our whole race," Douglass said to the president. He believed God had bestowed upon Johnson immense power and responsibility for shaping the future lives of African Americans after emancipation. Douglass echoed Downing's call for equality under the law, but he made a very specific appeal that Downing had not: He insisted on the absolute necessity of a constitutional guarantee of the right to vote for African American men. "We shall submit no argument on that point," Douglass firmly declared. African Americans shouldered all the responsibilities and burdens of citizenship. They paid taxes and fought in the Union army. They had every right also to "share in the privileges" of citizenship.[9]

Whatever limited goodwill existed at the outset of the meeting soon disappeared as Johnson spoke. The president first struck a defensive tone. He claimed (despite once being a slaveholder) to have always "been for the colored man." He intended now to pursue the policies that would "result in the amelioration and ultimate elevation" of all Americans, white and black alike. "I do not like to be arraigned by some who can get up handsomely rounded periods and deal in rhetoric, and talk about abstract ideas of liberty," Johnson sneered, words that surely stung Douglass, though the president did not mention him by name. "Now, it is always best to talk about things practically, and in a common-sense way," Johnson continued, with increasing condescension. He promised to act as "Moses" to African Americans, and lead them "from bondage to freedom." But he cared most about preventing an outright race war in the South. He therefore refused to adopt any policy that he thought might foster greater racial hostility. Johnson argued that immediately granting African American men the right to vote threatened to spark exactly that sort of violence, to the ultimate detriment of white and black southerners alike. Johnson further said he could not see how suffrage would in any practical way ameliorate the many real problems presently faced by former slaves.[10]

It took all the patience Douglass could muster to keep silent as Johnson spoke. But eventually he could not help but interrupt the president and plead his case for political equality. Douglass tried to get a word in but only annoyed Johnson, who shot back, "I am not quite through yet." Johnson went on to further lament the indignity long endured by poor white nonslaveholders, which he thought deserved far more attention than former slaves' quest for the vote. The Civil War already revolutionized the South's social order by setting free millions of African Americans. But granting the vote to black men was a radical step that poor white southerners would not—and should not—tolerate, Johnson said. Forcing universal suffrage would only exacerbate racial "enmity and hate" to the point of violence. He again concluded, bluntly, "I do not want to be engaged in a work that will commence a war of races." But then Johnson added, "Anything I can do to elevate the races, to soften and ameliorate their condition I will do."[11]

Johnson clearly now wanted the meeting to end. But a frustrated Douglass tried as politely as possible to challenge the president's rationale for not supporting black suffrage. If "you would grant us permission," Douglass said to Johnson, "of course we would endeavor to controvert some of the positions you have assumed." Downing tried tactfully to hold Douglass back, but to no avail. Douglass proceeded to argue that the only way to avoid the kind of race war Johnson most feared was to ensure African Americans enjoyed equal participation in the political process.[12]

The president interrupted Douglass before he could say much. "I merely wanted to indicate my views in reply to your address, and not to enter into any general controversy," Johnson said. He then obliquely suggested that it might be best if African Americans simply migrated wholesale from the South—a proposal that struck Douglass as absurd, especially considering how Black Codes limited the mobility of black southerners. The meeting finally came to a somewhat abrupt conclusion. As the National Convention of Colored Men delegates left the room, Douglass said, still in Johnson's earshot, "The President sends us to the people, and we will have to go and get the people right." The public battle over competing visions of equality had certainly commenced. The biblical prophets spoke words of truth to the politically powerful of their day. Douglass tried to do the same as he traveled to the Executive Mansion and boldly testified for black political equality to President Johnson.[13]

After Douglass's audience with the president ended on 7 February 1866, he intensified his public appeals for black suffrage. Over the next four years, he spoke and wrote on no topic at greater length than the need for a constitutional guarantee of universal suffrage regardless of race. "The great question is, What relation to the whites of this country shall the negro sustain?"

Douglass asked in March 1866 in a Washington, D.C., speech, delivered as Congress debated a bill to enfranchise African Americans in the District. To Douglass, the whole future of American society rested on the suffrage question. "Without the elective franchise, the negro would still be practically a slave," he continued. Without true political equality for African Americans, Douglass believed, all other forms of inequality would persist—economic, civil, intellectual, and religious. Power at the ballot box would radically transform the place of African Americans in the United States. The only lasting foundation of black freedom was the vote.[14]

Douglass argued that anyone who opposed black suffrage simply denied the full humanity of African Americans and rejected the principles of liberty and justice for all. As Congress debated authorizing black male suffrage in Washington, Douglass argued that every African American man deserved the right to vote "because physically, intellectually, morally, and religiously he is a man."[15] Douglass insisted that the most compelling arguments for the right to vote applied equally to all people, regardless of race. "All that can be urged in the face of any man's right to vote, can be urged as to his right to vote, no matter what his color," he explained. African Americans were fully human, made in God's image, just as their white brothers and sisters; their humanity qualified them to exercise the right to vote.[16]

Douglass saw the resistance to black suffrage as nothing less than a movement to demean a piece of God's precious creation and scoff at truths established by God. "One of the great evils of our country," Douglass explained at a September 1866 meeting of radical Republicans, "[is] to limit eternal and universal principles." Americans claimed to venerate a set of core political, religious, and moral principles—enshrined in their founding documents and sacred texts—but in practice they fell far short of truly adhering to them. "That has been the great error of the American people—to limit what in its very nature is illimitable; to circumscribe principles intended by the great Creator of the universe for the harmony of the universe, to be equally applicable to all the people of the country," Douglass argued. Americans may claim that all men are created equal and made in God's image, but they betrayed those lofty ideas by denying African Americans the right to vote. In the battle to end slavery, Douglass had long denounced proslavery Americans for failing to live according to the Christianity they professed. He did precisely the same thing in the battle over black suffrage, insisting that self-professed Christians who opposed universal suffrage simply opposed the moral and theological truths at the heart of the "true Christianity of Christ."[17]

The cause of racial equality won a significant triumph with the ratification of the Fourteenth and Fifteenth Amendments to the U.S. Constitution in 1868 and 1870. The Fourteenth Amendment guaranteed citizenship to former slaves and "equal protection of the laws." But the amendment did not explicitly include a guarantee of the right to vote for all citizens, regardless of race. Less than two years later, however, the ratification of the Fifteenth Amendment prohibited states from denying a citizen the right to vote "on account of race, color, or previous condition of servitude." The amendments together marked a major step forward for the cause of black civil and political equality. They made possible an unprecedented—though temporary—moment of black political participation and power in the Reconstruction-era South.

Douglass celebrated the ratification of the Fourteenth and Fifteenth Amendments. "At last, at last, the black man has a future," he rejoiced in April 1870 soon after the Fifteenth Amendment took effect. "The dismal death-cloud of slavery has passed away. Today we are free American citizens. We have ourselves, we have a country, and we have a future in common with other men." With the vote secured, African Americans could make real economic and educational progress. "It means that color is no longer to be a calamity; that race is to be no longer a crime," Douglass continued.[18] A year after the ratification of the Fifteenth Amendment, at a Republican Party meeting in Washington, D.C., Douglass credited "the favorings of Providence" for securing the vote for black men. The task now before the nation, Douglass said, was to "attempt to realize the Christian idea that of one blood God has made all nations to dwell on all the Christian earth."[19]

Though jubilant, Douglass realistically recognized that the black freedom struggle continued. The Constitution now guaranteed equality before the law and black male suffrage, but Douglass never believed the amendments solved all of America's deeper race problems. The Fifteenth Amendment "left many things undone," Douglass wrote in 1870, precisely because of "the nature of the evil it was designed to remove." The legacy of slavery still shaped relations between white and black Americans. Racial prejudice and hatred endured, a permanent threat to true equality in America. "Law on the statute book and law in the practice of the nation are two very different things, and sometimes very opposite things," Douglass warned.[20]

For that reason, he sought to maintain a prophetic witness against persistent forms of racial inequality and discrimination. Douglass again saw Christian churches as among the chief culprits in sustaining racial bigotry. The spirit of equality enshrined in the Constitution had not permeated America's churches. Douglass asked, "Over the gateway of what Christian church in America is it written that no distinction shall be here made on account of color or race?" The same religious hypocrisy that defined Christian slaveholding America persisted after slavery. "The time may come when practice and precept, life and profession will harmonize," Douglass continued in regards to America's churches, "but that time has not yet come, and is not even at the door."[21] Since his escape, Douglass had maintained an ambivalent attitude toward institutional Christianity. He remained forever indebted to the African American congregations of his early life, and maintained a deep reverence for the faith he encountered there. To his final days, he also continued to attend and speak at services hosted by AME and AME Zion churches. Yet Douglass had too much of a prophet's spirit to retain a formal affiliation with any single congregation or denomination—a decision he had effectively made by the late 1840s. He was too acutely aware of how easily institutions compromised the radical message of the Christian gospel. If Douglass largely practiced his faith apart from any particular institution, he did so precisely to maintain the integrity of his commitment to Christianity.

The persistent prejudice and discrimination practiced by America's churches tempered Douglass's hopes for the future prosperity and equality of African Americans. Most white churches might employ a black man "to sweep the holy dust from the velvet of the saintly pew," Douglass sarcastically wrote in 1870, but few would let the same black man sit in that pew on Sunday "to worship God for one moment."[22] If equality and harmony among the races could not take root in Christian churches, Douglass wondered, could it take root in the nation at large?

Nonetheless, Douglass never lost hope that racial equality could flourish in America after slavery. And he recognized that the quest for racial equality encompassed far more than the struggle for civil and political rights for African Americans alone. On a cold Boston day in December 1869, the year separating the ratifications of the Fourteenth and Fifteenth Amendments, Douglass made one of the most powerful and perceptive speeches of his life, addressed precisely to this point. The speech became known as "Our Composite Nationality." Douglass delivered the address not only in the wake of slavery's death, but also in a moment of rising Chinese immigration—two developments that helped transform the racial makeup of American democracy. It was an apt time to meditate on "the character and mission of the United States," Douglass said, and to consider especially a momentous question about America: "whether we are the better or the worse for being composed of different races of men."[23]

Frederick Douglass, 1870. *Courtesy of the Library of Congress.*

To Douglass, America's "composite nationality" was the source of the nation's deepest dilemmas and most enduring tensions. Many white Americans saw their nation's ethnic and racial diversity as a problem to solve, a demographic trend to reverse. But Douglass saw it as the potential source of America's greatness and goodness—if the country truly dedicated itself to "the principle of absolute equality." The institution of slavery had made a mockery of that principle for centuries. But now, after emancipation, new challenges to the principle had emerged in the treatment endured by recent Chinese immigrants. They were not enslaved, but they too found themselves deprived of full civil and political equality, and often forced into oppressive labor arrangements.[24]

Ardently committed to "the principle of absolute equality," Douglass insisted that Americans of all races and creeds must embrace Chinese immigrants as full citizens, empowered to vote and hold office and stand wholly equal under the law. Douglass here appealed to some of his most essential theological convictions. He said his vision of a harmonious "composite nationality" of true racial equality rested "upon the laws of nature and upon the idea of justice, to say nothing of a common Creator." God had created men and women of every race and equally endowed them with basic rights that were "eternal, universal, and indestructible."[25]

Douglass believed America would never fulfill its "mission in the world," given by God, if it failed to become a multiracial democracy of true equality. The United States should strive to be "the most perfect national illustration of the unity and dignity of the human family that the world has ever seen," Douglass argued. Yet to stand to the world as a beacon of these ideals, America had to commit itself to "the faithful application of the principle of perfect civil equality."[26] The Chinese immigrant and the recently freed black southerner—like men and women of all races—had to enjoy the full fruits of citizenship. As a prophet committed to equality, Douglass concluded that America's "composite nationality" was among its greatest assets. It empowered the nation to fulfill its mission, and cohered with its highest professed moral and political ideals.

As Douglass battled for racial equality in the Reconstruction era, he also remained heavily involved in the postwar women's rights movement. Douglass saw the quests for gender and racial equality as intimately connected. He believed the same theological and moral convictions he used in the black freedom struggle also supported the cause of women's suffrage. Even so, real tensions and tactical disagreements remained between Douglass and several leading women of the American Equal Rights Association, particularly Elizabeth Cady Stanton. By the time of the ratification of the Fifteenth Amendment, those tensions turned ugly, fraying the bonds that once tenuously united black and white activists within the association. Still, for the remainder of his life, Douglass took an uncompromising prophetic stand in support of women's suffrage.

Douglass had actively supported the cause of women's rights since at least 1848. That year, he attended the legendary Seneca Falls Convention, organized chiefly by Elizabeth Cady Stanton, the first major convention in America devoted to discussing the "social, civil, and religious condition and rights of woman." Douglass heartily endorsed the convention's Declaration of Sentiments. He also supported a far more controversial resolution introduced by Stanton calling for female suffrage. A significant number of attendees at the convention opposed the resolution, but not Douglass. He was the only man in attendance who spoke on behalf of the suffrage resolution, and he eventually helped secure its narrow formal approval by the convention.[27]

Once the Civil War ended and the women's rights movement resumed its efforts in full force, Douglass eagerly lent his support. He locked arms with the American Equal Rights Association at the moment of its founding. At the association's first meeting in May 1866, Douglass was chosen as one of its three vice presidents. In the years immediately following the Civil War, Douglass argued that the health of American democracy required granting women the right to vote. "I am for woman's rights because I am in favor of a republican form of government," Douglass explained in Boston. "Let government rest squarely and universally down upon the whole people." He assumed that the strength of American democracy rested on wide popular participation in the nation's civic life. In allowing women to vote, America could take advantage of the wisdom of its *entire* population, not merely half the population, Douglass believed. He hoped for the day when there would be "no conscience in the land that has not its appropriate opportunity for infusing itself into the government."[28]

Douglass's conviction that the American republic would flourish with equal participation from men and women rested on an even deeper theological assumption about human nature. Douglass optimistically affirmed that men and women possessed equal dignity and capability as human beings. He also insisted that a democratic society could only mitigate the more harmful elements of human nature if it placed the responsibilities of civic life in the hands of the greatest number of people. "When you want good government go to the mass," Douglass reasoned. "Individuals may be ignorant and vile, but the mass is comparatively pure, and always will be. The masses are well-intentioned. They may be ignorant, but they are always honest and true." Douglass therefore affirmed, "woman's right to vote rests on the same foundation that man's right to vote rests upon," for men and women shared the same nature, and democracies needed them both to flourish.[29]

The American Equal Rights Association existed to fight for universal suffrage, regardless of race and gender, but internal divisions threatened to undermine the movement's unity from its very beginning. Too closely linking together the causes of female and black male suffrage carried potential risks. If granting the vote to African American men required also granting it to women, many northerners in 1866 may have opted to do neither. For this reason, public opinion posed serious dilemmas to members of the American Equal Rights Association. If in the short-term the association could successfully achieve a constitutional guarantee of black suffrage but not female suffrage, should it do so? Should women who had devoted their lives to attaining the vote accept another delay in accomplishing their goal—in the hopes that a constitutional amendment granting African American men the right to vote would soon be followed by a similar amendment for women? Or was the cause of gender equality too great and long-delayed to be put on hold again, even compared to the dire need for racial equality after emancipation? The association's members did not agree on how best to answer those questions, and eventually their differences bred bitterness and hostility.

The association met in November 1866 in Albany, New York, on the eve of a statewide convention to revise New York's constitution. Association members hoped to convince the convention to guarantee universal suffrage. But debate erupted within the association during its meeting over the merits of prioritizing black suffrage over female suffrage. Some of the association's most prominent women talked openly about opposing the extension of the vote to African American men if the vote was not also simultaneously extended to women. While Douglass always affirmed a woman's right to vote, he insisted that in the immediate future black male suffrage was more desperately needed. "With them it is a desirable matter," Douglass said of women and the vote. But for African Americans, securing the vote was "a question of life and death." He explained by evoking the horrors of recent antiblack riots: "With us disenfranchisement means New-Orleans, it means Memphis, it means New-York mobs, it means being driven from the workshops and the schools."[30]

The association did not resolve this difference of opinion in 1866, and the chasm separating its members only grew over the next two years. At the association's 1867 meeting, Elizabeth Cady Stanton refused to support black male suffrage if not accompanied by female suffrage. "I would not trust him with all my rights; degraded, oppressed himself," Stanton said of former slaves. "He would be more despotic with the government power than even our Saxon rulers are." Sojourner Truth added, "There is a great stir about colored men getting their rights, but not a word about the colored women; and if colored men get their rights, and not colored women theirs, you see the colored men will be masters over the women, and it will be just as bad as it was before." Yet other members argued that it would be counterproductive and imprudent to refuse to support

The Hopeful Prophet

suffrage for only African American men. Abby Kelly Foster, a tireless white abolitionist who devoted much of her life to the work of the American Anti-Slavery Society, contended that black southerners occupied a far more abused "civil, social, and religious status" than white northern women. Their future lives and fortunes rested on the ability of black men to wield real political power, she said. "Have we any true sense of justice," Foster asked, "are we not dead to the sentiment of humanity if we shall wish to postpone his security against present woes and future enslavement till woman shall obtain political rights?"[31]

Tensions within the American Equal Rights Association reached a breaking point in 1869 over the Fifteenth Amendment, which extended suffrage to all men, regardless of race, but not to women. Acrimonious debate over the amendment debilitated the association at its May 1869 meeting in New York City. Fourteen states had ratified the amendment by the time the association met. Its members could not agree on whether to endorse or repudiate the amendment. Douglass spoke on several occasions at the meeting, making many of the same arguments he had made since 1866. He continued to affirm that so long as women were denied the vote, America's government remained of a "defective, unworthy, and an oppressive character." Yet he also insisted on the greater need, in the immediate future, for black suffrage. The very future of the race depended on the ability of its men to vote. "I must say that I do not see how any one can pretend that there is the same urgency in giving the ballot to women as to the negro," Douglass said at the association's first morning meeting, before evoking the horrors of recent racial violence across the South.[32]

Susan B. Anthony and Elizabeth Cady Stanton had stiffened in their opposition to any amendment that granted the vote to black men but not women. Both before and during the 1869 meeting, Anthony and Stanton resorted to crude racial stereotypes to ridicule the prospect of recently freed slave men voting before white women of an elite class and education. "If you will not give the whole loaf of justice and suffrage to an entire people, give it to the most intelligent first," Anthony said at the first day of the association's meeting. "If intelligence, justice, and moralities are to be placed in the government, then let the question of woman be brought first and that of the negro last." Ultimately, the association did not formally endorse the Fifteenth Amendment at its 1869 meeting, which was its final one. The association splintered into two competing organizations: the National Woman Suffrage Association, formed by Anthony and Stanton, and the American Woman Suffrage Association.[33]

Despite the bitter and often derogatory debate over the Fifteenth Amendment, for the rest of his life Douglass still argued strongly for women's suffrage. He continued to affirm the deep moral connection between the causes of black and female political equality. To speak a prophetic word on behalf of one movement compelled him to do the same for the other, he believed. As he had done since 1848, Douglass rooted his defense of a woman's right to vote in his understanding of human nature—the inherent dignity and ability of all people, men and women equally.

A woman, like a man, was "a moral and intellectual being, possessing a sense of good and evil, and a power of choice between them," Douglass wrote in October 1870. For that reason, women deserved an equal stake in the governance of their society. "Woman's natural abilities and possibilities, not less than man's, constitute the measure of her rights in all directions and relations," Douglass explained, "including her right to participate in shaping the policy and controlling the action of the Government under which she lives."[34] When a nation denied its women the right to vote it demeaned their inherent value and capabilities. "Women themselves are divested of a large measure of their natural dignity by their exclusion from such participation in Government," Douglass argued. In prohibiting women from voting, America effectively proclaimed that half its population did not possess the intelligence or virtue necessary for true self-governance. For that reason, restricting suffrage on the basis of gender "deprives [woman] of a part of her natural dignity," Douglass concluded.[35] He contended that if only the nation properly understood human nature—the equal dignity, goodness, and ability of men and women alike—it would enthusiastically embrace universal suffrage.

Douglass also continued to insist that preventing women from voting imperiled American democracy. At a women's suffrage rally in Boston in 1873, Douglass argued, "I believe that this government will never be in a healthy condition until all the good people under it, and all the bad people under it, also, shall have the right at least secured to them of bringing whatever of good or whatever of bad there is in them into the government." Douglass argued that democracies are strongest when popular participation is at its widest. "This government will never be what it ought to be until all the people who live under it have some method of diffusing or infusing themselves into the government," he explained.[36] Only then could the nation benefit from the full wisdom of its citizenry while also best mitigating the evil inherent in its citizenry. In an 1886 speech on female equality and suffrage, Douglass concluded that "government is wisest and strongest which is guided and controlled by the combined wisdom of all the men and all the women."[37]

After the Civil War and the end of slavery, Douglass frequently condemned American churches for perpetuating racial bigotry, and he also denounced them for discriminating against women. Douglass believed both racial and gender prejudice contradicted the great Christian affirmation of the dignity of all people, made in God's image. During his remarks on female suffrage and gender equality at the May 1888 meeting of the New England Woman Suffrage Association, Douglass addressed recent controversies over the role of women within the Methodist Episcopal Church. "There is still a Methodist Episcopal Conference confronting us and barring the way to woman's progress, as it once barred the way to emancipation," Douglass said. He had in mind two recent actions taken by the denomination's leaders. At the church's General Conference of 1880, an all-male delegation formally decided that women could not become ordained ministers. Eight years later, just prior to Douglass's address, the general conference refused to accept four women who had arrived at the meeting intending to participate as lay delegates.[38]

Reflecting on the recent Methodist General Conference actions, Douglass could not help but think of the support for slavery offered by many members of the Methodist Episcopal Church earlier in the century. "In some respects this woman suffrage movement is but a continuance of the old anti-slavery movement," he suggested. "We have the same sources of opposition to contend with, and we must meet them with the same spirit and determination." Douglass condemned the denomination for bigoted practices that amounted to "the degradation of woman, by denying her a voice and a vote" in the governance of the church. He lamented that America's churches, once bastions of proslavery sentiment, now sustained gender inequality by perpetuating discriminatory and degrading attitudes toward women. In this respect, the Methodist General Conference only reinforced Douglass's sense of alienation from institutional Christianity. As in the battle over slavery, the battle for gender equality compelled Douglass to turn his prophetic voice to the Christian church in the United States. He preached a simple message to American Christians on behalf of the nation's women: "Her rights of person are equal in all respects to those of man. . . . She is capable of forming an intelligent judgment as to the character of public men and public measures."[39]

For more than two decades, Douglass deftly appealed to the "true Christianity of Christ" to bolster his abolitionist appeals. After emancipation, he turned again to his deepest theological convictions about God and humanity to argue for full political and civil equality for all citizens, regardless of race or gender. As America's prophet, in the era of Reconstruction Douglass found ample opportunity to again defend the dignity and equality of all people— made in God's image, intelligent and good.

At the Dark Dawn of Jim Crow

Douglass did not quite feel like celebrating in 1889 as he had in years past. The Bethel Literary and Historical Association—an elite hub of black intellectual life in the nation's capital—had invited him to deliver an address on the twenty-seventh anniversary of emancipation in Washington, D.C. At least 1,500 people filled the historic Metropolitan AME Church to commemorate the great day of liberation. They prayed and sang hymns together, and then listened in rapt attention as the seventy-one-year-old Douglass spoke for two hours.

It did not take Douglass long to announce his true feelings: "I declare to you that, in my judgment, at no period since the abolition of slavery in the District of Columbia, have the moral, social, and political surroundings of the colored people of this country been more solemn and foreboding than they are this day." The rights and liberties attained by African Americans during the Civil War and Reconstruction seemed as imperiled as ever. The Thirteenth Amendment might have abolished slavery, but Douglass insisted "slavery can as really exist without law as with it." The same spirit of oppression that defined slavery could live on past the death of the institution. To make matters worse, there remained nothing in the "morals, manners, or religion" of the white South inherently opposed to "the re-establishment of slavery" or a racially discriminatory social order. The past decade in the American South presaged a future where African Americans would be denied any meaningful liberty and equality under the law. "It is easy to indulge in the illusions of hope," Douglass said. But the times demanded that brave black men and women everywhere "not shrink from looking truth squarely in the face, no matter what may be the consequences."[1]

In the final years of the nineteenth century, America again found itself at a great moral crossroads. Two paths lay before the nation. It had started down the path of iniquity and injustice, but Douglass hoped to help set right his nation's errors. All the seemingly difficult questions surrounding the future of American race relations really boiled down to one "all-commanding question," Douglass said. That question, simply, was "whether American justice, American liberty, American civilization, American law, and American Christianity can be made to include and protect alike and forever all American citizens in the rights which, in a generous moment in the nation's life, have been guaranteed to them by the organic and fundamental law of the land." What America needed, now more than ever, was to remain true to its best constitutional, political, and religious ideals, and thereby "conquer its prejudices." Douglass never assumed this would be an easy task. The "malignant prejudice of race" still infected America; it "poisoned the fountains of justice, and defiled the altars of religion." But Douglass believed an alternative path of justice and equality awaited the nation. This path rested on a "broad foundation laid by the Bible itself, that God has made of one blood all nations of men to dwell on all the face of the earth."[2]

A quarter century after the death of American slavery, the "irrepressible conflict" of the antebellum era still raged. The battle pitted in bitter conflict "two opposite civilizations," Douglass contended, "one created and sustained by slavery, and the other framed and fashioned in the spirit of liberty and humanity." He believed that the "spirit of justice, liberty, and fair play is abroad in the land," hastening the triumph of freedom in America. But it increasingly seemed as if the resurrected Slave Power might prevail. It had managed to keep alive racial oppression and inequality after emancipation—which made the commemoration at the Metropolitan Church in April 1889 an ambivalent celebration.[3]

Douglass accurately described the latest challenges facing African Americans in the twilight of the nineteenth century. When he spoke to the Bethel Literary and Historical Association audience in 1889, the Jim Crow order was rapidly descending upon the nation. America's "second founding" in the 1860s and 1870s witnessed truly revolutionary changes: first emancipation and then citizenship, suffrage, and equality under the law regardless of race. But in the final years of his life, Douglass watched as white southerners systematically dismantled the progress achieved through the Civil War. The onset of Jim Crow—with its racial segregation, disenfranchisement, and grotesque violence—compelled Douglass to raise again his voice for truth and justice. He spoke a final prophetic word to America, exhorting the nation to trade its hypocrisy and oppression for a true righteousness rooted in love and respect for all people.

In the decade following the end of Reconstruction, uncertainty clouded the future direction of American race relations. The years that separated the end of Reconstruction from the final years of the nineteenth century saw a strange blend of hopeful possibility and ominous inequality in the South. After the last Union troops departed the former Confederate states in 1877, white southerners did not immediately and wholly undo all the constitutional guarantees of black equality achieved during Reconstruction. But the exact sort of freedom black southerners would enjoy remained an open question. African American men in the South did not everywhere instantly lose the right to vote; in some states they continued to vote well into the 1880s. But white southern planters had perfected exploitative economic arrangements such as sharecropping that trapped the overwhelming majority of black southerners in the bondage of debt and destitution. Given also the constant threat of violence, and the lack of meaningful civil equality, it is no surprise that by the late 1870s some African American leaders advocated the mass migration of black southerners to the Western Plains states.[4] Westward exodus seemed to many to be the only hope left for survival. Even the great legal triumphs for equality looked lately endangered, if not about to collapse entirely. In October 1883 the Supreme Court declared unconstitutional the Civil Rights Act of 1875, which had banned racial discrimination in public accommodations such as hotels, theaters, and trains.[5] Douglass condemned the Court's decision for blatantly "defeating the manifest purpose of the Constitution, nullifying the Fourteenth Amendment, and placing itself on the side of prejudice, proscription, and persecution."[6]

Douglass was nearly sixty years old by the time the Reconstruction era ended. He had assumed the role of venerated elder statesman among African American activists. His influence, in many ways, remained as potent as ever, though not immune to challenges. In these years he stayed loyal to the Republican Party, often to the point of tension with other black leaders, who had growing doubts about the commitment of the white Republican leadership to African American equality and uplift. Each election season, Douglass reliably took to the stump again to plead with black voters to support Abraham Lincoln's party. He had also faced serious personal financial setbacks in the mid-1870s. In 1874, the Freedman's Savings and Trust Company, incorporated in 1865 to assist former slaves, collapsed in ruin while Douglass served as its president. That same year, his latest newspaper, the *New National Era*, folded after its subscriptions waned, costing Douglass thousands of dollars. Even so, he had become a quite wealthy man, certainly far wealthier than he could have imagined as a young slave boy on the Eastern Shore.[7]

In 1877, Douglass and his family moved to a twenty-one-room home in the Anacostia neighborhood of Washington, D.C., set on fifteen acres near the Potomac River. Douglass's financial prosperity inevitably raised new tensions in his work as a leader of his race. Would there come a time when he could no longer meaningfully speak for African Americans, the majority of whom lived not in comfort in Anacostia but amid inescapable poverty and oppression in the rural South? This tension did not undermine entirely Douglass's witness for black equality and opportunity in the final years of his life. But he could not completely escape the tension either. It remained a definitive part of his postwar public career.[8]

In the uncertain years after Reconstruction, Douglass wanted to remain hopeful about the future. "I have at length rid myself of all doubt as to the vindication of the principles of justice and liberty," he said in Baltimore in 1879. The progress made since emancipation would surely continue, unless "Christianity be an empty name with no vitality . . . and the Declaration of Independence prove a lie."[9] But Douglass still saw the challenges facing African Americans in their quest for freedom, justice, and prosperity. In a July 1875 speech in Washington, D.C., Douglass posed a question that proved to define the decades following Reconstruction: "If war among the whites brought peace and liberty to the blacks, what will peace among the whites bring?" Would the greater liberty and equality won by African Americans in the Civil War era truly endure in the postwar world, as bitter hostility between white northerners and southerners subsided? A real revolution had occurred in America since 1861, Douglass granted. But in 1875, as he meditated on what the future held, he could only conclude, "The signs of the time are not all in our favor."[10]

Still, Douglass never gave himself over to despair or resignation. Throughout the late 1870s and 1880s, he remained resilient. Douglass believed this required him to acknowledge the still dark reality of life for African Americans, rooted in persistent racial bigotry. In 1883, he argued that the black man still lived in a nation "where all presumptions are arrayed against him, unless we except the presumption of inferiority and worthlessness."[11] A year later, in a speech in Syracuse, New York, Douglass said white America had "made up its mind about the negro" and would not likely change it willingly any time soon. "Now the negro has been taken, described, and stamped as an indolent, careless, stupid, degraded, helpless, hopeless, and God-forsaken being," he explained.[12]

Douglass tried to attack exactly this sort of racial prejudice, for he assumed doing so was necessary for the long-term security of black freedom. In an 1881 article, he called racial bigotry a "moral disorder" that had diseased America from its very inception. But Douglass did not believe that racial prejudice was inevitable and ineradicable. Instead, he contended, "slavery created and sustained this prejudice against race and color." America's *race-based* system of slavery fostered the myth that people of darker skin color were inferior to people of a lighter skin color.[13] This lie lived on even after the death of the institution that created it. As long as it persisted, African Americans faced the possibility that the liberty and equality they had lately gained might be taken away.

As part of his effort to prevent this from happening, in the years immediately following Reconstruction Douglass took a keen interest in how Americans *remembered* the Civil War, especially its causes and consequences. This was no casual curiosity for Douglass. He considered winning the battle over the memory of the Civil War as absolutely essential to maintaining freedom and equality for African Americans. Douglass shuddered at the thought of what might result if white Americans outside the South forgot that slavery stood at the center of the war and that the Confederacy's cause was immoral.

Douglass resisted what he called "the doctrine of forgiveness and forgetfulness" between white northerners and white southerners, a dishonest and destructive way of remembering the war that refused to openly affirm that "rebellion was wrong and loyalty right . . . slavery was wrong and emancipation right." Americans must never forget "the stupendous wickedness" of rebellion and slavery, Douglass said. He pledged to "never forget the difference between those who fought for liberty and those who fought for slavery; those who fought to save the Republic and those who fought to destroy it."[14] For Douglass, much of the future of American race relations depended upon whether white Americans would remember that "there was a right side and a wrong side in the late war."[15] If white America forgot the causes of its Civil War, and embraced instead a simple spirit of "forgiveness and forgetfulness," then the war's greatest accomplishments might well wither away. Douglass worried that if Americans misremembered their Civil War, they would endanger the triumphs of emancipation and black freedom.

Douglass wanted to remain hopeful about the future for African Americans. "I cannot believe that the Almighty Power that has brought us so near the promised land will now abandon us," he wrote to Presbyterian minister Francis Grimké in 1886.[16] But when Douglass wrote these words, America was passing into a nadir of race relations, the full onset of Jim Crow in all its terror. By the end of the century, in the American South there reigned a systematic legal regime of racial discrimination and inequality—all intended to uphold white supremacy and relegate black southerners to an inferior social status.

The disenfranchisement of African American voters was a first key piece of the imposition of Jim Crow. After the fall of Reconstruction, white political leaders initially resorted to violence or intimidation to keep black voters from the polls. Eventually, white southerners codified into law an array of obstacles that effectively stripped African Americans of the vote, including literacy tests and poll taxes. The loss of meaningful political power left black southerners in an increasingly imperiled position in the South. On the heels of the disenfranchisement laws came vast efforts to racially segregate southern society. No dimension of public life was beyond the reach of the segregation laws; they governed public schools, restaurants, hotels, restrooms, hospitals, and theaters, among many other places. But perhaps the most harrowing element of the Jim Crow era was the violence committed against black southerners. In the 1890s, the final decade of Douglass's life, it is estimated that white mobs lynched nearly 200 African Americans each year.

Douglass closely monitored the ever-worsening racial conditions in the South. Throughout the late 1880s and early 1890s, he spoke with great fervor against Jim Crow. The times demanded searing honesty from him, a courageous and unflinching account of the reality of race relations in America. In April 1888, at a speech marking the twenty-sixth anniversary of emancipation in Washington, D.C., Douglass felt compelled not to glory in the past but to address "the deplorable condition of the Negro in the Southern states." He told his audience that he refused "to prophesy smooth things, to be joyful and glad, to indulge in the illusions of hope," for there "comes a time when it is best that the worst should be made known."[17] Life for black southerners presently made emancipation nothing more than a "stupendous fraud," Douglass proclaimed. The former slaveholding aristocracy wielded as much social and economic power as ever before. They had devised innumerable laws and practices to ensure their continued economic exploitation of African Americans. The region's Black Codes and laws regulating sharecropping kept black southerners perpetually impoverished and in bondage—a "disgrace and a scandal to American civilization." White southerners routinely subverted the Fourteenth and Fifteenth Amendments, depriving African Americans of any meaningful political power or equality under the law. Meanwhile, the federal government passively watched as this reign of injustice hardened, doing little to protect the rights of black citizens.[18]

It infuriated Douglass that most white Americans referred to deteriorating southern race relations as "the Negro problem," as if blame rested on black southerners and not the white architects of Jim Crow. "The true problem is not the negro, but the nation," Douglass contended in an 1890 speech in Washington, D.C., at an AME church. "Not the law-abiding blacks of the South, but the white men of that section, who by fraud, violence, and persecution, are breaking the law, trampling on the Constitution, corrupting the ballot-box, and defeating the ends of justice." Douglass easily summarized the real problem, as he understood it: "The United States Government made the negro a citizen, will it protect him as a citizen?"[19]

What some called the Negro problem, Douglass called a national existential dilemma: Would America live up to its highest religious and political principles, as enshrined in its Constitution and sacred scriptures? In a private letter Douglass wondered if "the white man can and will yet rise to that height of justice, humanity, and Christian civilization as will permit Indians, Chinamen and Negros to enjoy an Equal chance in the race of life among them?"[20] Throughout the late 1880s and early 1890s, Douglass had a hard time offering an optimistic answer to that question. But he tried to remain hopeful that Americans could still correct even the latest errors and injustices of Jim Crow. "I have seen dark hours in my life, and I have seen the darkness gradually disappearing and the light gradually increasing," he said in an October 1890 speech after recounting the disheartening reality of life for black southerners. "And I remember that God reigns in eternity, and that whatever delays, whatever disappointments and discouragements may come, truth, justice, liberty, and humanity will ultimately prevail."[21]

Yet, they had not presently prevailed, as each lynching of a black American grimly confirmed. Douglass denounced the murders by white lynch mobs as a "cruelty which might well shock the sensibility of the most benighted savage." The nation's lynching epidemic was a symptom of a deep moral disease, Douglass wrote in 1892. "Its presence is either an evidence of governmental depravity, or of a demoralized state of society." All that really stood behind each lynching, whatever its purported justification, was the same tired old "prejudice and hatred" white southerners had always felt toward African Americans. Douglass asked how the white Christian South could possibly preach "the sacredness of human life while it cheapens it and profanes it by the atrocities of mob law." Every lynching was an act of blasphemy, an utter betrayal of American law and the perfect law of the Lord.[22] Douglass concluded that African Americans in the age of Jim Crow "are yet, as a people, only half free." The promises of freedom contained in the Constitution remained unfulfilled: "We stand to-day only in the twilight of American liberty."[23]

The Hopeful Prophet

Douglass lived only to see the onset of Jim Crow. But few Americans were better suited to condemn the segregation, disenfranchisement, and violent assault of African Americans. He had devoted his entire life to the cause of black liberty and justice, only at the end to see that cause again imperiled. In the first half of the 1890s, the last five years of his life, Douglass reprised his role as America's prophet for a final time. Two moments at the end of Douglass's life capture the prophetic witness against Jim Crow that he bore until he breathed his last: first, his response to the 1893 World's Columbian Exposition; and, second, the final great speech of his life, "Lessons of the Hour," delivered in January 1894. On both occasions, Douglass spoke with fiery authority against the bigotry and injustice of Jim Crow—denouncing racial oppression as both un-Christian and un-American.

Organizers of the World's Columbian Exposition in Chicago claimed to commemorate the 400th anniversary of Christopher Columbus's arrival in North America. But more than anything, the six-month-long fair celebrated the great progress and ingenuity that had transformed America in the second half of the nineteenth century. The Chicago Fair, like its European predecessors, hosted many exhibits meant to enlighten and edify by displaying the latest technological advancements and fashionable knowledge. The fairgrounds also beckoned potential visitors with all kinds of entertainment, from orchestras to George Ferris's grand wheel. The center of the Exposition grounds became known as the White City—for the main fair buildings, designed in the neoclassical style, featured facades of plaster and cement painted white, matched by pearly stucco ornamentation.[24]

The fair came to Chicago at the same moment Jim Crow came to America. Naturally, the racial discrimination and conflict prevalent throughout the nation in the 1890s also enveloped the Columbian Exposition. African American leaders initially had grand hopes for the fair. They wanted to use the occasion to display to the world (and to white Americans) the achievements and abilities of their race. But serious impediments to that dream quickly appeared. Not a single African American was appointed to the administrative body responsible for planning and governing the fair. Many fair jobs were closed to African American applicants, especially on the guard patrol. Exposition exhibits designed and proposed by African Americans underwent particularly intense scrutiny, and many were rejected outright. White-produced exhibits purporting to capture the history and character of America often either marginalized black Americans or included demeaning depictions of them.[25]

Not surprisingly, many African American activists, closely following events surrounding the fair, protested the racial discrimination and exclusion.

They feared that keeping silent would give a false impression to the world about the past and present nature of American race relations. One of the leading black voices of protest against the fair was Ida B. Wells, the legendary journalist and activist. Born a slave in Mississippi in 1862, Wells moved to Memphis, Tennessee, after receiving a college education. In Memphis she began her trailblazing career as a newspaper editor and investigative reporter. Her editorials in the late 1880s denounced segregation laws and advocated for civil and political equality. Her career took a courageous turn after a white Memphis mob lynched three of her black friends, made lately prosperous by a successful grocery store they owned. Wells began a thorough investigation of lynchings across the South. Lynch mobs usually justified their executions by claiming that they punished a black man for sexually assaulting a white woman. The white South almost universally accepted this "rape myth," but Wells's investigations debunked it completely. In works such as *Southern Horrors: Lynch Law in All Its Phases* (1892) and *The Red Record* (1895), she showed that black lynch victims had not raped white women but instead had challenged the political and economic superiority of white men, the real reason for their grisly murders. By the time of the World's Columbian Exhibition, Wells had made a name for herself as perhaps the nation's leading antilynching activist.

Wells wanted visitors from around the world to know about the racial discrimination committed by the fair's organizers. She also hoped to educate the international audience about the plight of people of color in the United States. Wells eventually published a brief pamphlet, *The Reason Why the Colored American Is Not in the World's Columbian Exposition,* and planned to hand out copies for free to fairgoers. Wells intended to print copies in several different languages, but limited funds forced her to print the pamphlet only in English, which was ready for distribution in the late summer of 1893.[26]

Despite its title, only one of the pamphlet's six short essays addressed the discrimination African Americans faced from the fair's organizers. Ferdinand Lee Barnett, a lawyer and newspaper publisher who married Ida B. Wells in 1895, penned the chapter that documented how, in Barnett's words, "from the very first steps of the Exposition work the colored people were given to understand that they were *persona non grata*," especially when it came to governing the fair and selecting its exhibitions.[27] The pamphlet's five other essays together outlined the accomplishments of African Americans since emancipation and the challenges they still faced. Irvine Garland Penn, an educator and prominent Methodist layman, contributed a chapter listing the many educational, artistic, religious, and commercial successes of black Americans in the three decades after the Civil War. Wells wrote three essays—on post-Reconstruction Black Codes and segregation laws, on the convict lease system, and on the significant rise in lynchings over the past decade. In her essays, Wells succeeded in succinctly capturing for a foreign readership the essence of life for black southerners in the Jim Crow era.[28]

Wells convinced Douglass to write the pamphlet's introduction. Douglass had spent significant time at the Columbian Exposition as Haiti's official commissioner. (In 1889, President Benjamin Harrison had appointed Douglass as America's minister-resident and consul-general to Haiti, a post he filled for two years, during a time of internal political turmoil in the Caribbean nation.) In his introduction, Douglass explained that because the "colored people of America are not indifferent to the good opinion of the world," the pamphlet's authors set out to honestly describe "our first years of freedom and citizenship," with all its triumphs and misfortunes. This required "plain speaking of wrongs and outrages endured, and of rights withheld, and withheld in flagrant contradiction to boasted American Republican liberty and civilization." Douglass had done exactly this his entire public life, but such an honest testimony of black life in America took on new urgency in the early 1890s.[29]

Douglass devoted most of his introduction to summarizing the character and legacy of slavery. The perverse institution had "possessed the power of blinding the moral perception, stifling the voice of conscience, blunting all human sensibilities and perverting the plainest teaching of the religion we have here professed," a consequence that still affected American Christianity and the nation's moral sensibilities. However, Douglass hoped that the world would marvel at the progress African Americans had made since emancipation. For centuries they had been enslaved, beaten, murdered, and trapped in ignorance and destitution. In three short decades, in the face of continued bigotry, African Americans made remarkable strides toward "a higher position" of greater prosperity, education, and virtue.[30]

Douglass confessed that he wished he could report a great "moral progress" among the American people since emancipation, the banishment of all "race hate" and inequality, but it simply had not occurred. To African Americans, the World's Columbian Exposition in Chicago stood as a microcosm of the nation. Using his favorite biblical metaphors for hypocrisy, Douglass labeled the fair (like the nation) a "whited sepulcher," whose gleaming facade thinly covered an inner deadness. Visitors to the Chicago fair would find "splendid display of wealth and power," testaments to the nation's prosperity and progress. But all the exhibits and the dazzling stucco-whiteness of the fair's main buildings could not mask the racial inequality and oppression that still rotted out the heart of America.[31]

"The Americans are a great and magnanimous people and this great exposition adds greatly to their honor and renown," Douglass concluded, "but in the pride of their success they have cause for repentance . . . for shame as well as for glory." Douglass pledged to use the public platform provided by the fair to preach a prophetic message that America and the world desperately needed to hear: "Let the truth be told, let the light be turned on ignorance and prejudice, let lawless violence and murder be exposed."[32]

The piece of the fair that provoked the greatest controversy among African American activists was the "Colored People's Day" scheduled for 25 August 1893. The fair's organizers, following a suggestion from a black Boston delegation, had planned the special day to commemorate black Americans' achievements since emancipation. Many black leaders reacted to the plan with decided suspicion, if not outright opposition. To them, the day appeared only to perpetuate the segregationist spirit and relegate African Americans to a decidedly minor place in the larger American story told by the fair. Others feared that the day's actual events might only reinforce derogatory stereotypes of African Americans before an international audience. Ida B. Wells, for one, strongly opposed the Colored People's Day and called upon African Americans to join her in boycotting it.[33]

Douglass had his concerns about the day, but he opted not to support the boycott. He thought the better response would be to do all he could to make the day a true celebration of African Americans. Douglass agreed to preside over the day's main events and deliver a keynote address. The ceremony showcased several talented young black artists, including the violinist Joseph Douglass, Frederick's grandson, and the poet Paul Laurence Dunbar. Despite threatened boycotts, the crowd that day featured many distinguished African American leaders, including Methodist bishop Henry McNeal Turner.[34]

When it came time for Douglass to speak, he began to read a prepared address, "The Race Problem in America." Soon after he started, a handful of white hecklers shouted at him, and he briefly stumbled over his words. The taunting seemed to have gotten the better of the elder Douglass. But he then set aside his text, fixed his gaze on his audience, and spoke with a stern authority that drowned out the white men's catcalls. Douglass orated for an hour on America's persistent race problem, the nation's inability to treat justly and equitably all people. He denounced the religious and political hypocrisy that kept America, a supposed land of Christianity and liberty, from truly extending freedom and opportunity to all its citizens.

The Hopeful Prophet

"There is no Negro problem," Douglass roared. "The problem is whether the American people have loyalty enough, honor enough, patriotism enough, to live up to their own Constitution." When Ida B. Wells later read about the address, she praised Douglass for ignoring her call to boycott. His words and the day's festivities, she said, did "more to bring our case to the attention of the American people than anything else which had happened during the fair."[35]

The core of Douglass's Colored People's Day address previewed the message of the final great speech of his life, "Lessons of the Hour." Douglass had begun a draft of the address in the fall of 1893, but he delivered the finest version of the speech on 9 January 1894 in Washington, D.C., at the Metropolitan AME Church. The crowd that gathered that day to hear Douglass included Jeremiah Rankin, the president of Howard University, and a host of former black elected officials, including onetime Mississippi senator Blanche K. Bruce.[36]

It was only fitting that Douglass's last magnificent speech was one of his most prophetic. Douglass delivered to Jim Crow America a word of rebuke and warning and a call to atonement. He denounced as un-Christian the atrocity of lynching. He cautioned that the unjust and oppressive treatment of African Americans threatened the nation's future—for God would not forever tolerate such gross offenses. He pleaded with America to adhere to the religious and political principles it claimed to cherish. If it did so, the sin and terror of Jim Crow would end; if it did not, untold apocalyptic terror awaited.

Douglass proposed in "Lessons of the Hour" to offer "a colored man's view" of the present state of race relations and violence in the South. What some called "the Negro problem" Douglass again called the American problem, for it concerned "the honor or dishonor, glory or shame, happiness or misery of the whole American people." The time had come to tell the full, grisly truth of "the epidemic of mob law and persecution" against black Americans—rampant in the South but present in the northern states as well. "The contagion is spreading," Douglass warned, "extending and over-leaping geographical lines and state boundaries, and if permitted to go on it threatens to destroy all respect for law and order."[37] Jim Crow mob violence threatened to dismantle the very values and institutions that should define democratic America, especially the rule of law.

Having announced his topic, Douglass unleashed as furious a prophetic fire as he had ever delivered. Although the injustice had changed—Jim Crow violence instead of slavery—Douglass's rhetorical tactic remained the same. He forced Americans to confront the gross disjuncture between the Christianity they professed and the violent oppression they committed against African Americans. "We claim to be a Christian country and a highly civilized nation," Douglass scoffed, "yet, I fearlessly affirm that there is nothing in the history of savages to surpass the blood chilling horrors and fiendish excesses perpetrated against the colored people by the so-called enlightened and Christian people of the South." The white lynch mobs reminded Douglass of bloodthirsty "buzzards, vultures, and hyenas" barbarically gloating over their prey. At the heart of Douglass's condemnation of the racial violence of the Jim Crow era was a simple but searing point: People who routinely lynched fellow human beings were not Christians.

White southerners had concocted an elaborate set of rationales for the mob lynchings. Douglass did his part in "Lessons of the Hour" to expose as utterly false the most commonly cited justification—that the lawless executions occurred in response to sexual assault by black men against white women. Following Ida B. Wells's exhaustive investigative reporting, Douglass contended that there was no evidence, in the past or present, of rampant sexual assault by black men against white women. Like Wells, he insisted that the rape allegation was a complete sham justification. Once a black man was accused of raping a white woman, Douglass said, "no matter by whom or in what manner, whether well or ill-founded, whether true or false," he would certainly face "immediate death."[38] The fact that lynch mobs denied their victims a trial by jury—and the presumption of innocence—only further proved the falsehood of the rape accusations, Douglass contended. He believed the charges of sexual assault were meant not only to excuse lynchings but also "to blast and ruin the negro's character as a man and a citizen."[39] The way white mobs justified the violence they committed reflected the very heart of the Jim Crow South, its effort to cast African Americans as neither full citizens nor full human beings.

For a century or more, white southerners had devised all sorts of excuses for their violent persecution of African Americans, Douglass argued. First, they appealed to the threat of slave insurrection. After emancipation, they trumpeted the prospect of "negro supremacy" in the region's political life. Following the fall of Reconstruction, white southerners warned of black "assault upon defenseless women," only the latest in a long tradition of hollow rationales for racial violence. Practically the whole history of the South—perhaps the entire nation—could be told by charting the evolving justifications white southerners used to sanctify their violence against black southerners, slave or free.

The one trait uniting white persecutors across the decades, and certainly exhibited by Jim Crow–era lynchers, was an "absolute contempt" for the lives of African Americans. "The sacredness of life which ordinary men feel does not touch them anywhere," Douglass said of lynch mobs. To Douglass, the latest spasm of lynchings, and the long tradition of racial violence that preceded it, was rooted in a terrible theological heresy. Lynchers denied the dignity and humanity of their victims, people created in God's image, and thereby grossly defied fundamental claims of the Christian faith.[40]

Douglass denounced with particular harshness the "better classes of the Southern people" who refused to speak out against lynch violence. "The mob-ocratic murderers are not only permitted to go free, untried and punished, but are lauded and applauded as honorable men and good citizens," Douglass said. He contended that much of the mob violence would end if the white South's political, religious, and business leaders spoke out against the lawlessness. But instead, "press, platform, and pulpit are either generally silent or they openly apologize for the mob." Urbane and educated white Christian ministers were particularly culpable for the continued lynchings, Douglass argued. In their strategic silence, as much as their outright endorsement of the lynch mobs, such ministers betrayed their calling. Douglass referred specifically to Bishop Atticus G. Haygood, a Georgian Methodist. In some ways, Haygood was progressive on race issues for a white southerner of his time. He strongly supported black educational efforts and opposed the South's convict lease system, among other discriminatory labor practices that nearly amounted to reenslavement.[41] In an 1893 article, "The Black Shadow in the South," Haygood condemned the "mob law" responsible for lynchings: "This is not civilization; it is at best barbarism," he wrote. Haygood even went so far as to call lynching "a crime against God and man," though chiefly because it defied the rule of law. But Haygood still blamed the lynchings on African American men and the sexual violence they committed. "Unless assaults by negroes on white women and little white girls come to an end, there will most probably be still further displays of vengeance that will shock the world," Haygood wrote, repeating a myth that Ida B. Wells had by then exposed as baseless.[42]

Douglass saw in Haygood a prime example of how even well-meaning white southerners reiterated the same demeaning lies about African Americans that enabled Jim Crow violence. Douglass lamented that Haygood and other leading white ministers failed to speak boldly against the dehumanizing, un-Christ-like practice of lynching. When white Americans like Haygood labeled the nation's racial turmoil the "negro problem," they tried thereby to absolve themselves of any guilt or complicity in it. Douglass vehemently rejected the label because it "implies that the negro is the cause of whatever trouble there is in the South," he said. It was a label that obfuscated the real nature of the problem. It "shields the guilty, and blames the innocent," and comforted white Americans, northerners and southerners alike, because it "makes the negro responsible and not the nation."[43] So long as white Americans affixed the name "the negro problem" on the oppression of Jim Crow, they would never deal honestly with the injustice and inequality destroying their nation.

Douglass called America to task for failing to confront and resolve its racial problems. If the nation continued its present course, Douglass warned, apocalyptic judgment awaited. God would not forever tolerate America's present course of racial oppression. If the crimes and injustices of Jim Crow continued, Douglass expected "a national punishment which would cause the earth to shudder."[44] The time had arrived for America to face directly its national racial problems. The only question that remained, according to Douglass, was "whether, after all, with our Declaration of Independence, with our glorious free constitution, whether with our sublime Christianity, there is enough of national virtue in this great nation to solve this problem, in accordance with wisdom and justice."[45] Was there time enough left for America to vindicate its highest ideals and purge itself of another great national sin, racial bigotry and violence?

Douglass believed there was. He never lost hope that America could trade prejudice and hatred for justice, compassion, and equality. The nation simply needed to live according to the political and religious principles it claimed to venerate. How could the American people "conquer their prejudices" and "cultivate kindness and humanity"? Douglass answered, "Let the great Northern press and pulpit proclaim the gospel of truth and justice against war now being made upon the negro. . . . Let the organic law of the land be honestly sustained and obeyed."[46] If America truly abided by the spirit of true Christianity and the letter of the Constitution it would promptly abandon the injustice and violence of Jim Crow.

Though seventy-five years old in January 1894, Douglass spoke to the Metropolitan Church audience with the vigor and endurance and intensity of a man half his age. The crowd that day caught a glimpse of what it must have sounded like in the early 1840s to hear the passionate young fugitive slave plead the abolitionist cause to Christian America. "But could I be heard by this great nation," Douglass said at the end of his speech,

I would call to mind the sublime and glorious truths with which, at its birth, it saluted a listening world. Its voice then, was as the tramp of an archangel, summoning hoary forms of oppression and time honored tyranny, to judgment. Crowned heads heard it and shrieked. Toiling millions heard it and clapped their hands for joy. It announced the advent of a nation, based upon human brotherhood and the self-evident truths of liberty and equality. Its mission was the redemption of the world from the bondage of ages. Apply these sublime and glorious truths to the situation now before you. Put away your race prejudice. Banish the idea that one class must rule over another. Recognize the fact that the rights of the humblest citizen are as worthy of protection as are those of the highest, and your problem will be solved; and, whatever may be in store for it in the future, whether prosperity, or adversity; whether it shall have foes without, or foes within, whether there shall be peace, or war; based upon the eternal principles of truth, justice and humanity, and with no class having any cause of compliant or grievance, your Republic will stand and flourish forever.[47]

Douglass died a year later, having never seen in America the Promised Land for which he yearned and fought. But his prophetic words yet live, an eternal witness to truth and justice.

Unraveling the Mysteries of God's Providence and Progress

Frederick Douglass wrote three autobiographies during his long life, and he never quite told his story in precisely the same way. His autobiographies grew longer and more detailed over time, which make all the more fascinating the *omissions* in the later ones. Certain passages included in *Narrative of the Life of Frederick Douglass* (1845) and *My Bondage and My Freedom* (1855) are missing entirely from the *Life and Times of Frederick Douglass* (1881, 1892). One of the more striking examples is how Douglass altered his account of his removal from Maryland's Eastern Shore to Baltimore at age eight. In *Narrative of the Life of Frederick Douglass*, he called the unexpected move "the first plain manifestation of that kind providence which has ever since attended me, and marked my life with so many favors." Douglass granted that some people might think him "superstitious, and even egotistical" for regarding his twist of fate as God's doing—"a special interposition of divine Providence," as he called it. But that did not dampen Douglass's deep "thanksgiving and praise" to God for the unexpected blessing early in his life.[1]

In *My Bondage and My Freedom*, Douglass changed the story only slightly. "I regard my removal from Colonel Lloyd's plantation as one of the most interesting and fortunate events of my life," Douglass wrote. Unlike in his first autobiography, Douglass also quoted William Shakespeare's *Hamlet* to explain the move: "There's a divinity that shapes our ends, rough-hew them how we will." Douglass again admitted that his opinion might be deemed "irrational by the wise, and ridiculous by the scoffer," but he still looked to that pivotal moment in his life as "a special interposition of Divine Providence in my favor."[2]

Readers of *Life and Times of Frederick Douglass* found a dramatically different version of the same event. After recounting again the story of Thomas and Lucretia Auld's decision to send him to Baltimore to live with Hugh and Sophia Auld, Douglass simply concluded: "I may say here that I regard my removal from Colonel Lloyd's plantation as one of the most interesting and fortunate events of my life. Viewing it in the light of human likelihoods, it is quite probable that but for the mere circumstance of being thus removed, before the rigors of slavery had fully fastened upon me; before my young spirit had been crushed under the iron control of the slavedriver; I might have continued in slavery until emancipated by the war." Douglass deleted entirely any mention of "a special interposition of Divine Providence" or "a divinity that shapes our ends." He seemingly now concluded that God had played no role in the first truly transformative moment of his life, which set him on the long path to freedom.[3]

The way this section of *Life and Times of Frederick Douglass* differed from Douglass's earlier autobiographies might appear to be proof that Douglass radically altered his theology over the course of his life. It seems as if, at least by 1881, Douglass had adopted an understanding of God's character and presence in the world that he did not hold four decades earlier as a recent convert to Methodism. In his classic intellectual biography *The Mind of Frederick Douglass*, Waldo Martin argued that by the onset of the Civil War Douglass had traded his "traditional God-centered religious philosophy" for a "liberal human-centered religious philosophy." That is, according to Martin, Douglass came to believe that God's "direct involvement in human affairs was minimal," and that human beings alone overwhelmingly—if not completely—shaped the course of history.[4]

At first glance, the way Douglass wrote out God from a key portion of his final autobiography seems to confirm Martin's argument.[5] But the passages quoted above from the autobiographies, taken alone, can be misleading. By and large, Douglass did not trade a "God-centered" faith for a "human-centered" one, as if the complex substance of his deepest religious convictions must be pigeonholed into one of those two categories. Instead, Douglass's understanding of who God was and how God worked in the world remained largely unchanged over the course of his life.

The continuity in Douglass's faith is especially apparent in his theology of progress and providence—his understanding of how and why progress occurs in history and who is responsible for it. Douglass accepted a millennialist-tinged, progressive vision of history. But who exactly achieves progress—God or human beings or both in some mysterious way? How fully did God preordain history—the history of an individual or particular race or entire nation? Was God responsible especially for the great progress of emancipation? In the final quarter century of his life, Douglass often pondered these questions, especially in three particular speeches: an 1870 address on emancipation at the final meeting of the American Anti-Slavery Society; an 1883 speech titled "It Moves," delivered at an African Methodist Episcopal church in Washington, D.C.; and an 1893 version of "Self-Made Man," an oration Douglass delivered dozens of times after 1859. Taken together, these three speeches reveal that Douglass largely held fast his entire life to the understanding of providence and progress that he had worked out as a young man.

In the antebellum era, as a leading abolitionist orator, Douglass spoke often of God's active work in history to ensure the destruction of American slavery. He also insisted that human beings, particularly radical activists like the abolitionists, played an essential role in achieving meaningful reform in society. After the Civil War, Douglass at times appeared far more hesitant to credit God for all progress in history, including emancipation. He certainly spoke more about the preeminent power people possessed to shape their lives and their world.

Yet any apparent changes in Douglass's later theology had less to do with some new understanding of God and far more to do instead with the new social and political challenges confronting African Americans after emancipation. Douglass feared that a certain passive spirit might spread among African Americans, especially former slaves, if they embraced too-simplistic notions of providence. He worried that members of his race might laxly confront their postwar problems if they expected God's imminent deliverance and protection. The passages in Douglass's later speeches and writings that appear to show a newfound "liberal human-centered religious philosophy" should be read as part of an effort to exhort African Americans to vigilant action in the quest for justice and equality. Douglass's understanding of God did not significantly change in the years before and after the Civil War. But the realities of life as an African American did, which compelled Douglass to speak to his people in newly appropriate ways about providence and progress.

On 9 April 1870, the American Anti-Slavery Society met for a final time at the Apollo Hall in New York City. A jubilant spirit filled the hall, as attendees gathered to celebrate the final triumph of their decades-long work. The Thirteenth Amendment, ratified December 1865, abolished slavery. Less than three years later, in July 1868, the Fourteenth Amendment guaranteed the full "privileges and immunities" of citizenship to all persons born or naturalized in the United States. The amendment compelled states to extend to each of their citizens the equal protection of the law, and it forbid states from depriving citizens of "life, liberty, or property, without due process of law."

By March 1870, after the ratification of the Fifteenth Amendment, the Constitution prohibited the federal or state governments from denying a person the right to vote based "on account of race, color, or previous condition of servitude." The Reconstruction Amendments carried forward the work of emancipation begun during the Civil War; they guaranteed, to an unprecedented degree, freedom and equality under the law in America. Abolitionists found reason to rejoice in the amendments. Many also looked upon the constitutional triumphs as an occasion to give thanks to God and reflect on the nature of progress in history.

The American Anti-Slavery Society executive committee had earlier decided to disband the society after the ratification of the Fifteenth Amendment. Society members now met to formally ratify the decision. They first heard from Wendell Philips, their president, who advised them "to thank God and throw their strength into other channels."[6] Members prayed, sang hymns, and considered several formal resolutions from the executive committee. One of the resolutions expressly thanked God for bringing to completion the work of emancipation. Eventually, members officially voted to end the society. But before then, several leading abolitionists spoke—including Douglass, who could not help but respond to the earlier resolution thanking God.[7]

In his remarks, Douglass appeared to bluntly reject the notion that God secured emancipation in America. He instead credited groups like the American Anti-Slavery Society. At first glance, Douglass's speech seems like undeniable evidence that he was shifting away from a "traditional God-centered religious philosophy."[8] But Douglass only rebelled against simplistic providential thinking, the kind that quickly credited God for all human progress without adequately considering the social and theological implications of such a claim. By 1870, Douglass worried especially about the negative consequences that might befall African Americans if they adhered to a misguided providential mindset. For despite the great triumph of the ratification of the Reconstruction Amendments, Douglass saw in 1870 that African American civil and political equality still faced a decidedly uncertain future.

Douglass resisted a too-easy view of God's providential role in the world because he thought it did not deal honestly with the problem of evil: If God was responsible for ensuring that justice and goodness triumphed on earth, why did God continue to allow evil and suffering? To Douglass, the even more pertinent problem in 1870 was finding a way for African Americans to avoid the worst consequences of adhering to an excessively providential mindset. Would confidence in God's deliverance foster passivity among African Americans and their white allies, who still faced many obstacles to true racial equality?

"I am living in an entirely new atmosphere," Douglass acknowledged at the beginning of his address to the American Anti-Slavery Society. "Who could have imagined ten years ago, or even seven years ago, what has occurred?" Three amendments to the U.S. Constitution had abolished slavery, proclaimed African American full citizens of the nation, and guaranteed black men the right to vote. Douglass praised several important figures within the American Anti-Slavery Society, its key founders and financiers and leaders. These tireless men and women, Douglass said, proved pivotal to abolitionism's triumph.[9]

Douglass then turned his attention to the resolution from earlier in the day that, in his words, "proposes to give thanks to God, and none especially to men." Here, Douglass the reformer-theologian turned caustic: "I like to thank men. I like to thank the people I see. Those people who give all their thanks to God I have a suspicion of.... I have no sort of sympathy with that kind of religion that expresses its devotion to God by neglect of their fellows.... I want to express my love to God and gratitude to God, by thanking those faithful men and women, who have devoted the great energies of their souls to the welfare of mankind. It is only through such men and such women that I can get any glimpses of God anywhere. I want, not to fall down and worship them, but to express my gratitude and my affection for them."[10]

Many attendees in Apollo Hall that day applauded Douglass during this part of his speech. But others condemned him for it. A group of AME clergy and laity in Philadelphia met a month later and responded directly to Douglass's claims. "While we love Frederick Douglass, we love truth more," one minister said. "We admire Frederick Douglass, but we love God more." The gathered Philadelphians then adopted a formal resolution, plainly aimed at Douglass, that pledged to not "acknowledge any man as a leader of our people who will not thank God for the deliverance and enfranchisement of our race."[11]

In the decades prior to the Civil War, and even as late as 1865, Douglass frequently affirmed God's active work in ensuring the destruction of American slavery. Had his opinion on the matter really shifted dramatically by 1870? The key to understanding Douglass's comments comes earlier in the speech. Near the start of his address, Douglass admitted that only one thing gave him pause for concern on this day of celebration: "The black man is now absolutely thrown on his own responsibility." After emancipation and enfranchisement, African American men were now "stripped of every apology for any sort of lack of manhood or of usefulness in society." He continued: "We must depend on ourselves, make our own record, make our own future. I have no doubt that we will, or at least but few shadows of doubt."[12]

The Hopeful Prophet

Douglass appealed to African Americans to seize each new opportunity for uplift and equality, and not simply assume God would bestow upon them the blessings of prosperity and freedom. After the Civil War, Douglass constantly worried about the consequences of allowing a certain providentialism to inculcate a lax attitude—as if God ordained entirely the unfolding course of history, and left human beings little power over their own lives. Douglass had this sort of theology in mind when he said, "Those people who give all their thanks to God I have a suspicion of."[13] By 1870, Douglass sometimes even expressed almost the exact opposite opinion: that human effort played the chief role in determining history's direction, especially in American emancipation. He expressed this view in the hopes of best preparing African Americans to deal successfully with the problems and opportunities they faced in Reconstruction. "It is true that we are no longer slaves, but it is equally true that we are not yet quite free," Douglass explained in an August 1869 speech. "We have been turned out of the house of bondage, but we have not yet been fully admitted to the glorious temple of American liberty. We are still in a transition state and the future is shrouded in doubt and danger."[14]

Douglass certainly did not deny God's existence in 1870, or even reject entirely the idea that God remained at work in the affairs of the earth. Nor did he think of human agency and divine providence as two opposing forces. The work of God and the work of human beings could remain mysteriously united in shaping events toward the same ends. In the work of abolitionists Douglass said he caught "glimpses of God."[15] Not only did abolitionists live according to God's justice and righteousness, but they also labored as God labored, for freedom. Twenty years later, during a speech in Boston, Douglass made a similar point: "While I believe there are eternal forces in motion, carrying on the course of truth and justice in this world, still, when I am looking around to give thanks, I recognize a two-fold duty, to express gratitude to God and to good men—who are God in the flesh."[16] Douglass's controversial words at Apollo Hall in 1870 did not constitute a radical or decidedly new theological pronouncement. Instead, Douglass merely called righteous men and women everywhere to play a role in the next long chapter of the black freedom struggle.

For that reason, late in life Douglass spoke often on what he labeled "the philosophy of reform." By that he meant simply how and why a people progressed, how and why they improved themselves and their world. As a veteran of the abolitionist and women's rights movements, as well as the struggle against Jim Crow, Douglass cared about the philosophical underpinnings of his vision of reform and progress. In November 1883, he offered his most extensive statement on the matter, in a speech titled "'It Moves,' or the Philosophy of Reform."

Frederick Douglass, ca. 1880. *Courtesy of the Library of Congress.*

Douglass delivered the address in Washington, D.C., at the Metropolitan AME Church's Bethel Hall. The audience that November evening consisted of members of the Bethel Literary and Historical Association, a learned society of African American Washingtonians founded two years prior by AME bishop Daniel Payne. In the oration, Douglass, the veteran activist, assumed the role of senior philosopher of reform. Along the way, he contemplated first-order theological questions. When Douglass discussed his "philosophy

The Hopeful Prophet

of reform," he could not help but address God's character, the nature of truth, and God's presence in the world.

The speech was immediately controversial. As Douglass finished, the Reverend Walker Henderson Brooks, pastor of the Nineteenth Street Baptist Church, charged him with heresy for suggesting that the latest geological evidence likely confirmed that the Earth was much older than what one might conclude from a literal reading of the Book of Genesis. Douglass fired back that he had no desire to attack religion generally or Christianity in particular, simply certain "human misrepresentations of it." Newspaper accounts of the evening reported that most audience members sided with Douglass and thought Brooks had been needlessly confrontational.[17] But the quibble over geology and Genesis was, in the end, far removed from the main intention of Douglass's speech, which was to offer a nuanced account of how both human effort and divine providence achieved reform—that is, progress—in history.

Douglass prepared his "It Moves" speech during a long season of personal turmoil. In August 1882, his wife, Anna, died at the age of sixty-nine. His political influence had been waning among the Republican Party elite. When James A. Garfield was elected president in 1880, he replaced Douglass as marshal for Washington, D.C., a bitter slight that Douglass bore silently. By the summer of 1883, Douglass suffered from severe depression, nearly to the point of mental and emotional collapse. He briefly came under the full-time care of a physician. Then, in October, the cause to which Douglass devoted his life endured a major setback when the Supreme Court declared unconstitutional the Civil Rights Act of 1875. In this season of depression and disappointment, Douglass turned once again to familiar questions about God's presence in a world so full of suffering.

As Douglass stood before the gathered crowed at Bethel Hall, he first acknowledged that some people flatly denied the possibility of any sort of real progress in society. Some said a fixed, unchangeable balance between good and evil remained on earth, hindering true improvement; others said that, if anything, the world grew worse, increasing in evil. Douglass rejected both perspectives because they rested on a false understanding of "the essential nature of man" and known "historical facts and experience."[18]

Douglass's philosophy of reform started instead from a decidedly progressive vision of history. "Happily for us the world does move, and better still, its movement is an upward movement," he said. Kingdoms, empires, and nations rise and fall, "but mankind as a whole must ever move onward, and increase in the perfection of character." Douglass affirmed that the story of human history was, in the grandest sense, a story of protracted conflict between "good and evil, truth and error, enlightenment and superstition." Douglass detected some variation of this fundamental conflict in all the major advancements in science and medicine, politics and law, religion and philosophy in Western history, as well as in the evolving status of women and African Americans in the United States. The conflict between forces of good and evil endured. But Douglass insisted that the bitter struggle ultimately worked toward a benevolent end, guiding humanity toward a state of greater perfection.[19]

For Douglass, the real question was not *if* progress occurred in history but *why*. Who—or what—was responsible for the essentially progressive spirit of history? "Whence comes the disposition or suggestion of reform," Douglass asked. "Is it human or is it divine, or is it both?" Douglass contended that the true engine of reform "was not found in the clouds, or in the stars, or any where else outside of humanity itself." Human beings were responsible for achieving progress on earth. Douglass explained: "So far as the laws of the universe have been discovered and understood, they seem to teach that the mission of man's improvement and perfection has been wholly committed to man himself. So is he to be his own savior or his own destroyer. He has neither angels to help him nor devils to hinder him."[20]

Douglass never uttered a more seemingly straightforward affirmation of a "human-centered religious philosophy." He appeared in the speech to have left no real room for God in history. He affirmed without any qualification that "man's improvement and perfection has been wholly committed to man himself." Yet taken in its entirety, Douglass's address was far more nuanced, and full of evidence that he still believed God played an essential role in realizing progress in the unfolding events of human history.[21]

A deep theological quandary kept Douglass from simply affirming God's providential role in progress. Any faith that too quickly and simplistically credited God with reform—the triumph of goodness and justice on earth—had not adequately confronted the problem of evil, Douglass thought. God did not predictably "protect the weak against the strong, the simple against the cunning, the oppressed against the oppressor, the slave against his master," he said. Evil endured on earth, despite the prayers and pleas of the oppressed.[22] It was a lesson hard learned by former slaves. For that reason, Douglass scoffed at anyone who merely hoped for divine deliverance from evil and did nothing to resist injustice and work for liberation. He had his suspicions that many of the African American ministers in his audience at Bethel Hall reflexively adopted this mindset, to the ultimate detriment of their race.

If human beings remained responsible for their own uplift, in what sense exactly were they responsible—in what way exactly did they reform and improve their societies? In answering this question, Douglass revealed that he had not written God out of the process of progress in history, even though he spoke in slightly different ways about God's role in that process. Douglass believed "all reform is an effort to bring man more and more into harmony with the laws of his own being and with those of the universe." Progress in history was another name for more fully conforming the reality of human existence to the eternal truths woven into the cosmos—such as justice, equality, liberty, and love. For this reason, God remained present in the work of reform, for Douglass affirmed the divine origin of these eternal truths. God established them, not humanity. Reformers discerned the truth emanating from the divine, and then labored to see it more fully realized in the societies in which they lived.[23]

Although evil persisted on earth, and the wicked often prospered while the saintly suffered, Douglass still believed a certain moral law remained inherent in the universe. The truth that constituted this moral order was sometimes mysterious, impenetrable, and perplexing. But as fixed eternal law it remained in force—just as the law of gravity governed motion in the universe. "If the smallest particle of matter in any part of the universe is subject to law," Douglass explained, "it seems to me that a thing so important as the moral nature of man cannot be less so."[24] Douglass envisioned the cosmos as "a stupendous whole, a system of law and order, eternal and perfect," as he said at an 1881 speech in Harpers Ferry celebrating John Brown.[25] An eternal, perfect moral law remained at the heart of the universe; it defined a truly righteous, just, and flourishing life.

Any real reform in society came ultimately by more fully comprehending and abiding by the "eternal and perfect" moral law that gave order to the cosmos. "All genuine reform must rest on the assumption that man is a creature of absolute, inflexible law, moral and spiritual," Douglass explained, "and that his happiness and well-being can only be secured by perfect obedience to such law." The task of the reformer was to "first discover the law and to enforce compliance by all his power of precept and example."[26] Reformers proclaimed the truth—that is, the moral order of the universe—and implored their fellow human beings to live according to it. Douglass never doubted that the truths of the cosmos aligned with the black freedom struggle. "The moral government of the universe is on our side," Douglass said in an April 1883 speech, "and cooperates, with all honest efforts, to lift up the down-trodden and oppressed in all lands, whether the oppressed be white or black."[27]

To bolster his argument, Douglass cited Theodore Parker, the American transcendentalist. Paraphrasing Parker, Douglass said, "All the space between man's mind and God's mind is crowded with truth that waits to be discovered and organized into law, for the government and happiness of mankind."[28] Douglass quoted the same line quite often in the speeches of his later life. Parker was a religious radical, a Massachusetts minister and reformer whose theological views left him alienated from the Unitarian establishment of his native state. His most infamous sermon was "The Transient and Permanent in Christianity," which he first delivered in 1841. In it, Parker attempted to disentangle the "permanent" moral and religious truths of Christianity from the "transient" and imperfect scriptures and doctrinal traditions of the faith. Parker refused to bow to any Christian authority, even to Christ himself. "It is hard to see why the great truths of Christianity rest on the personal authority of Jesus, more than the axioms of geometry rest on the personal authority of Euclid, or Archimedes," Parker once wrote.[29]

Douglass never followed Parker completely in his rebellion against historic Christian orthodoxy. Yet Douglass found in Parker's writings a compelling account of the nature of truth, progress, and the moral character of the universe. Douglass paraphrased Parker to reiterate his chief argument: Reform consisted ultimately of comprehending and applying the eternal moral law of the cosmos. Douglass therefore concluded: "All reform, whether moral or physical, whether individual or social, is the result of some new truth or of a logical inference from an old and admitted truth." Humanity progressed when it renounced error and ignorance and wholly embraced truth, aided along the way by reformers of great moral vision.[30]

Douglass opened his speech in an unusual way, by referencing Galileo Galilei's conflict with the Catholic Church over his heliocentric view of the universe. Under intense pressure from the Church, Galileo infamously renounced his views. Yet, according to a likely apocryphal legend, after professing that planetary bodies orbited around the earth, which remained stationary, Galileo supposedly uttered of the earth, "yet it moves." Galileo's story reminded Douglass of the biblical account of Peter's denial of Christ. Douglass thought that both men, under "terrible pressure," ultimately "denied and repudiated the grand and luminous truth" they had discovered.[31] As "reformers," both testified to eternal truths, scientific and religious, respectively. Yet as reformers, both men were flawed, unable to bear fully the consequences of proclaiming the truth they had discovered.

Douglass saw in the lives of Galileo and Peter two honest examples of the place of human effort in the process of reform. "The instruments of reform are not necessarily perfect," Douglass concluded. But the triumph of truth and progress did not depended solely on the courage, insight, and endurance of reformers alone. Douglass said of Galileo and Peter: "Though neither was as strong as the truth they had denied, the world is vastly better off for their lives, their words and their works."[32] Both men testified boldly, though imperfectly, to truth. Despite their failures, what they proclaimed endured. Even in their weaknesses, truth remained resilient. As it spread, humanity progressed.

Douglass believed that the ultimate "mission of the reformer is to discover truth, or the settled and eternal order of the universe."[33] But progress in history did not depend simply on fallible reformers alone. God established the moral law of the universe, and God desired for human beings to know it. As reformers discovered new truths hidden between their minds and God's, they labored for humanity's progress. Therefore, both divine power and human effort carried forward the process of reform. God established the truth and order of the cosmos; reformers endeavored to discover and more fully realize it in their societies. Though wrapped in mystery, true progress depended upon both God and human beings.

A decade after his "It Moves" speech, Douglass traveled to Carlisle, Pennsylvania, to address the students of the city's Indian Industrial School. On a March day in 1893, Douglass delivered for the last time his famous "Self-Made Man" speech, which he first wrote in 1859 and had given more than fifty times since then. Douglass usually gave the speech to African American religious or educational organizations. He left most of it unchanged from 1859 to 1893, except for the passages periodically added or revised after the Civil War that addressed the new circumstances facing African Americans after emancipation.[34]

"Self-Made Man" was the quintessential statement of Douglass's particular vision of black uplift and self-improvement.[35] He assumed that the advice offered in the speech—relevant not only to African Americans but also to the Native American students at Carlisle—would become only more pertinent during the Jim Crow era. The final version of Douglass's speech also sheds important light on his later theology, particularly his understanding of the relationship between divine providence and human effort in shaping a person or a people's destiny. Read alongside the "It Moves" speech, the final delivered version of "Self-Made Man" confirms that in emphasizing human agency in effecting reform, Douglass did not mean to reject God's active presence in history. Instead, the shifts in rhetoric reflected a renewed effort on Douglass's part to exhort racial minorities to not passively tolerate the injustice of Jim Crow but instead to strive for true freedom, equality, and prosperity.

Douglass began his well-honed speech in Carlisle with lofty words about human nature and potential. "From man comes all that we know or can imagine of heaven and earth, of time and eternity," Douglass proclaimed. "He is the prolific constituter of manners, morals, religions and governments." Human beings can comprehend—and create—what is good and true and beautiful. At times, there seemed to be no limits to humanity's "marvelous powers and possibilities." Everyone shared this glorious ability and potential, which forged a common bond among all people, united "like waves to the ocean."[36]

Nevertheless, the students of the Indian Industrial School had gathered to hear Douglass speak not about humanity in general but about a particular type of exceptional individuals, the "self-made men." Douglass defined his subject as "men who, under peculiar difficulties and without the ordinary helps of favoring circumstances, have attained knowledge, usefulness, power and position." Enjoying neither noble birth nor inherited wealth, self-made men began life in destitution and triumphed despite the "open and derisive defiance of all the efforts of society." They were typically self-educated, an indication of their scorned status among social elites and the gatekeeping establishment. "If they have travelled far, they have made the road on which they travelled," Douglass said. "If they have ascended high, they have built their own ladder." Self-made men were utterly "indebted to themselves for themselves."[37]

How exactly did self-made men achieve their success? Douglass credited neither chance nor innate ability; a man became self-made not by accident or sheer genius alone. Douglass also detested when someone ascribed "their good or ill fortune directly to supernatural intervention." He rejected any vision of human nature or success that made a person "a very insignificant agent in his own affairs."[38] In the same way that Douglass rejected any too-simplistic providential explanation of progress, he also rejected the notion that God alone determined a person's achievements or misfortunes in life.

Instead of raw talent or divine favor, Douglass credited a tireless work ethic as the essential reason why a person became a self-made man: "We may explain success mainly by one word, and that word is WORK!" The tenacious man who labored relentlessly for success stood the best chance of achieving it in life. Douglass explained: "When we find a man who has ascended heights beyond ourselves, we may know that he has worked harder, better, and more wisely than we. He was awake while we slept. He was busy while we were idle." Douglass hoped to inspire his listeners to adopt this spirit of "patient, enduring, honest, unremitting and indefatigable work."[39]

On the surface, Douglass's "Self-Made Man" speech was far less theological than "It Moves." But it too reflected Douglass's deepest assumptions about God's providential presence in history, particularly in relation to a person's freedom to shape his or her life. Douglass did not reject the notion of supernatural intervention in the world. He simply believed that "faith, in the absence of work, seems to be worth little, if anything." He had no patience for anyone who justified inaction by crudely appealing to providence, as if God alone entirely determined someone's fate. Douglass mocked this mindset by imagining a preacher who would rather "pray for knowledge than tax his brain with study and application."[40] Such a minister would only leave a congregation spiritually malnourished. On an earlier occasion, Douglass said bluntly, "The Lord is good and kind but is of the most use to those who *do* for themselves."[41]

The "Self-Made Man" speech of 1893 showed how Douglass's concerns about the problems facing African Americans after emancipation influenced the way he talked about providence and progress in history. Douglass believed that long-term prosperity and equality for African Americans depended significantly on their ability to embrace the spirit of strenuous labor he extolled in "Self-Made Man." "A poor people are always a despised people," Douglass said in St. Michaels, Maryland, in 1877. "To be respected they must get money and property. Without money there's no leisure; without leisure no thought, without thought no progress."[42] Throughout his thirty years after the Civil War, Douglass worried that African Americans might not attain true progress if they held to a misguided understanding of providence. Douglass never denied entirely that God remained at work in the world. But a certain mystery surrounded God's activity, and human beings still possessed immense power to shape their own lives. Douglass advised African Americans at the onset of Jim Crow to live as if their every action determined the degree of freedom and equality they would enjoy.

One year before he delivered the "Self-Made Man" speech for the last time, Douglass released his final autobiography, a revised and expanded version of *Life and Times of Frederick Douglass*. "My part has been to tell the story of the slave," Douglass there explained. "The story of the master never wanted for narrators. The masters, to tell their story, had at call all the talents and genius that wealth and influence could command." Douglass wrote to testify not merely to his own experiences but to the experiences of all his enslaved brothers and sisters, toiling in America for more than two centuries. "To those who have suffered in slavery I can say, I, too, have suffered," Douglass continued. "To those who have battled for liberty, brotherhood, and citizenship I can say,

I, too, have battled. And to those who have lived to enjoy the fruits of victory I can say, I, too, live and rejoice."[43]

Douglass said he wrote his autobiographies not merely to speak for fellow former slaves but also to inspire them. The institution of slavery tried to trap slaves in ignorance, destitution, and self-loathing servility. Now free, ex-slaves could move on to lives of education, prosperity, and self-respect. "A way is open to welfare and happiness to all who will resolutely and wisely pursue that way," Douglass promised. But the burden of achieving this success remained on African Americans alone: "Neither institutions nor friends can make a race to stand unless it has strength in its own legs."[44]

Douglass, in effect, here appealed to members of his race to become self-made men. Quite abruptly in the final lines of his autobiography, he tried to strengthen his appeal by resorting to a theological argument: "All the prayers of Christendom cannot stop the force of a single bullet, divest arsenic of poison, or suspend any law of nature." As he often said in his "Self-Made Man" speech, Douglass suggested that former slaves had to do more than simply pray or hope for prosperity after emancipation. A man who failed to work tirelessly and then pleaded to God for riches and blessings was like a man who foolishly drank poison and then asked God for miraculous healing. Both men acted on a misguided understanding of providence.[45]

Sometimes the wicked prospered and the righteous languished. God's will often remained inscrutable. Douglass advised African Americans to labor mightily for themselves and their race, and not merely wait for God's provision. He thought this sort of religiously inspired passiveness on the part of African Americans was no better than the "Christian" submission that proslavery ministers once demanded of slaves. As Douglass put it, in religious matters he encountered too many former slaves "strutting about in the old clothes of the masters."[46] A new era of freedom had begun that demanded a correct understanding of God's nature and activity in the world.

Just before he defiantly proclaimed, "All the prayers of Christendom cannot stop the force of a single bullet," Douglass wrote, "Races, like individuals, must stand or fall by their own merits." At the end of his life, Douglass made many strident theological claims that appeared to reject conventional Christian notions of divine providence. He seemed to say that human beings were on their own in this world, and not even the faithful benefited consistently from God's gracious protection. In reality, Douglass had not abandoned his long-standing conception of an active and benevolent God—a vision first forged during his suffering as a slave. Instead, Douglass now tried simply, after emancipation, to speak a meaningful word to fellow African

Americans. "I have urged upon them self-reliance, self-respect, industry, perseverance, and economy," Douglass wrote, "to make the best of both worlds, but to make the best of this world first because it comes first." To former slaves who thought they had "means of procuring special favor and help from the Almighty," Douglass simply advised, "the universe is governed by laws which are unchangeable and eternal. . . . what men sow they will reap."[47]

Even as he chided members of his race to work for their own uplift, as if their prosperity depended upon their labor alone, Douglass still affirmed that God remained at work in history. In early 1886, Douglass wrote a revealing letter to Francis J. Grimké, a Presbyterian minister and prominent race leader in Washington, D.C., who eventually helped establish the National Association for the Advancement of Colored People. Douglass honestly expressed his anxieties about what the future held for African Americans. A nation that tolerated the routine lynching of black men would hardly accept full civil and political equality for African Americans. But despite his despair, Douglass found reason for hope in the Lord who brought the Israelites out of the house of bondage in Egypt, and had set free long-captive American slaves: "I am consoled with the thought that God reigns in eternity—and that deliverance will finally come."[48]

[CONCLUSION]

Frederick Douglass Is Not Dead!

Douglass spent the final day of his life as he had spent so many days, in the company of like-minded activists devoted to making America a land of true liberty and equality. On the morning of 20 February 1895, Douglass traveled from Anacostia to Metzerott Hall, in the heart of Washington, D.C., to attend the triennial meeting of the National Council of Women. Veterans of the women's rights movement had formed the council in 1888. Its diverse membership had many goals, but according to the preamble of the council's first constitution it remained chiefly dedicated "to the overthrow of all forms of ignorance and injustice, and to the application of the Golden Rule to society, custom and law."[1] Douglass enthusiastically supported the council's mission. On the late February day that would be his last, he sat on the platform at Metzerott Hall and listened attentively to the council's proceedings, which featured Susan B. Anthony, May Wright Sewall, and Anna H. Shaw. It had been nearly fifty years since Douglass attended his first women's rights meeting in Seneca Falls. His devotion to the movement had not wavered.[2]

Sometime shortly after 5:00 p.m. Douglass returned home and dined with his wife, Helen. After finishing the meal, as he waited for a carriage to take him to speak that evening at the Hillside African Church in Anacostia, Douglass recounted the day's events. While imitating one of the speakers, Douglass collapsed to the floor. Helen rushed to call a doctor, who arrived in time only to watch helplessly as Douglass breathed his last. When the *New York Times* reported Douglass's death the next morning, it fittingly commented, "It is a singular fact, in connection with the death of Mr. Douglass, that the very last hours of his life were given in attention to one of the principles to which he has devoted his energies since his escape from slavery."[3]

On the morning of 25 February, Douglass's body lay in state at the Metropolitan AME Church in Washington, D.C. For roughly four hours, thousands of people passed by Douglass's oak casket to pay their final respects. "Not since the unveiling of the Lincoln Emancipation Statue in 1878 has there been such a general gathering of colored people to pay tribute to a benefactor of their race," reported the *New York Times*. An honor guard of members of a Maryland division of the Sons of Union Veterans stood watch over Douglass's casket. It lay on the dais of the church's grand auditorium, decorated for the occasion with a sole black drape resting near the pulpit. Around the casket and pulpit sat dozens of floral bouquets and wreaths—sent by local black schools, women's groups, the government of Haiti, and even from a son of Thomas Auld, Frederick's former master.[4]

Shortly after 2:00 p.m. the funeral procession entered the sanctuary, packed to capacity with 2,000 mourners. The Reverend John Thomas Jenifer, Metropolitan's pastor, led the procession, which included not only family members and intimate friends but also Massachusetts senator George Frisbie Hoar, former Ohio senator John Sherman, Associate Justice of the Supreme Court John Marshall Harlan, and several leading women's rights activists, including Susan B. Anthony. The list of honorary pallbearers and official delegates from major American cities read like a who's who of prominent black ministers.[5]

Once the processors took their seats, the funeral began with a rendition of "Nearer, My God, to Thee." Alexander Crummell, an Episcopal priest born to free black parents in New York City one year after Douglass, then delivered the opening prayer. Crummell's and Douglass's lives had unfolded on parallel but decidedly separate tracks. As Douglass scrapped together dirty and discarded pieces of scripture on the streets of Baltimore, Crummell received a quite exceptional education at a progressive Quaker-run school for black children. About the time Douglass escaped to freedom, Crummell was denied admission to the Episcopal General Theological Seminary in New York City because of his race. Even so, he was eventually ordained a priest in 1844 and soon began his pastoral career in Philadelphia. Not long after Douglass wrapped up his speaking tour of Great Britain, Crummell left Philadelphia for England, too. By 1853, he had graduated from Queen's College, Cambridge. Crummell spent the next twenty years as a missionary and educator in Liberia, before returning to Washington, D.C., to eventually help establish and lead the capitol's first independent black Episcopal church.[6]

Crummell's prayer served also as a eulogy, and one that fittingly evoked the character of the fallen Douglass. "Deep and marvelous are Thy ways,

O Lord, and we cannot always understand them," he began. Yet, even though God remained wrapped in so much mystery, "we know Thy graciousness, and we acknowledge Thy great loving kindness." Crummell believed that amid death it was essential to look to the Lord and remember again the "outpourings of Thy favors." Crummell especially thanked God "for the mission, to the societies of men, of patriots and prophets," people like Douglass who "served their generation, and glorified God." In Douglass's consequential public career, Crummell detected "the light of Thy goodness and the glory of Thy beneficence."[7]

Crummell ended his prayer with a final word of thanksgiving: "We thank Thee, O God, our Father, for the gift of this great preacher and prophet of Justice and Freedom!" In the immediate wake of Douglass's death, Crummell was hardly the only observer to remember Douglass as a great prophetic figure. The *Springfield (Mass.) Republican* praised Douglass for effectively using "the intense fervor of the prophet's indignation" for the cause of justice in America. Howard University professor George W. Cook called Douglass "a man of prophetic vision," who always gave "reasonable assurance of a triumphant cause." The white abolitionist editor and poet Theodore Tilton wondered:

How does it happen that, in every clime,
When any groaning nation of the earth
Hath need of some new leader of a race,
Or some true prophet of a better time,
The Heavens elect him for his lowly birth,
Ere they uplift him to his lofty place?

Crummell added simply that Douglass possessed "constant apprehension of truth," a fierce devotion to liberating his people from bondage and his nation from iniquity. In that righteous work, he surely showed his prophetic spirit.[8]

After Crummell finished his prayer, AME Zion bishop J. W. Hood read Psalm 90. The psalm, traditionally attributed to Moses, begins by praising the Lord as "our dwelling place in all generations." It then speaks of God as the almighty Lord who "hast set our iniquities before thee, our secret sins in the light of thy countenance." The psalm ends with a plea—a yearning to understand and participate in the merciful work of the Lord: "Let thy work appear unto thy servants, and thy glory unto their children. And let the beauty of the Lord our God be upon us: and establish thou the work of our hands upon us."[9]

The choir sang another anthem, and then came a string of eulogies. Hugh T. Stevenson, pastor of the Baptist Church of Anacostia, praised Douglass as "a prince among the orators of the world," surpassed by none in his ability to "sway men by the power of his eloquence." Jeremiah Rankin, president of Howard University, likewise said that Douglass's "voice was of unequaled depth and volume and power." Yet beneath the compelling oratory was "a great-hearted, generous, forgiving natured soul, which feared not the face of man and believed in the living God." Rankin called Douglass a man "whose foundations of truth and righteousness were established in God," a man deeply marked by "the spirit of God's kingdom." Several other black ministers briefly eulogized Douglass, as did a representative of the Haitian government.[10]

Then Susan B. Anthony rose and read a letter from the seventy-nine-year-old Elizabeth Cady Stanton. Despite their differences, at times bitter, in earlier decades, Stanton now called Douglass "the only man I ever knew who understood the degradation of disfranchisement for women." She remembered with gratitude his great service to the women's rights movement, starting in 1848 at Seneca Falls. "Frederick Douglass is not dead! His grand character will long be an object lesson in our national history," Stanton concluded. "His lofty sentiments of liberty, justice and equality, echoed on every platform over our broad land, must influence and inspire many coming generations!"[11]

Jenifer delivered the afternoon's main eulogy. Like Douglass, Jenifer was born a slave in Maryland and eventually made it to Baltimore. He converted to Christianity at the Sharp Street Methodist Church in April 1856. Three years later, Jenifer fled to New Bedford, Massachusetts, as Douglass had done more than twenty years earlier, where the two men met in 1862. As the Civil War raged, Jenifer began his pastoral career at an AME church in California. He then studied under the great Methodist bishop Daniel Payne at Wilberforce University in Ohio, before serving several AME congregations throughout the 1870s and 1880s, first in Arkansas and then Boston, Rhode Island, Chicago, and eventually the Metropolitan Church. The two men's friendship deepened considerably after Jenifer's arrival in Washington, D.C.[12]

Jenifer chose two scriptures for his eulogy, II Samuel 3:38 ("Know ye not that there is a prince and a great man fallen this day in Israel?") and Revelation 14:13 ("And I heard a voice from heaven saying, Write, Blessed are the dead that die in the Lord, from henceforth; yea, saith the Spirit, that they may rest from their labors: and their works do follow them"). Jenifer first praised Douglass as "a representative ever faithful to his people, their champion, wise counselor and fearless defender." Reflecting on all Douglass had said and written and accomplished, Jenifer concluded, "such a life as his is itself an oration," a faithful witness to the truth. The day's funeral was but an "echo" of the great man's voice.[13]

As a seasoned eulogist, Jenifer ably recounted Douglass's long life and venerated his many accomplishments. But Jenifer also spoke at great length and insight about the substance of Douglass's faith and its effect on his public career. Jenifer approvingly quoted a recent edition of the *Washington Post* that had claimed, "Freedom to Mr. Douglass meant not only freedom of the person. He believed in and was a brilliant champion for the vast liberty of the soul." Jenifer quickly added that the sort of liberty Douglass cherished "was not license" but was instead the freedom that comes in abiding in the righteous path—the liberty to pursue and uphold truth. Douglass doubted his entire life that "spiritual liberty," thus defined, could be found and maintained within the American church. This conviction, Jenifer rightly intimated, was key to understanding the very essence of Douglass's faith.[14]

Douglass forever cherished the true Christianity of Christ, and for that reason he "broke with the American Church, and with American Christian dogma," Jenifer explained. Both church and dogma too readily defended "the enslavement and bondage of a brother." Jenifer suggested that Douglass's tortured relationship with the American church most fully captured the prophetic moral zeal at the heart of his faith. In his commitment to justice and righteousness, Douglass did not hesitate to condemn what he discovered in America's churches. His obligation, as a prophet, was to speak against injustice and oppression wherever it existed.[15]

Jenifer rightly claimed of Douglass, "Christ to him was larger than Creed, and his Christianity transcended his Churchianity." No man who had been born a slave, suffered under evangelical masters, and long heard proslavery sermons could equate faithfulness to the true gospel of Christ with blind loyalty to a church or creed. The African American citizens of Marshall, Missouri, affirmed the same point in a formal resolution they adopted after Douglass's death. "He sought the good and he condemned the bad," the resolution proclaimed, and he remained "religious in spite of creeds." Many Americans, like Jenifer and the black residents of Marshall, first remembered precisely this prophetic element of Douglass's religion. Francis J. Grimké, a black Presbyterian minister in Washington, D.C., described Douglass's faith as rooted in the deep conviction that there "was no colorphobia in Christ, and there is none in Christianity, whatever may be the practice of so-called Christian men and women." Several weeks after Jenifer's eulogy, the *Christian Recorder*, the nation's leading black Methodist newspaper, similarly said of Douglass: "His religion was not a religion of creeds, churches, hymnals and prayer books, but he believed in precept, the life and practice as taught by the Master of 'doing unto others as we would have others do unto us.' It was the 'cups of cold water in His name,' 'feed the hungry,' 'clothe the naked,' not in professions of church phraseology and beautiful song, but in the example with love to our fellows and our neighbors as ourselves, which, after all, is the greatest and only evidence of our love to God."

Douglass found little of that true love of God and humanity in the American church in the eras of slavery and Jim Crow. On each Sunday, congregants gathered together throughout the nation to profess their faith in Christ. Yet, according to the *Christian Recorder*, Douglass saw such hollow professions only as "a license not to practice the teachings of Christ," which few churchgoers truly did as they departed their pews.[16]

Still, Jennifer hoped no one would mistake Douglass's hostility toward the American church for rejection of Christianity altogether. Douglass never renounced his conversion or his devotion to the true way of Christ. He had suffered much, doubted often, and passed through deep valleys of misery. But Douglass did not abandon the faith that gave him freedom and meaning. Jenifer said that the elderly Douglass had several times mentioned how it still uplifted his weary soul to hear the hymn:

> Jesus my Saviour, to Bethlehem, came,
> Born in a manger to sorrow and shame;
> Oh it was wonderful! How can it be?
> Seeking for me, for me.

To the family and friends who had gathered to mourn and remember, Jenifer offered a final word of assurance: Their beloved Douglass now surely stood at heaven's gates and heard proclaimed, "Well done, thou good and faithful servant; enter thou into the joy of thy Lord."[17]

When Frederick Douglass died, his contemporaries found many reasons to celebrate his life. Across the nation, eulogies and obituaries fondly remembered Douglass not simply as an orator, activist, and editor but also as a prophet. It was Douglass's prophetic zeal that lent power to his voice; it was his dedication to using his voice for freedom's sake that lent greatness to his life. Well-spoken and well-written words enraptured Douglass. He loved their sound and force. Near the end of his life, in an August 1891 address, Douglass marveled, "Great is the miracle of human speech—by it nations are enlightened and reformed; by it the cause of justice and liberty is defended, by it evils are exposed, ignorance dispelled, the path of duty made plain, and by it those that live to-day are put into the possession of the wisdom of ages gone by."[18] There, Douglass well described how he long endeavored to use the miracle of his own prophetic voice. For seventy-seven years, Douglass saw how easily America could surrender itself to bigotry and bondage, injustice and inequality. He responded by trying to speak words of wisdom and truth to the nation. In doing so, from his first speeches in Massachusetts in the early 1840s to his final public appearances in 1895, Douglass's faith shaped his voice and vision of the world. His prophetic Christianity supplied him with so many of his deepest convictions—about who God was, what God was doing in the world, and the true meaning of grand words like liberty, justice, and equality. Douglass's religious convictions were not tightly guarded private matters. Instead, they gave direction and meaning to his public life as an abolitionist and civil rights leader.

Douglass's powerful prophetic words to America, especially its Christians, might sometimes sound hopelessly hostile, as if fueled by nothing more than disparaging hate. But *hope*, not hate, fueled Douglass—not anger alone but also *love*. He did not lose faith in the true Christianity of Christ and the justice of the God of the oppressed. Less than a decade removed from the lash of Christian masters like Thomas Auld, Douglass still insisted, "I love the religion of our blessed Saviour.... I love that religion that is based upon the glorious principle, of love to God and love to man."[19] Nor did Douglass lose faith in America's highest moral and political ideals. In the dark wake of the Supreme Court's *Dred Scott* decision in 1857, Douglass still affirmed that the Constitution and Declaration of Independence together provided a glorious "platform broad enough, and strong enough, to support the most comprehensive plans for freedom."[20]

The burden Douglass carried throughout his long life was the power to see clearly all the ways America fell short of upholding its professed religious, political, and moral ideals—while also not losing all affection for those same ideals and the nation of his birth. This tension was at the heart of Douglass's work as a prophet. He possessed both deep affection for and deep alienation from America and American Christianity. He cherished the words of the Bible and the Declaration of Independence. Precisely for that reason he never fully overcame his estrangement from slaveholding and Jim Crow America, and the Christianity practiced there.

Yet as America's prophet, Douglass ultimately longed not for devastating apocalyptic judgment against America, but for its creative redemption. He yearned to see the United States redeemed from its bigotry and hypocrisy, not destroyed for it. He forever bore slavery's scars, a bitter reminder of Americans' capacity for oppression, but he did not bear the scars as one who had no hope. Instead, Douglass spoke to his nation as the prophet Isaiah once spoke to his people: "Cease to do evil, learn to do good; seek justice, correct oppression; defend the fatherless, plead for the widow. Come now, let us reason together, says the Lord: though your sins are like scarlet, they shall be as white as snow."

Acknowledgments

It is an honor now to express my sincerest gratitude:

To my former students, for the days we spent together learning from Douglass.

To many colleagues, for helping me better understand Douglass's life and times.

To two anonymous readers of my manuscript, for their generous assistance in improving this book.

To Mark Simpson-Vos and the University of North Carolina Press staff, for their incomparable work in making my life as an author an utter delight.

To my wife, Mackenzie, for encouraging me when I most need it and loving me when I least deserve it.

A dozen or so volumes of Douglass's collected works lined a wall of my study for several months. Stacked in two piles, they were nearly as tall as my daughter, Pearl, then two years old. She sometimes eyed them with wonder, slowly flipped their pages, and then slammed shut their covers and grabbed one of her own cherished books instead. Douglass's *Narrative* may be no match now for *Brown Bear, Brown Bear, What Do You See?* But I eagerly await the day Pearl and Jack read Douglass for the first time. I dedicate this book to them, my beloved children—confident that, once grown, they will find the courage to answer Douglass's call to justice and mercy.

Notes

ABBREVIATIONS

FDP   John W. Blassingame, ed., *The Frederick Douglass Papers*, ser. 1, vols. 1–5 (New Haven, Conn.: Yale University Press, 1979, 1982, 1985, 1991, 1992)

FDS   Philip S. Foner and Yuval Taylor, eds., *Frederick Douglass: Selected Speeches and Writings* (Chicago: Lawrence Hill, 1999)

LTFD Frederick Douglass, *Life and Times of Frederick Douglass*. In *Frederick Douglass: Autobiographies*, edited by Henry Louis Gates Jr. (New York: Library of America, 1994)

LWFD Philip S. Douglass, ed., *The Life and Writings of Frederick Douglass*. 5 vols. (New York: International, 1950, 1952, 1955, 1975).

MBMF Frederick Douglass, *My Bondage and My Freedom*. In *Frederick Douglass: Autobiographies*, edited by Henry Louis Gates Jr. (New York: Library of America, 1994)

NFD   Frederick Douglass, *Narrative of the Life of Frederick Douglass, an American Slave*. In *Frederick Douglass: Autobiographies*, edited by Henry Louis Gates Jr. (New York: Library of America, 1994)

INTRODUCTION

1. "What to the Slave Is the Fourth of July?," *FDP*, ser. 1, vol. 2, 368.

2. All biblical citations in the manuscript are taken from the King James Version.

3. "What to the Slave Is the Fourth of July?," *FDP*, ser. 1, vol. 2, 377–78.

4. The most noteworthy Douglass biographies include Quarles, *Frederick Douglass*; Huggins, *Slave and Citizen*; Preston, *Young Frederick Douglass*; and McFeely, *Frederick Douglass*. Douglass's religion occupies a curious place in these biographies. Only William McFeely thoroughly considers the substance of Douglass's faith in the years prior to the Civil War. But none of the biographies fully explore how Douglass's religious convictions shaped his public career, and none analyze Douglass's faith in the final thirty years of his life.

5. To date, the leading intellectual biographies of Douglass are Martin, *The Mind of Frederick Douglass*; and Blight, *Frederick Douglass' Civil War*. Blight succeeds more than Martin in capturing the essence of Douglass's faith, but his analysis is limited to the Civil War era. My critiques of Martin's interpretations are found in chapter 10. Over the past thirty years, a small literature has emerged on Douglass's religion, and, though illuminating, it remains fragmented; no one has attempted a full religious biography of Douglass—covering both the antebellum and postbellum years (which remain especially neglected in the existing literature). See Van Deburg, "Frederick Douglass: Maryland Slave to Religious Liberal"; Andrews, "Frederick Douglass, Preacher"; Hunt, "The Faith Journey of Frederick Douglass"; Gibson, "Faith, Doubt, and Apostasy"; Williamson, *The Narrative Life*; Davis, *Frederick Douglass*; and Ernest, "Crisis and Faith in Douglass's Work."

6. I have here adopted the influential definition of evangelicalism provided in Bebbington, *Evangelicalism in Modern Britain*.

7. Brueggemann, *The Prophetic Imagination*, 3, 116.

8. For a more detailed introduction to this black prophetic tradition, see Hobson, *The Mount of Vision*; Moses, *Black Messiahs and Uncle Toms*, chap. 2; Howard-Pitney, "The Enduring Black Jeremiad"; and Howard-Pitney, *The Afro-American Jeremiad*.

9. *NFD*, 97.

10. "The Negro Problem," *FDP*, ser. 1, vol. 5, 456.

CHAPTER 1

1. *NFD*, 23–24.

2. Preston, *Young Frederick Douglass*, 8–15.

3. McFeely, *Frederick Douglass*, 9.

4. *MBMF*, 145; Preston, *Young Frederick Douglass*, 35–37.

5. *NFD*, 18; Preston, *Young Frederick Douglass*, 22–30.

6. Preston, *Young Frederick Douglass*, 37–40; *MBMF*, 148–50.

7. *MBMF*, 157.

8. Ibid., 152, 155. The pathos of the section of Douglass's biographies narrating his mother's death relies on an implicit appeal to conventional nineteenth-century American conceptions of the "good death." Drew Gilpin Faust has shown how "Victorian ideals of domesticity" reinforced the assumption that a hallmark of a good death was dying "among family assembled around the deathbed," who would hear the dying person's final words and assess the state of his or her soul. See Faust, *This Republic of Suffering*, 6–17.

9. *MBMF*, 149, 157, 142.

10. Ibid., 160; Preston, *Young Frederick Douglass*, 41–48; McFeely, *Frederick Douglass*, 14.

11. Ibid., 164–65.

12. *NFD*, 19; *MBMF*, 174–77.

13. *MBMF*, 176.

14. *NFD*, 30–31; Preston, *Young Frederick Douglass*, 72.

15. *NFD*, 31–32; *MBMF*, 203–4.

16. "To Thomas Auld," *FDS*, 113.

17. Ibid., 113.

18. *MBMF*, 178–79.

19. Preston, *Young Frederick Douglass*, 80–82; McFeely, *Frederick Douglass*, 23–24.

20. *NFD* 36; *MBMF*, 212–13.

21. *NFD*, 36.

CHAPTER 2

1. *MBMF*, 214.

2. Rockman, *Scraping By*, 27.

3. *MBMF*, 214–15; Preston, *Young Frederick Douglass*, 87.

4. *MBMF*, 215, 221.

5. Ibid., 219–20.

6. McFeely, *Frederick Douglass*, 27–28; Preston, *Young Frederick Douglass*, 87–92.

7. *MBMF*, 217.

8. Ibid., 218, 224.

9. *MBMF*, 225; Preston, *Young Frederick Douglass*, 98–99.

10. *MBMF*, 226.

11. Bingham, *The Columbian Orator*, 240.

12. *MBMF*, 225–26.

13. Bingham, *The Columbian Orator*, 241.

14. *MBMF*, 226–27.

15. Ibid., 231.

16. Hatch, *The Democratization of American Christianity*, 102–10.

17. Ibid.; Newman, *Freedom's Prophet*, 158–82.

18. Melton, *A Will to Choose*, 68–73; McFeely, *Frederick Douglass*, 37–38.

19. *MBMF*, 231.

20. Ibid.; Preston, *Young Frederick Douglass*, 97; McFeely, *Frederick Douglass*, 38.

21. *MBMF*, 231–32.

22. Ibid., 232–33.

23. Ibid., 233.

24. *MBMF*, 232; Preston, *Young Frederick Douglass*, 96.

25. *MBMF*, 232.

26. Ibid., 245.

CHAPTER 3

1. For an extended introduction to the history of religion, especially Christianity, among enslaved persons in the American South in the antebellum era, see Raboteau, *Slave Religion*; Frey and Wood, *Come Shouting to Zion*; Clarke, *Dwelling Place*; Irons, *The Origins of Proslavery Christianity*; and Harvey, *Through the Storm, through the Night*, 49–67.

2. *MBMF*, 244, 248; *NFD*, 50–51; Preston, *Young Frederick Douglass*, 106–7.

3. *NFD* 50; *MBMF*, 247.

4. *MBMF*, 250–51.

5. Ibid., 252–53, 306.

6. Ibid., 252.

7. Ibid., 254.

8. Ibid., 254, 299.

9. Ibid., 254.

10. *NFD*, 55; *MBMF*, 256; Preston, *Young Frederick Douglass*, 116–17.

11. *MBMF*, 266–67; *NFD*, 57–58.

12. *MBMF*, 267.

13. Ibid., 265.

14. *MBMF*, 260–64; Preston, *Young Frederick Douglass*, 119–21.

15. *MBMF*, 264; *NFD*, 58.

16. *NFD*, 59.

17. Ibid., 59.

18. Ibid., 61.

19. *MBMF*, 274.

20. Ibid., 275–76.

21. Ibid., 277–78.

22. Ibid., 279–81.

23. Ibid., 280–81.

24. Ibid., 282.

25. *MBMF*, 283–85; *NFD*, 64–65.

26. *MBMF*, 284–85, 287; *NFD*, 64–65.

27. *MBMF*, 286.

28. Ibid., 293.

29. Ibid., 293–94.

30. Ibid., 298–300, 302

31. *MBMF*, 323–25; McFeely, *Frederick Douglass*, 51–57.

32. *MBMF*, 328; Preston, *Young Frederick Douglass*, 143.

33. Preston, *Young Frederick Douglass*, 143–44; *MBMF*, 328.

34. Preston, *Young Frederick Douglass*, 144–45; *MBMF*, 332–33.

35. *MBMF*, 333–34; Preston, *Young Frederick Douglass*, 145.

36. Preston, *Young Frederick Douglass*, 145–46; *MBMF*, 333–34.

37. Preston, *Young Frederick Douglass*, 148–49.

38. Ibid., 149–50.

39. *MBMF*, 342–43; McFeely, *Frederick Douglass*, 64–65.

40. *MBMF*, 344–45; McFeely, *Frederick Douglass*, 69.

41. Preston, *Young Frederick Douglass*, 154–55; *LTFD*, 642–46.

42. *MBMF*, 350; Preston, *Young Frederick Douglass*, 156.

43. *MBMF*, 353; McFeely, *Frederick Douglass*, 73.

CHAPTER 4

1. *LTFD*, 654.

2. McFeely, *Frederick Douglass*, 76–80.

3. *MBMF*, 359–60.

4. Ibid., 360; McFeely, *Frederick Douglass*, 81.

5. *MBMF*, 361.

6. Ibid., 361.

7. Ibid., 361.

8. Andrews, "Frederick Douglass, Preacher," 596.

9. *MBMF*, 362.

10. For more on the life and career of Garrison, see Mayer, *All on Fire*.

11. For a classic but still compelling account of "the dynamics of moral suasion" among abolitionists, see Stewart, *Holy Warriors*, 50–73. Manisha Sinha aptly summarizes Garrison's vision of moral suasion as committed above all else to "the conversion of white Americans, convincing them to recognize African Americans as their 'fellow countrymen.'" Sinha, *The Slave's Cause*, 223.

12. *MBMF*, 362.

13. Andrews, "Frederick Douglass, Preacher," 596; *MBMF*, 360.

14. McFeely, *Frederick Douglass*, 83; *MBMF*, 363.

15. *MBMF*, 364; McFeely, *Frederick Douglass*, 86–87.

16. *MBMF*, 364; McFeely, *Frederick Douglass*, 88.

17. Quoted in McFeely, *Frederick Douglass*, 88; *MBMF*, 365.

18. *MBMF*, 365–66; McFeely, *Frederick Douglass*, 92.

19. "I Have Come to Tell You Something about Slavery," *FDP*, ser. 1, vol. 1, 3–4.

20. "The Union, Slavery, and Abolitionist Petitions," *FDP*, ser. 1, vol. 1, 5–6.

21. "American Prejudice and Southern Religion," *FDP*, ser. 1, vol. 1, 9–13.

22. "The Church and Prejudice," *FDS*, 3–4.

23. *LTFD*, 671–76.

24. "Abolitionists and Third Parties," *FDP*, ser. 1, vol. 1, 14.

25. Douglass to William Lloyd Garrison, 27 October 1844, in McKivigan, *The Frederick Douglass Papers*, ser. 3, vol. 1, 33.

26. "My Slave Experience in Maryland," *FDS*, 14.

27. McFeely, *Frederick Douglass*, 105–6.

28. "The Anti-Slavery Movement, the Slave's Only Earthly Hope," *FDP*, ser. 1, vol. 1, 22.

29. McFeely, *Frederick Douglass*, 116–17.

30. *NFD*, 97.

31. Ibid., 97.

32. Ibid., 98.

33. Ibid., 99–100.

CHAPTER 5

1. *MBMF*, 370.

2. Douglass to William Lloyd Garrison, 1 September 1845, in McKivigan, *The Frederick Douglass Papers*, ser. 3, vol. 1, 47–50; *MBMF*, 370–71.

3. For an extended speaking itinerary, see *FDP*, ser. 1, vol. 1, xcvi–cii.

4. *MBMF*, 378.

5. "An Appeal to the British People," *FDS*, 32–33.

6. Ibid., 36–37.

7. "Slavery, the Free Church, and British Agitation against Bondage," *FDP*, ser. 1, vol. 1, 328.

8. "An Appeal to the British People," *FDS*, 37.

9. "I Am Here to Spread Light on American Slavery," *FDP*, ser. 1, vol. 1, 44.

10. "Baptists, Congregationalists, the Free Church, and Slavery," *FDP*, ser. 1, vol. 1, 104.

11. "The Horrors of Slavery and England's Duty to Free the Bondsman," *FDP*, ser. 1, vol. 1, 380.

12. "American Prejudice against Color," *FDP*, ser. 1, vol. 1, 60.

13. "To Horace Greeley," *FDS*, 37.

14. "Remarks at Soiree in Honor of Messrs. Douglass and Buffum," *LWFD*, 5:35.

15. "Irish Christians and Non-fellowship with Man-Stealers," *FDP*, ser. 1, vol. 1, 35.

16. For more on the sectional division of America's leading Protestant denominations, see Goen, *Broken Churches, Broken Nation*.

17. "The Horrors of Slavery and England's Duty to Free the Bondsman," *FDP*, ser. 1, vol. 1, 380.

18. For an extended study of Chalmers and his vision for the Free Church of Scotland, see Brown, *Thomas Chalmers and the Godly Commonwealth*.

19. McFeely, *Frederick Douglass*, 134.

20. Quoted in ibid., 129.

21. "The Free Church of Scotland and American Slavery," *FDP*, ser. 1, vol. 1, 146–47, 151, 155.

22. "The Free Church Connection with the Slave Church," *FDP*, ser. 1, vol. 1, 159.

23. Ibid., 161.

24. "Emancipation Is an Individual, a National, and an International Responsibility," *FDP*, ser. 1, vol. 1, 257.

25. "Send Back the Blood-Stained Money," *FDP*, ser. 1, vol. 1, 241.

26. "America's Compromise with Slavery and the Abolitionists' Work," *FDP*, ser. 1, vol. 1, 213.

27. "Send Back the Blood-Stained Money," *FDP*, ser. 1, vol. 1, 243.

28. Ibid., 243.

29. "American Slavery, American Religion, and the Free Church of Scotland," *FDP*, ser. 1, vol. 1, 298.

30. *MBMF*, 382.

31. For a thorough introduction to the Evangelical Alliance, see Randall and Hilborn, *One Body in Christ*.

32. Maclear, "The Evangelical Alliance and the Antislavery Crusade," 154–64.

33. For a helpful overview of the Evangelical Alliance controversy, see the footnotes in *FDP*, ser. 1, vol. 1, 435–39, 444–49.

34. Maclear, "The Evangelical Alliance and the Antislavery Crusade," 160.

35. "Slavery, the Evangelical Alliance, and the Free Church," *FDP*, ser. 1, vol. 1, 448; "Defenders of Slavery and the Evangelical Alliance," *FDP*, ser. 1, vol. 1, 454.

36. "American Slavery, American Churches, and the Evangelical Alliance," *FDP*, ser. 1, vol. 1, 423.

37. "Slavery, the Evangelical Alliance, and the Free Church," *FDP*, ser. 1, vol. 1, 440, 449.

38. Ibid., 451, 442.

39. "The Slaveholders' Maneuverings at the Evangelical Alliance, *FDP*, ser. 1, vol. 1, 439.

40. "Farewell Speech to the British People," *FDS*, 56, 58, 61.

CHAPTER 6

1. McFeely, *Frederick Douglass*, 146–58.

2. *MBMF*, 392.

3. Many historians have analyzed Douglass's shifting opinions on violence and the Constitution, but they largely have failed to explore the underlying theological ideas that helped guide this evolution. See, for example, McFeely, *Frederick Douglass*, 168–69; Blight, *Frederick Douglass' Civil War*, 31–33, 92–100; and Huggins, *Slave and Citizen*, 58–65.

4. Douglass to Thomas Van Rensselaer, 18 May 1847, in McKivigan, *The Frederick Douglass Papers*, ser. 3, vol. 1, 212.

5. "Love of God, Love of Man, Love of Country," *FDP*, ser. 1, vol. 2, 101.

6. "Country, Conscience, and the Anti-Slavery Cause," *FDP*, ser. 1, vol. 2, 60.

7. *LTFD*, 705.

8. Douglass to C. H. Chase, 9 February 1849, in McKivigan, *The Frederick Douglass Papers*, ser. 3, vol. 1, 355.

9. "Is the Constitution Pro-slavery?" *FDP*, ser. 1, vol. 2, 223.

10. For more on Gerrit Smith and his orbit of abolitionists, see Friedman, "The Gerrit Smith Circle."

11. Gerrit Smith to Douglass, 16 March 1849, in McKivigan, *The Frederick Douglass Papers*, ser. 3, vol. 1, 371.

12. Gerrit Smith to Douglass, 30 March 1849, in McKivigan, *The Frederick Douglass Papers*, ser. 3, vol. 1, 377.

13. *North Star*, 30 March 1849.

14. "The Bible Opposes Oppression, Fraud, and Wrong," *FDP*, ser. 1, vol. 1, 128–29. For a compelling account of the wider theological implications of this antislavery biblical hermeneutic, see Oshatz, *Slavery and Sin*.

15. *North Star*, 5 April 1850.

16. Ibid.

17. "To Gerrit Smith," *FDS*, 171–72.

18. *FDS*, 173.

19. *North Star*, 15 May 1851.

20. "To Gerrit Smith," *FDS*, 175.

21. *LTFD*, 706.

22. "Love of God, Love of Man, Love of Country," *FDP*, ser. 1, vol. 2, 103–4.

23. Richard Carwardine has shown how unpopular the act was among northern ministers and churchgoers. Douglass's religion-inspired opposition to the act was not unusual. Still, these same northern Christians were far less united over how to respond to the act. Some, like Douglass, called for outright resistance, but many more did not. See Carwardine, *Evangelicals and Politics in Antebellum America*, 176–80.

24. "Northern Ballots and the Election of 1852," *FDP*, ser. 1, vol. 2, 418.

25. "An Appeal to Canada," *FDP*, ser. 1, vol. 2, 330.

26. "Do Not Send Back the Fugitive," *FDP*, ser. 1, vol. 2, 248.

27. "Resistance to Blood-Houndism," *FDP*, ser. 1, vol. 2, 276.

28. Ibid., 275–76.

29. "Slavery's Northern Bulwarks," *FDP*, ser. 1, vol. 2, 279–81.

30. *Frederick Douglass' Paper*, 17 April 1851.

31. *FDS*, 178–79.

32. *Frederick Douglass' Paper*, 25 September 1851.

33. *Frederick Douglass' Paper*, August 1852.

34. *North Star*, 22 December 1848.

35. *North Star*, 21 January 1848.

36. *North Star*, 17 March 1848.

37. "Brethren, Rouse the Church," *FDP*, ser. 1, vol. 2, 92.

38. "Slavery's Northern Bulwarks," *FDP*, ser. 1, vol. 2, 284–85.

39. *North Star*, 5 September 1850.

40. *Frederick Douglass' Paper*, August 1852.

41. "Northern Ballots and the Election of 1852," *FDP*, ser. 1, vol. 2, 419.

42. *Frederick Douglass' Paper*, 30 October 1851.

43. "An Abolitionist Measure of American Churches and the Free Soil Party," *FDP*, ser. 1, vol. 2, 199.

44. "Too Much Religion, Too Little Humanity," *FDP*, ser. 1, vol. 2, 180.

45. "The Folly of Racially Exclusive Organizations," *FDP*, ser. 1, vol. 2, 110.

46. *North Star*, 13 October 1848.

47. "On Robert Burns and Scotland," *FDP*, ser. 1, vol. 2, 170.

48. "Love of God, Love of Man, Love of Country," *FDP*, ser. 1, vol. 2, 101; "Freedom, the Eternal Truth," *FDP*, ser. 1, vol. 2, 352.

49. For example, see "Lecture on Slavery," *North Star*, 5 December 1850.

50. *Frederick Douglass' Paper*, 11 December 1851.

51. *North Star*, 8 February 1850.

52. *North Star*, 9 November 1849.

53. "What to the Slave Is the Fourth of July?," *FDP*, ser. 1, vol. 2, 363–64.

54. Ibid., 363.

55. Ibid., 368.

56. Ibid., 371.

57. Ibid., 373.

58. Ibid., 375–76.

59. Ibid., 377–78.

60. Ibid., 383–84.

61. Ibid., 386–87.

CHAPTER 7

1. Quoted in *FDP*, ser. 1, vol. 2, 420.

2. "No Peace for the Slaveholder," *FDP*, ser. 1, vol. 2, 421–23.

3. *Douglass' Monthly*, May 1861.

4. In this respect, Douglass's ideas bore many hallmarks of the Protestant millennialism prevalent among nineteenth-century Americans. For more on this quintessential element of American culture in Douglass's day, see Moorhead, *American Apocalypse*; and Wright and Dresser, *Apocalypse and the Millennium in the American Civil War Era*.

5. "The Present Condition and Future Prospects of the Negro People," *FDS*, 259.

6. "The Claims of Our Common Cause," *FDS*, 271.

7. "An Inside View of Slavery," *FDP*, ser. 1, vol. 3, 6–7.

8. "The Anti-Slavery Movement," *FDS*, 331.

9. "Freedom in the West Indies," *FDP*, ser. 1, vol. 3, 241.

10. *Frederick Douglass' Paper*, 27 July 1855.

11. "Aggressions of the Slave Power," *FDP*, ser. 1, vol. 3, 127.

12. Ibid., 127.

13. "To William Still," *FDS*, 398.

14. Varon, *Disunion!*, 251–59. Richard Carwardine suggests that the act "radicalized many political moderates" among northern Christians, especially evangelicals, precisely because it threatened "to introduce slavery into territories regarded since 1821 as forever free." Even more important to these evangelical critics was the fact that the act, in Carwardine's words, "put freedom and pure religion on the defensive, and altered the moral orientation of the republic," a fear Douglass certainly shared. Carwardine, *Evangelicals and Politics in Antebellum America*, 236–37.

15. *Frederick Douglass' Paper*, 24 November 1854.

16. *Frederick Douglass' Paper*, 26 May 1854.

17. "We Are in the Midst of a Moral Revolution," *FDP*, ser. 1, vol. 2, 483.

18. *Frederick Douglass' Paper*, 24 February 1854.

19. *Frederick Douglass' Paper*, 26 May 1854.

20. *Frederick Douglass' Paper*, 24 November 1854.

21. Varon, *Disunion!*, 295–304.

22. "The Dred Scott Decision," *FDS*, 345.

23. Ibid., 346–47.

24. Ibid., 347–48.

25. Ibid., 349–50.

26. *Douglass' Monthly*, November 1859.

27. *LTFD*, 715–16.

28. Ibid., 717–19.

29. *FDS*, 372–73.

30. "John Brown and the Slaveholders' Insurrection," *FDP*, ser. 1, vol. 3, 315.

31. *Douglass' Monthly*, November 1859; "To James Redpath," *FDS*, 396.

32. *Douglass' Monthly*, November 1859.

33. "To James Redpath," *FDS*, 396.

34. *Douglass' Monthly*, November 1859.

35. *Douglass' Monthly*, October 1860.

36. *Douglass' Monthly*, December 1860.

37. *Douglass' Monthly*, May 1861.

38. "Hope and Despair in These Cowardly Times," *FDP*, ser. 1, vol. 3, 424.

39. Ibid., 424–27.

40. *Douglass' Monthly*, April 1862.

41. *Douglass' Monthly*, March 1862.

42. *Douglass' Monthly*, July 1861.

43. "Do Not Forget Truth and Justice," *LWFD*, 3:340.

44. *Douglass' Monthly*, September 1861.

45. *Douglass' Monthly*, May 1861.

46. "America before the Global Tribunal," *FDP*, ser. 1, vol. 3, 451.

47. *Douglass' Monthly*, September 1861.

48. "The Slaveholders' Rebellion," *FDP*, ser. 1, vol. 3, 541.

49. *Douglass' Monthly*, September 1861.

50. "Fighting the Rebels with One Hand," *FDP*, ser. 1, vol. 3, 477.

51. *Douglass' Monthly*, May 1861.

52. *Douglass' Monthly*, June 1861.

53. *Douglass' Monthly*, June 1861.

54. *Douglass' Monthly*, January 1863.

55. "The Mission of the War," *FDS*, 554.

56. Ibid., 554–66.

57. "Our Work Is Not Done," *FDS*, 548.

58. "The Present and Future of the Colored Race in America," *FDP*, ser. 1, vol. 3, 576.

59. "To E. Gilbert," *LWFD*, 3:403.

60. "A Friendly Word to Maryland," *FDP*, ser. 1 vol. 4, 42–49.

61. *Douglass' Monthly*, November 1862.

CHAPTER 8

1. For a survey of the Reconstruction-era fight for woman's suffrage, including the work of the American Equal Rights Association, see Dudden, *Fighting Chance*.

2. "Equal Rights for All," *FDP*, ser. 1, vol. 4, 173.

3. For an introduction to the religious dimensions of late-nineteenth-century American social and political issues, especially African American civil and political equality, see Stowell, *Rebuilding Zion*; Foster, *Moral Reconstruction*; Blum, *Reforging the White Republic*; Blum and Poole, *Vale of Tears*; and Harvey, *Freedom's Coming*, 5–46. Taken together, these works suggest Douglass was perfectly ordinary among Americans in the long era of Reconstruction in bringing his core moral and religious convictions to bear on his opinions about racial and gender equality.

4. "The Need for Continuing Anti-Slavery Work," *FDS*, 579.

5. "The Douglass Institute," *FDS*, 582.

6. "The Need for Continuing Anti-Slavery Work," *FDS*, 578.

7. "The Claims of Our Race," *FDP*, ser. 1, vol. 4, 97.

8. Ibid., 97–98.

9. Ibid., 98–99.

10. Ibid., 99–100.

11. Ibid., 101–3.

12. Ibid., 104.

13. Ibid., 105–6.

14. "The Issues of the Day," *FDP*, 119–20.

15. Ibid., 119.

16. "We Are Here and Want the Ballot-Box," *FDP*, ser. 1, vol. 4, 131–32.

17. Ibid., 126.

18. "At Last, at Last, the Black Man Has a Future," *FDP*, ser. 1, vol. 4, 266–67, 271.

19. "We Need a True, Strong, and Principled Party," *FDP*, ser. 1, vol. 4, 283.

20. *New National Era*, 6 October 1870.

21. Ibid.

22. "To A. M. Powell," *FDS*, 608.

23. "Our Composite Nationality," *FDP*, ser. 1, vol. 4, 241.

24. Ibid., 245–47.

25. Ibid., 252.

26. Ibid., 253.

27. McFeely, *Frederick Douglass*, 155–56.

28. "Women's Rights Are Not Inconsistent with Negro Rights," *FDP*, ser. 1, vol. 4, 182.

29. Ibid., 182, 184–85.

30. "Let No One Be Excluded from the Ballot Box," *FDP*, ser. 1, vol. 4, 147.

31. Stanton, Anthony, and Gage, *History of Woman Suffrage*, 2:214, 193, 216.

32. "We Welcome the Fifteenth Amendment," *FDP*, ser. 1, vol. 4, 216.

33. Ibid., 216.

34. *New National Era*, 20 October 1870.

35. Ibid.

36. "Nobody Can Be Represented by Anybody Else," *FDP*, ser. 1, vol. 4, 396.

37. "Who and What Is Woman?," *FDP*, ser. 1, vol. 5, 256.

38. "I Am a Radical Woman Suffrage Man," *FDP*, ser. 1, vol. 5, 381.

39. Ibid., 381–82, 387.

CHAPTER 9

1. "The Nation's Problem," *FDP*, ser. 1, vol. 5, 406, 420–21.

2. Ibid., 409, 413.

3. Ibid., 423.

4. Classic accounts of southern history in the decades between the end of Reconstruction and World War I include Woodward, *Origins of the New South*; Ayers, *The Promise of the New South*; and Litwack, *Trouble in Mind*.

5. McFeely, *Frederick Douglass*, 312–18.

6. *LTFD*, 966.

7. McFeely, *Frederick Douglass*, 277–86.

8. Ibid., 296.

9. "The South Knows Us," *FDP*, ser. 1, vol. 4, 497.

10. "The Color Question," *FDP*, ser. 1, vol. 4, 417.

11. "The United States Cannot Remain Half-Slave and Half-Free," *FDS*, 658.

12. "An Inspiration to High and Virtuous Endeavor," *FDP*, ser. 1, vol. 5, 165.

13. "The Color Line," *FDS*, 648, 653.

14. "We Must Not Abandon the Observance of Decoration Day," *FDP*, ser. 1, vol. 5, 44, 46–47.

15. "There Was a Right Side in the Late War," *FDS*, 632.

16. "To Francis Grimké," *LWFD*, 4:447.

17. "I Denounce the So-Called Emancipation as a Stupendous Fraud," *FDS*, 712.

18. Ibid., 712.

19. "The Negro Problem," *FDP*, ser. 1, vol. 5, 443–44.

20. "To W. H. Thomas," *FDS*, 705.

21. "The Negro Problem," *FDP*, ser. 1, vol. 5, 456.

22. "Lynch Law in the South," *FDS*, 746–49.

23. "Southern Barbarism," *FDS*, 696.

24. Paddon and Turner, "African Americans and the World's Columbian Exposition," 19–36.

25. Ibid., 19–36.

26. Ibid., 19–23.

27. Rydell, ed., *The Reason Why the Colored American Is Not in the World's Columbian Exposition*, 67.

28. Paddon and Turner, "African Americans and the World's Columbian Exposition," 19–22.

29. Rydell, ed., *The Reason Why the Colored American Is Not in the World's Columbian Exposition*, 7.

30. Ibid., 9, 15.

31. Ibid., 7–9.

32. Ibid., 15–16.

33. Ibid., 19, 31–32.

34. McFeely, *Frederick Douglass*, 370–71; Paddon and Turner, "African Americans and the World's Columbian Exposition," 32.

35. McFeely, *Frederick Douglass*, 371; Paddon and Turner, "African Americans and the World's Columbian Exposition," 32.

36. "Lessons of the Hour," *FDP*, ser. 1, vol. 5, 575–76.

37. Ibid., 577.

38. Ibid., 578.

39. Ibid., 588.

40. Ibid., 590.

41. Ibid., 579.

42. Haygood, "The Black Shadow in the South," 167–68.

43. "Lessons of the Hour," *FDP*, ser. 1, vol. 5, 602.

44. Ibid., 599.

45. Ibid., 602.

46. Ibid., 604.

47. Ibid., 607.

CHAPTER 10

1. *NFD*, 35–36.

2. *MBMF*, 212–13.

3. *LTFD*, 523.

4. Martin, *The Mind of Frederick Douglass*, 178. Martin echoed William L. Van Deburg, who a decade earlier had posited that Douglass's faith evolved from an evangelical Methodism to a "religious liberalism" defined by "the rejection of God's power and the veneration of man and his reforms." Van Deburg, "Frederick Douglass: Maryland Slave

to Religious Liberal," 43. David Blight, in contrast, argues that Douglass held fast to a providential view of history throughout the Civil War. See Blight, *Frederick Douglass' Civil War*. John Ernest also questions Martin's argument in "Crisis and Faith in Douglass's Work."

5. Subsequent scholarship that affirms Martin's argument includes Hunt, "The Faith Journey of Frederick Douglass"; Gibson, "Faith, Doubt, and Apostasy"; and Hutchins, "Rejecting the Root."

6. "The Anti-Slavery Society," *New York Times*, 10 April 1870.

7. "A Reform Absolutely Complete," *FDP*, ser. 1, vol. 4, 259.

8. Martin, *The Mind of Frederick Douglass*, 178.

9. "A Reform Absolutely Complete," *FDP*, ser. 1, vol. 4, 260–63.

10. Ibid., 264.

11. Quoted in Van Deburg, "Frederick Douglass: Maryland Slave to Religious Liberal," 38.

12. "A Reform Absolutely Complete," *FDP*, ser. 1, vol. 4, 262.

13. Ibid., 264.

14. Ibid., 231.

15. Ibid., 264.

16. "Good Men Are God in the Flesh," *FDP*, ser. 1, vol. 5, 434.

17. "'It Moves,' or the Philosophy of Reform," *FDP*, ser. 1, vol. 5, 124.

18. Ibid., 129.

19. Ibid., 129–30.

20. Ibid., 137.

21. Ibid., 137.

22. Ibid., 137.

23. Ibid., 137.

24. Ibid., 138.

25. *FDS*, 635.

26. "'It Moves,' or the Philosophy of Reform," *FDP*, ser. 1, vol. 5, 139.

27. *FDS*, 657.

28. "'It Moves,' or the Philosophy of Reform," *FDP*, ser. 1, vol. 5, 139. For a convincing explanation of the origins of Douglass's paraphrase of Parker, see Stauffer, Trodd, and Bernier, *Picturing Frederick Douglass*, 148n70.

29. Parker, *Discourse on the Transient and Permanent in Christianity*, 16.

30. "'It Moves,' or the Philosophy of Reform," *FDP*, ser. 1, vol. 5, 142.

31. Ibid., 125.

32. Ibid., 127.

33. Ibid., 142.

34. "Self-Made Men," *FDP*, ser. 1, vol. 5, 545–46.

35. For an introduction to this element of Douglass's postwar public activity, especially the "Exodusters" issue, see McFeely, *Frederick Douglass*, 291–303.

36. "Self-Made Men," *FDP*, ser. 1, vol. 5, 548–49.

37. Ibid., 550.

38. Ibid., 554.

39. Ibid., 554–56.

40. Ibid., 555.

41. "Coming Home," *FDP*, ser. 1, vol. 4, 480.

42. Ibid., 480.

43. *LTFD*, 912–13.

44. Ibid., 913.

45. Ibid., 913.

46. Ibid., 913.

47. Ibid., 914.

48. "To Francis J. Grimké," *LWFD*, 4:429.

CONCLUSION

1. Robbins, *History and Minutes of the National Council of Women of the United States*, 12.

2. *New York Times*, 21 February 1895.

3. Ibid.; Douglass, *In Memoriam*, 17–19; McFeely, *Frederick Douglass*, 381–83.

4. *New York Times*, 26 February 1895; Douglass, *In Memoriam*, 19–21.

5. *New York Times*, 26 February 1895; Douglass, *In Memoriam*, 19–21.

6. Douglass, *In Memoriam*, 22.

7. Ibid., 22–24.

8. Ibid., 24, 290, 276–77, 150.

9. Ibid., 24.

10. Ibid., 29–31, 35–37.

11. Ibid., 43–44.

12. Wright, *Centennial Encyclopaedia of the African Methodist Episcopal Church*, 129–30; Douglass, *In Memoriam*, 26.

13. Douglass, *In Memoriam*, 25

14. Ibid., 26–27.

15. Ibid., 27.

16. Ibid., 27, 106, 191, 325.

17. Ibid., 27–29.

18. "Great Is the Miracle of Human Speech," *FDP*, ser. 1, vol. 5, 476–77.

19. "American Slavery, American Religion, and the Free Church of Scotland," *FDP*, ser. 1, vol. 1, 282.

20. "The Dred Scott Decision," *FDS*, 350.

Bibliography

PRIMARY SOURCES

Archival Materials
Library of Congress, Manuscript Division, Washington, D.C.
    Frederick Douglass Papers

Newspapers

Christian Recorder

Douglass' Monthly

Frederick Douglass' Paper

Harper's Weekly

Liberator

New National Era

New York Times

North Star

Washington Bee

Published Primary Sources
Andrews, William L., ed. *The Oxford Frederick Douglass Reader*. New York: Oxford
    University Press, 1996.
Bell, Howard Holman, ed. *Minutes of the Proceedings of the National Negro Conventions,
    1830–1864*. New York: Arno, 1969.
Blassingame, John W., ed. *The Frederick Douglass Papers*. ser. 1, vols. 1–5. New Haven,
    Conn.: Yale University Press, 1979, 1982, 1985, 1991, 1992.
Blassingame, John W., and Mae G. Henderson, eds. *Antislavery Newspapers and
    Periodicals*. Boston: G. K. Hall, 1980.
Bingham, Caleb. *The Columbian Orator: Containing a Variety of Original and Selected
    Pieces*. Boston: Manning and Loring, 1799.
Douglass, Frederick. *Life and Times of Frederick Douglass*. In *Frederick Douglass:
    Autobiographies*, edited by Henry Louis Gates Jr. New York: Library of America, 1994.
————. *My Bondage and My Freedom*. In *Frederick Douglass: Autobiographies*, edited by
    Henry Louis Gates Jr. New York: Library of America, 1994.

————. *Narrative of the Life of Frederick Douglass*. In *Frederick Douglass: Autobiographies*, edited by Henry Louis Gates Jr. New York: Library of America, 1994.

Douglass, Helen., ed. *In Memoriam: Frederick Douglass*. Philadelphia: J. C. Yorston, 1897.

Foner, Philip S., ed. *Frederick Douglass on Women's Rights*. Westport, Conn.: Greenwood, 1976.

————, ed. *The Life and Writings of Frederick Douglass*. 5 vols. New York: International, 1950, 1952, 1955, 1975.

Foner, Philip S., and Yuval Taylor, eds. *Frederick Douglass: Selected Speeches and Writings*. Chicago: Lawrence Hill, 1999.

Haygood, Atticus G. "The Black Shadow in the South." *Forum* 16 (October 1893): 167–75.

McKivigan, John R. *The Frederick Douglass Papers*. ser. 3, vol. 1. New Haven, Conn.: Yale University Press, 2009.

Parker, Theodore. *Discourse on the Transient and Permanent in Christianity*. Boston: Freeman and Bolles, 1841.

Robbins, Louis Barnum, ed. *History and Minutes of the National Council of Women of the United States*. Boston: E. B. Stillings, 1898.

Rydell, Robert, ed. *The Reason Why the Colored American Is Not in the World's Columbian Exposition*. Urbana: University of Illinois Press, 1999.

Sernett, Milton C. *Afro-American Religious History: A Documentary Witness*. Durham, N.C.: Duke University Press, 1985.

Stanton, Elizabeth Cady, Susan B. Anthony, and Matilda Joslyn Gage, eds. *History of Woman Suffrage*. 6 vols. Rochester, N.Y.: Charles Mann, 1887.

SECONDARY SOURCES

Books

Abzug, Robert H. *Passionate Liberator: Theodore Dwight Weld and the Dilemma of Reform*. New York: Oxford University Press, 1980.

Ahlstrom, Sydney. *A Religious History of the American People*. New Haven, Conn.: Yale University Press, 1972.

Ayers, Edward L. *The Promise of the New South: Life after Reconstruction*. New York: Oxford University Press, 1992.

Bay, Mia. *To Tell the Truth Freely: The Life of Ida B. Wells*. New York: Hill and Wang, 2009.

Bebbington, David. *Evangelicalism in Modern Britain: A History from the 1730s to the 1980s*. London: Unwin Hyman, 1989.

Berlin, Ira. *The Long Emancipation: The Demise of Slavery in the United States*. Cambridge, Mass.: Harvard University Press, 2015.

————. *Many Thousands Gone: The First Two Centuries of Slavery in North America*. Cambridge, Mass.: Harvard University Press, 1998.

Blackett, Richard J. M. *Beating against the Barriers: Biographical Essays in Nineteenth-Century Afro-American History*. Baton Rouge: Louisiana State University Press, 1986.

————. *Building an Antislavery Wall: Black Americans in the Atlantic Abolitionist Movement, 1830–1860*. Baton Rouge: Louisiana State University Press, 1983.

Blassingame, John W. *The Slave Community*. New York: Oxford University Press, 1972.

Blight, David. *Frederick Douglass' Civil War: Keeping Faith in Jubilee*. Baton Rouge: Louisiana State University Press, 1989.

Blum, Edward J. *Reforging the White Republic: Race, Religion, and American Nationalism, 1865–1898*. Baton Rouge: Louisiana State University Press, 2005.

Blum, Edward J., and W. Scott Poole, eds. *Vale of Tears: New Essays on Religion and Reconstruction*. Macon, Ga.: Mercer University Press, 2005.

Bontemps, Arna. *Free at Last: The Life of Frederick Douglass*. New York: Dodd, Mead, 1971.

Brown, Steward J. *Thomas Chalmers and the Godly Commonwealth in Scotland*. New York: Oxford University Press, 1982.

Brueggemann, Walter. *The Prophetic Imagination*. 2nd ed. Minneapolis: Fortress, 2001.

Buccola, Nicholas. *The Political Thought of Frederick Douglass: In Pursuit of American Liberty*. New York: New York University Press, 2012.

Carwardine, Richard. *Evangelicals and Politics in Antebellum America*. New Haven, Conn.: Yale University Press, 1993.

Clarke, Erskine. *Dwelling Place: A Plantation Epic*. New Haven, Conn.: Yale University Press, 2005.

Coles, Howard. *The Cradle of Freedom: A History of the Negro in Rochester, Western New York and Canada*. Rochester, N.Y.: Oxford Press, 1941.

Cook, Charles. *A Brief Account of the African Christian Church in New Bedford*. New Bedford, Mass.: Benjamin T. Congdon, 1834.

Cornish, Dudley. *The Sable Arm: Black Troops in the Union Army, 1861–1865*. New York: W. W. Norton, 1966.

Culver, Dwight W. *Negro Segregation in the Methodist Church*. New Haven, Conn.: Yale University Press, 1953.

Davis, Reginald F. *Frederick Douglass: A Precursor of Liberation Theology*. Macon, Ga.: Mercer University Press, 2005.

DuBois, Ellen Carol. *Feminism and Suffrage: The Emergence of an Independent Women's Movement in America, 1848–1869*. Ithaca, N.Y.: Cornell University Press, 1978.

Dudden, Faye E. *Fighting Chance: The Struggle over Woman Suffrage and Black Suffrage in Reconstruction America*. New York: Oxford University Press, 2011.

Ernest, John. "Crisis and Faith in Douglass's Work." In *The Cambridge Companion to Frederick Douglass*, edited by Maurice S. Lee, 60–72. New York: Cambridge University Press, 2009.

Faust, Drew Gilpin. *This Republic of Suffering: Death and the American Civil War*. New York: Alfred A. Knopf, 2008.

Fields, Barbara. *Slavery and Freedom on the Middle Ground: Maryland during the Nineteenth Century*. New Haven, Conn.: Yale University Press, 1985.

Foner, Eric. *Reconstruction: America's Unfinished Revolution, 1863–1877*. New York: Harper and Row, 1988.

Fordham, Monroe. *Major Themes in Northern Black Religious Thought, 1800–1860*. New York: Exposition, 1975.

Foster, Gaines M. *Moral Reconstruction: Christian Lobbyists and the Federal Legislation of Morality, 1865–1920*. Chapel Hill: University of North Carolina Press, 2002.

Fredrickson, George. *The Inner Civil War: Northern Intellectuals and the Crisis of the Union*. New York: Harper and Row, 1965.

Frey, Sylvia R., and Betty Wood. *Come Shouting to Zion: African American Protestantism in the American South and British Caribbean to 1830*. Chapel Hill: University of North Carolina Press, 1998.

Friedman, Lawrence J. *Gregarious Saints: Self and Community in American Abolitionism, 1830–1870*. New York: Cambridge University Press, 1982.

Gibson, Donald B. "Faith, Doubt, and Apostasy: Evidence of Things Unseen in Frederick Douglass's *Narrative*." In *Frederick Douglass: New Literary and Historical Essays*, edited by Eric J. Sundquist, 84–98. New York: Cambridge University Press, 1990.

Glatthaar, Joseph T. *Forged in Battle: The Civil War Alliance of Black Soldiers and White Officers*. New York: Free Press, 1990.

Glaude, Eddie S., Jr. *Exodus! Religion, Race, and Nation in Early Nineteenth-Century Black America*. Chicago: University of Chicago Press, 2000.

Glymph, Thavolia. *Out of the House of Bondage: The Transformation of the Plantation Household*. New York: Cambridge University Press, 2008.

Goen, C. C. *Broken Churches, Broken Nation: Denominational Schisms and the Coming of the Civil War*. Macon, Ga.: Mercer University Press, 1985.

Graham, Leroy. *Baltimore: The Nineteenth Century Black Capital*. Washington, D.C.: University Press of America, 1982.

Harvey, Paul. *Freedom's Coming: Religious Culture and the Shaping of the South from the Civil War through the Civil Rights Era*. Chapel Hill: University of North Carolina Press, 2005.
———. *Through the Storm, through the Night: A History of African American Christianity*. Lanham, Md.: Rowman & Littlefield, 2011.

Hatch, Nathan O. *The Democratization of American Christianity*. New Haven, Conn.: Yale University Press, 1989.

Hobson, Christopher Z. *The Mount of Vision: African American Prophetic Tradition, 1800–1950*. New York: Oxford University Press, 2012.

Howard-Pitney, David. *The Afro-American Jeremiad: Appeals to Justice in America*. Philadelphia: Temple University Press, 1990.

Huggins, Nathan Irvin. *Slave and Citizen: The Life of Frederick Douglass*. Boston: Little, Brown, 1980.

Irons, Charles F. *The Origins of Proslavery Christianity: White and Black Christianity in Colonial and Antebellum Virginia*. Chapel Hill: University of North Carolina Press, 2008.

Johnson, Paul E. *A Shopkeeper's Millennium: Society and Revivals in Rochester, New York, 1815–1837*. New York: Hill and Wang, 1978.

Johnson, Walter. *Soul by Soul: Life inside the Antebellum Slave Market*. Cambridge, Mass.: Harvard University Press, 1999.

Kolchin, Peter. *American Slavery: 1619–1877*. New York: Hill and Wang, 1993.

Levine, Lawrence. *Black Culture and Black Consciousness: Afro-American Folk Thought from Slavery to Freedom*. Oxford: Oxford University Press, 1977.

Levine, Robert S. *The Lives of Frederick Douglass*. Cambridge, Mass.: Harvard University Press, 2016.
———. *Martin Delany, Frederick Douglass, and the Politics of Representative Identity*. Chapel Hill: University of North Carolina Press, 1997.

Levine, Robert S., and Samuel Otter, eds. *Frederick Douglass and Herman Melville: Essays in Relation*. Chapel Hill: University of North Carolina Press, 2008.

Litwack, Leon F. *Trouble in Mind: Black Southerners in the Age of Jim Crow*. New York: Knopf, 1998.

Mabee, Carleton. *Black Freedom: The Non-violent Abolitionists from 1830 through the Civil War*. New York: Macmillan, 1970.

Martin, Waldo E. *The Mind of Frederick Douglass*. Chapel Hill: University of North Carolina Press, 1984.

Masur, Kate. *An Example for All the Land: Emancipation and the Struggle over Equality in Washington, D.C.* Chapel Hill: University of North Carolina Press, 2010.

Mathews, Donald G. *Religion in the Old South*. Chicago: University of Chicago Press, 1977.

———. *Slavery and Methodism: A Chapter in American Morality, 1780–1845*. Princeton, N.J.: Princeton University Press, 1965.

Mayer, Henry. *All on Fire: William Lloyd Garrison and the Abolition of Slavery*. New York. W. W. Norton, 1998.

McFeely, William. *Frederick Douglass*. New York: W. W. Norton, 1991.

McKivigan, John R. *The War against Proslavery Religion: Abolitionism and Northern Churches, 1830–1865*. Ithaca, N.Y.: Cornell University Press, 1984.

McKivigan, John R, and Stanley Harrold, eds. *Antislavery Violence: Sectional, Racial, and Cultural Conflict in Antebellum America*. Knoxville: University of Tennessee Press, 1999.

McPherson, James M. *The Struggle for Equality: Abolitionists and the Negro in the Civil War and Reconstruction*. Princeton, N.J.: Princeton University Press, 1964.

Meier, August. "Frederick Douglass' Vision for America: A Case Study in Nineteenth-Century Protest." In *Freedom and Reform*, edited by Harold M. Hyman and Leonard W. Levy, 127–48. New York: Harper and Row, 1967.

———. *Negro Thought in America: 1880–1915*. Ann Arbor: University of Michigan Press, 1963.

Melton, J. Gordon. *A Will to Choose: The Origins of African American Methodism*. Lanham, Md.: Rowman and Littlefield, 2007.

Moorhead, James H. *American Apocalypse: Yankee Protestants and the Civil War, 1860–1869*. New Haven, Conn.: Yale University Press, 1978.

Moses, William J. *Black Messiahs and Uncle Toms: Social and Literary Manipulations of a Religious Myth*. University Park: Pennsylvania State University Press, 1982.

Newman, Richard S. *Freedom's Prophet: Richard Allen, the AME Church, and the Black Founding Fathers*. New York: New York University Press, 2008.

Noll, Mark. *The Old Religion in a New World*. Grand Rapids, Mich.: Eerdmans, 2002.

Oakes, James. *Freedom National: The Destruction of Slavery in the United States, 1861–1865*. New York: W. W. Norton, 2013.

———. *The Radical and the Republican: Frederick Douglass, Abraham Lincoln, and the Triumph of Antislavery Politics*. New York: W. W. Norton, 2007.

O'Meally, Robert G. "Frederick Douglass's 1845 Narrative: The Text Was Meant to Be Preached." In *Afro-American Literature: The Reconstruction of Instruction*, edited by Dexter Fisher and Robert Stepto, 192–211. New York: Modern Language Association of America, 1979.

Oshatz, Molly. *Slavery and Sin: The Fight against Slavery and the Rise of Liberal Protestantism*. New York: Oxford University Press, 2012.

Painter, Nell Irvin. *Exodusters: Black Migration to Kansas after Reconstruction*. New York: W. W. Norton, 1976.

Perry, Lewis. *Radical Abolitionism: Anarchy and the Government of God in Anti-slavery Thought*. Ithaca, N.Y.: Cornell University Press, 1973.

Preston, Dickson J. *Young Frederick Douglass: The Maryland Years*. Baltimore: Johns Hopkins University Press, 1980.

Quarles, Benjamin. *Frederick Douglass*. Washington, D.C.: Associated, 1948.

———, ed. *Frederick Douglass*. Englewood Cliffs, N.J.: Prentice-Hall, 1968.

Raboteau, Albert J. *Slave Religion: The "Invisible Institution" in the Antebellum South*. New York: Oxford University Press, 1978.

Rael, Patrick. *Eighty-Eight Years: The Long Death of Slavery in the United States, 1777–1865*. Athens: University of Georgia Press, 2015.

Randall, Ian, and David Hilborn. *One Body in Christ: The History and Significance of the Evangelical Alliance*. Carlisle, U.K.: Paternoster, 2001.

Rice, C. Duncan. *The Scots Abolitionists, 1833–1861*. Baton Rouge: Louisiana State University Press, 1981.

Rockman, Seth. *Scraping By: Wage Labor, Slavery, and Survival in Early Baltimore*. Baltimore: Johns Hopkins University Press, 2009.

Sinha, Manisha. *The Slave's Cause: A History of Abolition*. New Haven, Conn.: Yale University Press, 2016.

Stauffer, John. *The Black Hearts of Men: Radical Abolitionists and the Transformation of Race*. Cambridge, Mass.: Harvard University Press, 2002.

———. *Giants: The Parallel Lives of Frederick Douglass and Abraham Lincoln*. New York: Twelve, 2008.

Stauffer, John, Zoe Trodd, and Celeste-Marie Bernier, eds. *Picturing Frederick Douglass: An Illustrated Biography of the Nineteenth Century's Most Photographed American*. New York: Liverlight, 2015.

Stewart, James Brewer. *Holy Warriors: The Abolitionists and American Slavery*. New York: Hill and Wang, 1976.

Stowell, Daniel W. *Rebuilding Zion: The Religious Reconstruction of the South*. New York: Oxford University Press, 1998.

Takaki, Ronald T. *Violence in the Black Imagination*. New York: Oxford University Press, 1993.

Taylor, Alan. *The Internal Enemy: Slavery and War in Virginia, 1772–1832*. New York: W. W. Norton, 2013.

Tise, Larry E. *Proslavery: A History of the Defense of Slavery in America, 1701–1840*. Athens: University of Georgia Press, 1987.

Varon, Elizabeth. *Disunion! The Coming of the Civil War, 1789–1859*. Chapel Hill: University of North Carolina Press, 2008.

Wacker, Grant. *Religion in Nineteenth Century America*. New York: Oxford University Press, 2000.

Walker, Clarence E. *A Rock in a Weary Land: The African Methodist Episcopal Church during the Civil War and Reconstruction*. Baton Rouge: Louisiana State University Press, 1982.

Walker, Peter F. *Moral Choices: Memory, Desire, and Imagination in Nineteenth-Century American Abolition*. Baton Rouge: Louisiana State University Press, 1978.

Williamson, Scott. *The Narrative Life: The Moral and Religious Thought of Frederick Douglass*. Macon, Ga.: Mercer University Press, 2002.

Woodward, C. Vann. *Origins of the New South, 1877–1913*. Baton Rouge: Louisiana State University Press, 1951.

Wright, Ben, and Zachary W. Dresser, eds. *Apocalypse and the Millennium in the American Civil War Era*. Baton Rouge: Louisiana State University Press, 2013.

Wright, Richard R., ed. *Centennial Encyclopaedia of the African Methodist Episcopal Church*. Philadelphia: R. R. Wright, 1916.

Articles

Albrecht, Robert M. "The Theological Response of the Transcendentalists to the Civil War." *New England Quarterly* 38 (March 1965): 21–34.

Andrews, William L. "Frederick Douglass, Preacher." *American Literature* 54, no. 4 (December 1982): 592–97.

Aptheker, Herbert. "An Unpublished Frederick Douglass Letter." *Journal of Negro History* 44 (July 1959): 277–81.

Bell, Howard Holman. "National Negro Conventions of the Middle 1840s: Moral Suasion vs. Political Action." *Journal of Negro History* 42, no. 4 (October 1957): 247–60.

Blight, David. "Frederick Douglass and the American Apocalypse." *Civil War History* 31, no. 4 (December 1985): 309–28.

Brown, Ira. "Watchers for the Second Coming: The Millennial Tradition in America." *Mississippi Valley Historical Review* 39 (December 1952): 441–58.

Carson, Sharon. "Shaking the Foundation: Liberation Theology in *Narrative of the Life of Frederick Douglass*." *Religion and Literature* 24, no. 2 (Summer 1992): 19–34.

Carter, J. Kameron. "Race, Religion, and the Contradictions of Identity: A Theological Engagement with Douglass's 1845 *Narrative*." *Modern Theology* 21, no. 1 (January 2005): 37–65.

Clebsch, William. "Christian Interpretations of the Civil War." *Church History* 30 (June 1961): 212–22.

Cooper, Frederick. "Elevating the Race: The Social Thought of Black Leaders, 1827–50." *American Quarterly* 24 (December 1972): 604–25.

Demos, John. "The Antislavery Movement and the Problem of Violent Means." *New England Quarterly* 37 (December 1964): 501–26.

Friedman, Lawrence J. "The Gerrit Smith Circle: Abolitionism in the Burned-Over District." *Civil War History* 26 (March 1980): 18–38.

Fulkerson, Gerald. "Exile as Emergence: Frederick Douglass in Great Britain, 1845–1847." *Quarterly Journal of Speech* 60, no. 1 (February 1974): 69–82.

Gibson, Donald B. "Christianity and Individualism: (Re-)Creation and Reality in Frederick Douglass's Representation of Self." *African American Review* 26, no. 4 (Winter 1992): 591–603.

———. "Reconciling Public and Private in Frederick Douglass's *Narrative*." *American Literature* 57 (December 1985): 549–69.

Goldstein, Leslie Friedman. "Violence as an Instrument for Social Change: The Views of Frederick Douglass." *Journal of Negro History* 61 (January 1976): 61–72.

Harlow, Ralph Volney. "Gerrit Smith and the Free Church Movement." *New York History* 43 (July 1937): 269–87.

Howard-Pitney, David. "The Enduring Black Jeremiad: The American Jeremiad and Black Protest Rhetoric, from Frederick Douglass to W. E. B. Du Bois, 1841–1919." *American Quarterly* 38, no. 3 (1986): 481–92.

Hunt, James B. "The Faith Journey of Frederick Douglass, 1818–1895." *Christian Scholar's Review* 15, no. 3 (March 1986): 228–46.

Hutchins, Zachary McLeod. "Rejecting the Root: The Liberating, Anti-Christ Theology of Narrative." *Nineteenth-Century Literature* 68, no. 3 (December 2013): 292–322.

Maclear, J. F. "The Evangelical Alliance and the Antislavery Crusade." *Huntington Library Quarterly* 42 (Spring 1979): 141–64.

Moorhead, James. "Between Progress and Apocalypse: A Reassessment of Millennialism in American Religious Thought, 1800–1880." *Journal of American History* 71 (December 1984): 524–42.

Paddon, Anna R., and Sally Turner. "African Americans and the World's Columbian Exposition." *Illinois Historical Journal* 88, no. 1 (Spring 1995): 19–36.

Pease, William H., and Jane H. Pease. "Boston Garrisonians and the Problem of Frederick Douglass." *Canadian Journal of History* 2, no. 2 (September 1967): 29–48.

Quarles, Benjamin. "Letters from Negro Leaders to Gerrit Smith." *Journal of Negro History* 27, no. 4 (October 1942): 432–53.

Schor, Joel. "The Rivalry between Frederick Douglass and Henry Highland Garnet." *Journal of Negro History* 64, no. 1 (Winter 1969): 30–38.

Shepperson, George. "Frederick Douglass and Scotland." *Journal of Negro History* 38 (July 1953): 307–21.

———. "The Free Church and American Slavery." *Scottish Historical Review* 30 (October 1951): 126–43.

———. "Thomas Chalmers, the Free Church of Scotland, and the South." *Journal of Southern History* 17, no. 4 (November 1951): 517–37.

Van Deburg, William L. "Frederick Douglass and the Institutional Church." *Journal of the Academy of American Religion* 14 (June 1977): 515–37.

———. "Frederick Douglass: Maryland Slave to Religious Liberal." *Maryland Historical Magazine* 69, no. 1 (Spring 1974): 27–43.

Dissertations

Gardner, Bettye J. "Free Blacks in Baltimore, 1800–1860." PhD diss., George Washington University, 1974.

Goldstein, Leslie Friedman. "The Political Thought of Frederick Douglass." PhD diss., Cornell University, 1974.

Grayson, John Turner. "Frederick Douglass' Intellectual Development: His Concepts of God, Man, and Nature in the Light of American and European Influences." PhD diss., Columbia University, 1981.

Hinshaw, George Asher. "A Rhetorical Analysis of the Speeches of Frederick Douglass before and after the Civil War." PhD diss., University of Nebraska at Lincoln, 1972.

Mosher, Shawn J. "Frederick Douglass's Theology of Violence, 1841–1849." MA thesis, Baylor University, 2005.

Van Deburg, William L. "Rejected of Men: The Changing Religious Views of William Lloyd Garrison and Frederick Douglass." PhD diss., Michigan State University, 1973.

Index